Introduction

The papers collected together in this book were, with three exceptions, all presented at the silver jubilee course and conference of the National Association for Remedial Education (NARE), held at University College, Swansea, in late August, 1988. The theme of that conference has been adopted as the title of this book.

Planning for the conference began in the later part of 1985, some two and a half years after the implementation of the provisions of the 1981 Education Act. It covered a period when, in local education authorities throughout England and Wales, and in schools and training institutions, major challenges were seen to be vested in the need to implement a range of actions which, collectively, would ensure that within the expanded definition adopted by the 1981 Education Act, the special education needs of any pupil could be identified and appropriately met.

In this period, much activity at local authority level was driven by statutory obligations to children with moderate and severe learning difficulties or special needs. This led, inevitably perhaps, to preoccupation with the development of policy and procedures affecting statemented children. Integration, while not mandatory, was nevertheless high on the agenda of concern of LEAs planning for provision.

At the level of individual schools, both primary and secondary, at pre-school and in the post-compulsory phase, there was a growing recognition that an effective response to the legislation of special education needs would require a whole-school approach.

Most of the recent writings in regard to whole-school policies on special needs take as pivotal the institutionalisation of key concepts connected with their redefinition. Part of the legacy of the Warnock Report relates to notions of continuity and relativity when applied to special needs, notably the continuity of handicap in terms of experience of severity, and the relativity of handicap as a function of the task demanded and the context in which the disabled child is required to function.

This latter notion, in particular, puts powerful demands on teachers in terms of their own lesson planning and of the learning environment they seek to create for all children. Warnock sought to question the traditional model of attribution of special needs which reflected an essentially medical view or within-child view of causation. Transforming explanations of causation to ecologically sensitive global perspectives which view learning difficulties as educational outcomes constitutes a profound challenge to teachers in so far as the resolution of the learning difficulty has to be sought within the framework of the learning context itself.

The rhetoric of whole-school response has focused on the need for all teachers to consider the way in which their own teaching may be modified to enable greater accessibility to the mainstream curriculum by children recognised as having a learning difficulty. The issues raised here relate to ownership of children with special needs and a recognition that special needs policy was not simply tacked on to other school policies, but was necessarily embedded within all of them. There are clear parallels here with policies on race and gender and the implications for classroom practice are equally profound.

An emerging literature (for example, Evans 1986) concerns itself with demystifying practice, with supportive education, co-operative teaching and sharing expertise within an articulated conceptual framework where the ordinary classroom teacher becomes the key to children's learning difficulties. The organisational character of the learning environment is increasingly seen as the core of concern in responding to children's individual and special educational needs and efficacy as related to teachers' management of resources available and the repertoire of their pedagogic skills.

Ownership may be effected and professional roles extended in ways which empower teachers to respond effectively to the learning difficulties of children in their classes if they are helped to see the multidimensionality and multiprofessionality of children's special needs. They may also be encouraged to understand how particular behavioural and educational outcomes are forged through the complex interaction between formal and informal learning situations. Attached to each of these is a set of attitudes, values and practices which collectively contribute to the child's idiosyncratic concept of social reality. A historic challenge to practice relates to the way in which educators can help children to achieve success and to feel good about themselves even in situations where what they achieve is quantitatively different from the achievement of others.

In the classroom situation, the sharp end of practice, equality of opportunity in the strong sense will be achieved when each child is enabled to reach attainable goals. It is in realising this aim that classroom teachers and subject teachers require advice, guidance and support. To be truly effective requires more than empathy with the disabled or handicapped child, more than a disposition to work with them, more than a supportive and caring manner. Necessary and helpful though these qualities may be, they of themselves will not be sufficient to ensure equity for children with special needs in the classroom.

Relevant teaching expertise must relate to the identification of children's

Special educational needs: Policy and practice

Edited by
Roy Evans

Blackwell Education,
in association with the
National Association for Remedial Education

To teachers everywhere – especially those who bring their own special gifts to the education of children with learning difficulties

First published 1989

Published by Basil Blackwell Ltd
108 Cowley Road
Oxford OX4 1JF
England

Typeset in 10/12 pt Plantin by Colset Private Limited, Singapore
Printed in Great Britain by TJ Press, Padstow, Cornwall

British Library Cataloguing in Publication Data

Special educational needs: policy and practice.
  1. Special education
  I. Evans, Roy
  371.9

  ISBN 0-631-16902-4
  ISBN 0-631-16903-2 pbk

Contents

learning needs, perhaps as distinct from their learning difficulties, to the setting of realistic goals and prioritising among alternatives, and to designing tasks in such a way that teaching remains effective.

The demystification of practice which I referred to earlier relates to the extent to which ordinary classroom teachers can be helped to understand that teaching children with special needs does not require a different order of skill but rather that their repertoire of personal skills may need to be enhanced, and relevant information and support made available to them.

Throughout the 1980s the sharing of expertise and the delivery of support to schools and teachers have emerged as key issues in the drive towards development of effective practice. What has been at stake and what continues to be debated is the role of the ordinary teacher alongside the perceived roles of other professionals who are significant in the overall enterprise.

Liaison between the teacher and other professionals, between the school and other professional agencies, home–school liaison and the role of governing bodies have been and continue to be areas for exploration in terms of the development of effective practice.

These concerns were reflected in the papers submitted to the silver jubilee conference at Swansea. They are, in consequence, reflected in the papers which comprise this book. What is important to point out is that in the early stages of conference preparation, the Education Reform Act (ERA) was still over the horizon, and while the Great Education Reform Bill had become an Act of parliament by the time the conference took place, the implications for children with special educational needs of many of the provisions of the new Act were not clear, and at the time of writing many of the attendant regulations and advisory circulars are still at the consultative stage.

From a special needs perspective, the existence of a national curriculum, an entitlement curriculum for all children, should be viewed with optimism. It remains to be seen whether the disapplication or suspension of the requirements of the national curriculum in respect of some children with special needs will represent a humane and sensitive response in the light of the best advice available or whether the door will be opened to a new form of segregation driven by financial expediency and characterised by the cynical disregard of the principles on which the Warnock recommendations were based, and the 1981 reforms enacted.

Disapplication of the national curriculum for some pupils may prove to be an attractive option to some local authorities where resources are particularly scarce. Supporting an individual child within the mainstream curriculum is expensive, especially so in those local authorities where individual support teachers work with the child on a one-to-one basis. Withdrawal of such support will, however, have the effect of predetermining the outcome for some such children.

It will become increasingly necessary for us to reflect upon whether integration in the truest meaning of the term can continue to be a credible aim for education in England and Wales when set alongside the possibility enshrined within the ERA of suspending the requirements of the national curriculum for some children either temporarily or permanently.

While it is clear that all the requirements of the 1981 Education Act continue to apply, concern must exist as to whether the progress made in relation to special needs can be maintained in the face of competition born of the need to deliver and monitor a centrally determined curriculum.

In those schools where the policy on special needs is well articulated and embedded within the framework of the curriculum, the challenge of the future must be related to maintaining the resource base. In schools and colleges where the response to special educational needs has been less well articulated, the pressure of new legislation may put at risk the evolution of a coherent response.

Pessimism over the future can have an immobilising effect and the greatest danger to the profession is that we come to believe that the effects of financial delegation, local management of schools, open enrolment, and the publication of school effectiveness data will inevitably have an adverse effect on resources for children with special educational needs. To deny that, in some situations, these factors will conspire to produce a decline in the quality of what is on offer for such children, is to be less than realistic. It is, however, worth bearing in mind that where formulae for financial delegation have inbuilt elements for special needs, this can conceivably secure the resource base to a greater extent than has previously been possible. This is true in so far as it permits the local education authority to monitor individual schools' disbursement of that element of the resource for which it is accountable.

Here, as elsewhere, the role of the governing body is crucial. Developing the response to special educational needs in the new climate must mean that governing bodies recognise their legal responsibilities under the 1981 Education Act so that special educational needs remain high on their agenda of concern and action.

At the time of the silver jubilee conference a climate of concern existed which was based substantially on uncertainty and the lack of clear priority guidelines from the DES. This will be seen to be reflected in many of the papers that follow. These have been organised into three sections: Part 1, Policy into Practice; Part 2, Sharing Expertise; Part 3, Supporting and Developing the Curriculum.

Part 1 is introduced by Ronald Davie whose keynote paper serves to remind us of the philosophy underlying the 1981 Act and of the relevance of the 1988 Act to pupils who have significant difficulties with learning or adjustment. He raises some of the problems of successfully translating policy into practice. Important among these are the evident difficulties of inter-agency collaboration, a theme which is returned to on a number of occasions by different authors throughout the book.

Philip Robinson's paper on the 1988 Education Reform Act serves to remind us of key issues connected with the Act, notable among which is that of effectiveness. There is evident concern that misguided notions of effectiveness are likely to distort both the ways in which schools package their curriculum and the criteria we employ to evaluate the outcomes of its delivery.

Subsequent papers in Part 1 deal with special educational needs from pre-school through to further and adult education. Each stresses its own priorities, but throughout the need emerges for clear, confident statements of intent coupled with a readiness for co-operative collaborative working within the institutions and for the development of modes of working which are exemplified by a readiness to seek collaboration, share expertise and co-operate fully with all relevant agencies, statutory and voluntary, and in particular with the family.

Part 2 explores in more detail the ways in which expertise may be shared and provides some insights into the needs of those professionals and para-professionals who are intimately connected with the delivery of quality education to children with special needs.

In her opening paper, Gerda Hanko develops the theme by focusing on the group consultative training approach which is proposed as one way of developing the consultancy role of those in a position to help teachers meet their pupils' special needs.

Eva Gregory's paper extends the theme of sharing expertise by attempting an analysis of the reasons why difficulties arise when professionals try to collaborate. Starting from the premise that power, status, knowledge, and expertise are as relevant as the ethos and rules of an institution or the perceptions and values of various individuals, she uses systems theory to explore how it is that the perception of one professional group may come to dominate multi-professional assessment of the needs of the child and his family. Perhaps inevitably one of the main conclusions is that if we wish people to work collaboratively then we have to pay attention to this early on in their professional development and training. Implicit in such attention is the need to help professionals examine some of the assumptions that are embedded in their day-to-day work with children and with other professionals and with families.

John Atkinson in his chapter on the development of a whole-school approach to disruptive pupils argues that sufficient knowledge now exists for schools to investigate themselves as organisations and for teachers to analyse themselves as individuals when meeting such behaviour.

Much of what Atkinson has to say is relevant to the theme of Part 3 of this book; it has been included in Part 2 because of its significance in supporting the general contention that the development of effective practice is a collaborative, multi-faceted venture which challenges basic assumptions about individuals and the ways in which they interact with others.

The need for training towards co-operative and supportive working is also emphasised in John Harrington's paper on the role of school governors and in Terence Clayton's paper on the important role played by welfare assistants.

The remaining two papers in this section concern themselves with the support services, the role of the support teacher, and address basic issues connected with the manner in which support may be applied more effectively and the type of skills that could be developed profitably.

Overall, an improvement in the quality of decision-making concerning children's needs and appropriate provision to meet these needs is dependent, it has been argued, on the readiness with which all participants in the decision-making process are prepared to adopt a self-critical approach in respect of basic attitudes, values and practices which characterise their daily working and similarly affect the quality of interaction both intra- and inter-professionally.

In Part 3, an attempt has been made to reflect the range of innovation at different age phases and in different agencies that has emerged in response to the special needs legislation.

The emphasis is on *support*. The ultimate goal is to support the child effectively within an appropriate curriculum framework. To this end, supporting a school and supporting the individual class teacher becomes of itself an important objective. While this might be taken as the central message of this section, there is a further message in that it would be foolish to assume that there is any one way, or any right way, to provide this support. Much depends on the resources available in any school or local authority and how these are organised and distributed, and on the levels of expertise that exist.

The papers in this section are offered as examples of practice unified by a common concern yet differentiated by context. Readily identifiable in each description of practice are the effects of locality, which offers both opportunities and constraints.

Attention is drawn to the need for a problem-solving approach which enables the most effective use to be made of the resources available at the time. To insist that one approach to the provision of support can ever be more than 'an approach', is to ignore the power of contextual features which logically should influence decisions concerning the sort of action that is taken, when it is taken, and who should be involved in it.

Acknowledgements

Many people have contributed to the development of this book of edited papers. Some contributors will be identified as authors of the papers which comprise its contents. Others will be less easily identified, being the families, colleagues, secretaries and professional mentors upon whom most of us depend at different times and perhaps to different degrees. The national executive committee of the National Association for Remedial Education (NARE) has also played an important role in facilitating this work. Particular thanks must be directed to the association's silver jubilee conference committee for enabling the contributors to this book to come together at University College, Swansea, in August 1988, so that we all can share a broader vision of progress being made towards meeting the special educational needs of all children.

PART 1

Policy into Practice

1 Special educational needs: policy into practice

Ronald Davie

Introduction

The title I have given to my paper echoes the extended title of the conference. This general theme is perhaps even more relevant now to the field of special educational needs than it was two or three years ago when the initial decision about the conference topic was made.

Certainly, we have seen over the last seven years in Britain new educational legislation of a kind which is having a profound influence upon practice in education departments and schools – for better or for worse. Furthermore, the impact of the 1981 Education Act has meant that the field of special educational needs has been more affected than mainstream practice by these new policies. The 1988 Education Reform Act will, however, have widespread implications for all concerned with education.

There is no time in one relatively short paper to undertake any comprehensive review of the 1981, 1986 and 1988 Acts and their potential and actual effects on practice in the area of special needs. In any event, as I have indicated, some of this ground will be covered by others.

I intend therefore to pursue three main strands. First, I shall look at the philosophy underlying the 1981 Act and examine the evidence as to how well it is working in practice. Second, and more briefly, I shall ask some questions about the relevance of the 1988 Act to the particular needs of pupils in our schools who have significant difficulties with learning, or whose behaviour or adjustment gives cause for concern. Finally, I shall, largely by reference to these two Acts, share with you some thoughts about the problems of successfully translating policies into practice.

The 1981 Act in its basic conception found – and finds – favour, I believe, with the overwhelming majority of those in the field, and with almost all others, too. Of course, it inherited the credibility and goodwill of its precursor, the Warnock Report (DES 1978).

The three cornerstones of this legislation were: the attempt to break away from the categorisation of children, allied to the concept of a continuum of need; the importance attached to successful integration; and the belief that a partnership with parents was vital. These cornerstones remain as firm in principle now as when they were laid down in 1981, or when the blueprint was drawn in 1978. The edifice built upon those stones – the implementation of the Act – leaves much to be desired, however, as the research of Goacher *et al* (1988) makes clear.

I draw upon these research findings here mostly, of course, because of their direct relevance to our theme. In addition, I have as a consultant – and on behalf of the National Children's Bureau – been working with a team from the University of London Institute of Education over the past two years or so, to distil the lessons from this research for local and health authorities. This collaborative development project, involving most of the original researchers, has been producing training and other materials, trying them out in a few selected authorities, and also extending its dissemination networks in anticipation of the finished products.

Before picking out a few of the research findings, which highlight shortcomings, I should say that there was a great deal to commend and admire about the response to the Act from individual schools and authorities in very difficult circumstances, not the least of which was the failure of central government to provide any additional resources.

The yardsticks of progress are not easy to quantify, but over 70 per cent of LEAs reported a proportionate increase in expenditure from 1983 to 1986 on special educational needs; and over three-quarters of LEAs have increased their use of mainstream placements for children with special needs, both in the primary and secondary sectors. Many other changes were reported. Yet, only a minority (40 per cent) of LEAs had substantially increased the number of their administrative staff working in this area.

Despite the crudity of these yardsticks, it is clear that most authorities have been, and are making considerable efforts to give effect to the 1981 Act. Nevertheless, it is necessary to introduce some significant qualifying remarks about the current direction of policies and procedures in many authorities.

The new definition of special educational needs

The new definition of special educational needs centres on whether or not a child has 'a learning difficulty which calls for special educational provision to be made'. This learning difficulty has to be 'significantly greater . . . than for the majority of children of his age'; or, he has to have a 'disability which either prevents or hinders him from making use of educational facilities of a kind generally provided in schools maintained by the local education authority concerned . . .'.

This definition breaks away from the previous categorisations of handicap and attempts to introduce a subtler and a more relative concept. Predictably, perhaps, this has resulted in different interpretations. Thus, if we restrict our attention for the moment to pupils for whom a statement is made, the proportion ranges across LEAs from less than 1 per cent of the school population to nearly 3 per cent. Furthermore, in their returns to the research team, administrators in some LEAs spoke of 5 per cent as their target population for statements, while elsewhere it was considered that as many as 18 per cent could require a statement. Notwithstanding the relativity of the concept, this situation surely indicates a lack of clarity or mutual agreement about the nature of special educational needs, which cannot be allowed to continue. Since statements are seen in part as a form of protection for the child, we must seek to ensure that all who need this protection have it.

As was clear in the original Warnock Report (DES 1978), however, the proportion of children who fall within the general definition of special educational needs is around 20 per cent. It is not at all clear what extra resources and provision are currently being planned or provided for this larger group, nor whether the size of that group is broadly agreed, nor whether local authorities and schools are identifying in any way the children involved. Finally, it should be noted that the process of categorisation is still with us, although the names have changed: former ESN pupils now have severe or moderate learning difficulties, maladjusted pupils have emotional or behavioural difficulties and so on. Initials have crept back, too, – 'SLD', 'MLD', 'EBD'.

Integration

The second topic to be considered in this first section is integration. We do not need here to rehearse the contentious issues which surround integration, but it is sometimes assumed that the placement of a child in a mainstream school constitutes integration, or, in any event, that we all understand the same meaning of this term. Both assumptions are false. To quote briefly from the Warnock Report:

> ... it was apparent that professionals and administrators in education, health and social services held a wide range of views concerning what constitutes 'integration'. It also became clear that diametrically opposed opinions of and attitudes towards integration could quite easily be found within a local authority.

In four out of the five authorities studied in depth by the research team, 'the provision of a statement appeared in the majority of cases to coincide with a decision to transfer a child to a special school'. Furthermore, 'responses to the questionnaire indicated that this pattern is reflected nationally'.

This situation bears an uncomfortably close resemblance to the picture which obtained before the 1981 Act when children were assessed under the old SE procedures as in need of special educational provision. It does not appear to sit easily with an Act which requires local authorities to educate children with special educational needs in ordinary schools, provided that this is in the interests of the child, that it does not adversely affect the education of the other children and is compatible with the efficient use of resources.

Thus, as it seems to me, the burden of proof under the 1981 Act has shifted to demonstrating why a child with special educational needs should *not* be educated in an ordinary school with the necessary extra provision. If I am correct – and the statement is also seen in some measure as a form of protection of the parents' and child's rights in this matter – it is surely anomalous that this statement appears largely to have become a passport to special schooling.

Inter-agency collaboration

The next theme I would like to share with you is a very familiar one at the National Children's Bureau, namely, the difficulty of achieving effective co-operation and collaboration between education, health and social services. It is not appropriate here to analyse, nor even to state, the many reasons for this difficulty, but after scrutinising the research findings I have to say that LEAs have on the whole not seen the implications of the 1981 Act for social services departments or district health authorities. Here is the research team's summary of its findings from the detailed study of five education authorities:

> With one notable exception, a factor common to all these very different approaches to policy formulation was the negligible role allowed to health and social services personnel. The joint DES/DHSS nature of the Circular, the necessary involvement of health and social services professionals in the multi-professional assessment, and their part in providing for those with special educational needs, were apparently not seen as sufficient reason for including them in discussions.

This picture in the five authorities studied in depth was mirrored in the country as a whole. It was reflected predictably in the relatively low priority now given by social services to special educational needs. Although they receive notification from education of the intention to assess a child, they are uncertain of their role, and so, with other pressing priorities, they tend not to give it high priority. Only a third of LEAs had arranged any training for social services departments about the purpose and procedures of the 1981 Act, and only a few more (38 per cent) had arranged training for health authorities. Even more culpably, not all LEAs, it seems, informed social services or health authorities of the outcome of their procedures for statements.

As I have indicated above, the reasons for poor collaboration between services are complex and many-sided. The time has surely come for local authorities, at least, to develop and implement 'whole authority' policies and procedures on a range of topics, which would certainly include children with special needs and also child abuse.

Parents as partners

My last theme deriving from the research findings relates to the involvement of parents, which was envisaged as a central feature of the Act. Circular 1/83 was clear on this point:

> In looking at the child as a whole person, the involvement of the child's parents is essential. Assessment should be seen as a partnership between teachers, other professionals and parents in a joint endeavour to discover the nature of the difficulties and needs of individual children.

The research findings indicate that many authorities have a long way to go before their procedures come close to what one might reasonably describe as a partnership with parents. On the one hand, it seemed clear from the studies in five authorities that the Act's emphasis on partnership was recognised and in general accepted. On the other hand,

> changed practice had yet to begin in many areas of the LEA procedures. Previous patterns of working, sets of beliefs about parents and their willingness and capacity to play a larger part in decisions about their children with special educational needs, professional uncertainty and paternalism all had a part to play in the process.
>
> (Goacher *et al*)

For example, the information booklets prepared for parents had obviously been written with care and many of the right sentiments were expressed. A certain formality of tone and style often intruded, however, and in one case there was no indication that the LEA viewed parental contributions as valuable or desirable. Overall, the research team concluded that only in one of the five authorities was the information provided really accessible to parents. This authority also often gave details absent from others' booklets. For example, the social services department was included among those to be contacted during a statutory assessment, together with the reassurance:

> If a social worker is already helping your family, there is nothing to worry about; your social worker will discuss the assessment with you, and will *not* give any information without your permission.

The needs of ethnic minorities

In none of these five detailed study authorities were versions available in any language other than English, despite the fact that in one of them, 17 per cent of the population were from ethnic minority groups. The authorities responding to the national survey questionnaire all said that they would offer the services of an interpreter, if this appeared to be necessary. Only six stated that they would offer a translation of the documents.

The position in the borough with 17 per cent from ethnic minority groups is especially revealing in this context. The statementing officer had reported that no one had thus far requested the use of an interpreter. Yet, another research team in the same borough at the same time, carrying out a survey of parental responses to statements, had to rely heavily on interpreters for interviews with the parents. Clearly, the fact that ethnic minority parents do not request help cannot be taken to mean that they fully understand the information they receive.

Parents' views of assessments

Parents in general, it seems, are not yet happy about the way assessments are handled, to judge by interviews with a sample of 44 parents in the five authorities studied. For some of these parents, who had established a long-standing and good relationship with a teacher or psychologist, the assessment procedures were seen as positive, informative and helpful. But the majority were either dissatisfied or upset about a number of aspects of the way they had been treated during the assessment process.

What particularly upset them, in some cases, was the negative tone, as they saw it, of assessments. Some did not like to face a battery of professionals. Resentment was always present when parents felt either that there was a lack of openness or frankness on the part of the professionals or administrators, or that they were being coerced, or that their concern for and about their child was being called into question. Two short quotations illustrate the negative and the positive. One disgruntled mother said:

> They tell you nothing, give you the idea that there are no alternatives . . . they don't like to admit that they can't cater for every child's needs . . . they don't give anything freely . . . not even information.

In contrast, the father of a three-year-old rubella-damaged deaf girl had received a great deal of help from the LEA, the hospital consultant, and from social services and voluntary organisations. He commented:

> Everyone was very helpful. It has been very good all the way. We wouldn't have known where to start really.

Perhaps 'end of term' reports on individual authorities and schools after their first two and a half years or so of implementing the 1981 Act (when the research data were finally gathered) would range from commenting, 'Encouraging progress has been made', through the ubiquitous 'Could do better' to 'Disappointing work. A somewhat slack attitude!'

I move now to the second strand of my paper: a consideration of the 1988 Act. Since others will be dealing with this in some detail, I will restrict myself to brief comments on some of the major areas of concern in respect of special educational needs. First, however, I have to declare myself in favour of the general principle of a national curriculum, which has been described by Kenneth Baker as the central feature of the new Act.

As far as children with special educational needs are concerned, there are for me two main worries. I want to see a curricular framework which is flexible enough to permit sensible modifications and, where necessary, exemptions to be made in the interests of individual children with special needs. On the other hand, flexibility can operate to the disadvantage of these pupils if inappropriate compassion on the part of teachers leads to a lowering of expectations, and consequently of standards, for the individual child.

Whether this fine balance of flexibility and rigour can be achieved in the context of the national curriculum, I do not know. But it is one of several such equations in the Education Reform Act.

With the possible exception of grant-maintained status, for which I personally find it very difficult to see any merit or justification, the other provisions with potential threat for children with special needs (open enrolment and local financial management) are for me rather like the curate's egg. Everything, then, will depend upon the guidance and circulars produced by the Department of Education and Science, i.e. upon the way in which the Act is interpreted by the department and implemented at local level. The future, therefore, is in the balance.

When I look at these various provisions taken together, I see the possibility of benefits deriving for children from increased accountability in education and from a more consistent national curricular framework.

A fresh wind of educational change can so easily become a chill wind, however, and, if it does, the most vulnerable of our children will suffer. To use another metaphor, if the world of education becomes a jungle of market forces, I fear for the survival of children with special needs.

As I have indicated, I believe the future educational scene is critically poised in several important areas for children with special needs. I therefore would strongly urge NARE – and preferably in concert with others – to monitor events very closely over the next few years.

The government has shown some willingness in parliamentary debates on the Bill to accept the need to safeguard the position of special needs pupils. This occasionally resulted in amendments – more often it took the form of assurances from ministers about future intentions. Those words need now to be scrutinised closely as future events unfold and as the 'small print' of implementation is written. NARE, and other like bodies, must be watchful and quick to respond not only in their explicit task of safeguarding the interests of their members but also in their implicit duty of safeguarding the interests of the children with special needs whom their members are privileged to serve.

The final part of my paper concerns the difficulties of successfully translating policies into practice. My earlier comments drawing on research findings exemplified well the reality of gaps between intended policy and actual practice.

The issues here are not just related to policies, however, nor to new legislation. The difficulties of translating any kind of new knowledge into practice are formidable and complex. The processes involved are common to a wide range of information – from research findings to new professional or practical developments, from innovative ideas or policies to parliamentary legislation.

The common factors include the problems of good communication and dissemination; the perceived 'ownership' of the innovation by those whose practice is most affected; the firm and explicit adoption of the innovation; the experience of initial implementation; the other pressures bearing upon the organisation or individuals who are being asked to change; the resource implications; and the extent to which the innovation becomes firmly embedded into the structure of the organisation or the practice of the individual.

These, then, are the kinds of factors to be borne in mind when any new knowledge or innovation is intended to affect practice. The complexity of the processes involved are often underestimated by researchers, administrators and by politicians.

The implications of this for those three groups are that careful consideration needs to be given, for example, to the overall time scale envisaged, to the consultation process, to the effectiveness of the dissemination and to the resource implications.

In the context of the particular brief I have set for myself, I would like, in concluding, to return to the government's legislative programme and some of the lessons to be learnt from the experience of recent years in translating policy into practice.

The first thing which strikes one is the speed with which bodies are expected to respond or to change. One knows that governments have other considerations to bear in mind, including the legislative process itself. Nevertheless, there are dangers that too much haste puts at risk that necessary bond of mutual trust and co-operation between the policymaker and those who are called upon to implement policy. This government – any government – would do well to heed those dangers.

The second aspect which can be noted is the reluctance of government sometimes to appreciate or accept possible resource implications. Again, this debate goes beyond the educational field. I am not one who believes that extra resources necessarily solve problems or necessarily smooth the way to their solution. Nevertheless, the notion that every new advance or development in education can be made by utilising existing resources more effectively is simplistic and does not bear close scrutiny.

One sometimes hears it said that this or that innovation is not a matter of extra resources but of new attitudes or different ways of working. This ignores the reality that attitudinal change, changes in working practices or skills and institutional change *at the very least* need careful and often time-consuming planning and preparation if they are to be successfully achieved. And time is money.

My final plea is that those who create new policies take seriously and consider fully the perspectives and situations of the practitioner. In the field of special educational needs, perhaps more than in any other area of education, there is a skilled and committed body of practitioners who are no strangers to innovation. If they are properly consulted, resourced and involved in the process of change, those skills and that commitment can be harnessed to great effect in serving the interests of those children and services on whom their professional careers are focused. If they are not involved, resourced and committed to the change, the reality of practice at the grass roots is likely to be a pale shadow of what might have been.

2   Whose Act is it anyway?

Philip Robinson

The Education Reform Act was given the Royal Assent on the 29 July 1988. The Great Education Reform Bill that had been presented to the House of Commons seven months earlier with the soubriquet of 'GERBIL' had, like gerbils, grown. The original 147 clauses were expanded and added to, becoming the 238 of the legislation.

The Act marks the most significant shift in direction of the education service since that of 1944. Its passage through the House considerably enhanced the reputation of the Secretary of State as a skilled parliamentarian and strategist as the November proposals emerged almost intact the following summer.

The Secretary of State is clearly a beneficiary of the legislation; the powers bestowed on that office have grown considerably. School governors have increased powers and responsibilities and it is alleged parents will also benefit from the greater choices available and the clearer accountability of the system.

Local education authorities have less autonomy and become more the administrative arm of the Department of Education and Science, delivering a system of education within the well defined orbit of circulars and orders in council.

Teachers are not free to define the curriculum but this may be more a loss of face than substance. Teachers have always been constrained by the demands of examinations and the expectations of parents. There is not a school in the land that doesn't teach mathematics and English. The criticisms made by the informed opinion of Her Majesty's Inspectors have been that too often the curriculum is narrow and pedestrian rather than promoting the full development of individuals.

In his discussion on social justice the American philosopher John Rawls wrote:

All social primary goods – liberty and opportunity, income and wealth, and the basis of self respect – are to be distributed equally unless an unequal distribution of any or all of these goods is to the advantage of the least favoured. (1972, p 303)

To what extent does the Education Reform Act promote the advantage of the least favoured? What are the benefits for the poor, the homeless, the disadvantaged in the education world heralded by the new legislation? Any special educational provision for a child provided with a statement under the 1981 Education Act may exclude or modify the national curriculum. On the basis of the present issue of statements this would mean that about two per cent of the child population are judged as likely to fall outside the provision of the 1988 Act. For the rest, excepting those who attend independent schools, the Act may be judged on the extent to which it promotes the interests of all children.

An aim of educational policy in this and many other countries has been that of enhancing equality of opportunity. Embedded within discussions of human rights is the intention that we should not so organise our social institutions that they promote some people and inhibit others. The realisation of this aim has remained elusive; in all societies the children of the powerful do better than those of the powerless. If power is represented as being 'middle class', or a member of the 'party apparatchik', the consequence is the same, the distribution of educational opportunities is progressively in its favour, with more of its children attending secondary education and even more attending tertiary or higher education. Is the 1988 Act likely to promote or impede the achievement of equality of opportunity? I fear the latter, but first a little more on the term itself.

I still find it helpful to return to a point made by Tony Crosland in 1962. He argued that 'equality of opportunity' has a weak and a strong sense. In its weak version the phrase means equality of access. In this usage we have achieved the goal of equality the moment there is a school in reach of every child. No one is denied books, materials or teachers, so all have the same opportunities to use them as they might. Such a view ignores the tremendous structural inequalities within society; it assumes that ethnicity, gender and class do not influence educational achievements and that all schools are of the same character. Children are not, however, independent of the nexus of expectations, attitudes and values that surround them. In recognising this, Crosland introduced what he called 'a strong definition of equality of opportunity – equality of outcomes.

The concept of equality of outcomes does not mean that each person obtains the same number of marks in the same number of examinations, but that a representative individual of any group has the same probability of success as a representative individual of any other group. The probability of someone with blue eyes gaining five or more passes at GCSE is, I imagine, the same as that of someone with brown eyes. As has been often demonstrated, however, this is not the case if we take the representative individual from a group divided on the basis of skin colour, parental occupation, gender or, in England, whether he or she lives in the north or south of the country.

For each of these divisions we would find inequalities of outcome and it is in this sense that one can assert that we have failed to achieve equality of opportunity in England. The girl who is black and the daughter of working class parents faces at least a triple disadvantage compared with a white middle-class boy. The cause of her disadvantage rests in the social arrangements we make, yet there is a tradition of social analysis which attempts to blame the girl for her failure, as if it were simply her responsibility to overcome the conditions of class, race and gender to which she is subject. This is not to deny personal responsibility, but to recognise that in all social organisations individual responsibility is constrained by the social arrangements which obtain.

The political realisation of Crosland's view of equality was the publication in July 1965 of DES Circular 10/65 outlining the government's intention of ending selection at 11 plus and eliminating separatism in secondary education. The circular gave an expression to a motion passed in the House of Commons in January of that year when the House, 'conscious of the need to raise educational standards at all levels', regretted the separation of children into different types of secondary schools.

For the next decade or so most local authorities stumbled, enthused, muddled and reorganised their secondary schools into a comprehensive form. Some resisted outright and a few, Kingston upon Thames for example, remained in their pre-1965 form more than 20 years after the Crosland circular. The focus of change was organisational arrangements, in the sanguine belief that if the framework of the school was altered then the processes of education which it enshrined would also alter to support a strong definition of equality of opportunity.

The evidence to date on the relative success of this organisational change in many schools in England and Wales is ambiguous. Maughan and Rutter (1987) report on an extension of *Fifteen Thousand Hours* where the opportunity was taken of the existence of the original 1970 data set to follow the progress of some of the pupils throughout their secondary education in either comprehensive or grammar schools. They have the examination results of these pupils at 16 and are able 'to compare the progress of pupils of similar ability and background in the two school sectors' (1987, p 56).

Although the pupils chosen, 79 from the grammar schools and 81 from the non-selective, had broadly similar attainments when they were aged ten, those who went to the grammar schools scored slightly higher than those who went to comprehensives. The grammar school pupils had a mean reading score of 11.2 when they were aged ten and the comprehensive pupils 10.7. The mean non-verbal IQ scores were 107.1 and 104.6 respectively. The outcomes, for example the number gaining five or more 'O' level equivalent passes, were much in favour of those attending grammar school, with 48.7 per cent gaining five plus 'O' level equivalents as against 14.7 per cent in the non-selective schools. One is not comparing like with like, however, and the grammar schools had a slightly more advantaged intake, less ambiguity as to the goals of the school and had not suffered the upset of reorganisation.

Other comparisons of the two systems, by Reynolds and Sullivan (1987), Sutherland and Gallagher (1987), and by Steedman (1983), are inconclusive on the grounds that they are not comparing like with like but the outcomes of a well established and resourced system with one still grappling with its identity and purpose.

An important series of research projects that does allow some judgment to be made between selective and non-selective schools in the comprehensive system has been undertaken at the Centre for Educational Sociology at Edinburgh University. The results give some support to the advocates of comprehensive secondary schooling that the system will reduce class inequalities and lead to an improvement in overall educational achievement.

This research (McPherson and Willms, 1988), draws upon surveys of Scottish school leavers. On three occasions, 1976, 1980 and 1984, data were gathered from a random sample of young people who left school in those years. The first cohort experienced the formation of comprehensive schools in Scotland, the second their early development and the third had, by and large, attended schools in a settled comprehensive system. McPherson and Willms conclude: 'Since the mid-1970s, the reorganisation that was initiated in 1965 has contributed to a rise in examination attainment and to a fall in the effect on attainment of social class'.

Over the eight years of the project the reduction in inequality between different socio-economic groups was consequent upon an improvement in scores attained at the bottom end of the distribution and not the levelling down of those at the top. McPherson and Willms assert that 'comprehensive reorganisation was a precondition to the translation into educational gains of the potential for educational improvement of other changes, economic, social and educational, that have occurred since the mid 1960s'.

The contribution of the comprehensive system to the improvement in attainment measured in terms of performance in the examinations for the Scottish Certificate of Education (SCE) at 16, 17 and 18, comes as a result of several factors. These include the abolition of selection at 12 years (the age of transfer from primary to secondary in Scotland) which gave all pupils formal access to certificate courses, and the raising of the school leaving age to 16, which prevented pupils leaving school before the stage of first public examinations.

The research evidence also suggests that the pupil of average socio-economic status tends to higher achievement in 'uncreamed schools', that is schools where high ability pupils are not sent to selective schools, and where the school has had the opportunity to establish itself. This latter finding is in accord with the view that within school factors – that mélange of characteristics embedded with concepts like 'school ethos' and 'climate' – are important in contributing to outcomes.

It is of interest to note that even Maughan and Rutter report one non-selective school with a low ability intake whose pupils' achievement is broadly comparable with the grammar school averages. They continue:

This school was the one with the most positive process score in our earlier study: it achieved good results for all its pupils despite a relatively poor balance in its intakes, and this seemed to reflect a very positive and cohesive ethos, supportive of academic attainment for all children, combined with a clear concern for their other needs. (1987, p 64–5)

The move towards a comprehensive system was one in which it was hoped artificial organisational barriers to the development of all pupils would be removed. The poor would at least have a common school with the advantaged in society, enjoy a common programme and though this in itself did not mark equality of outcomes it did secure equality of access. As the reorganised schools began to settle and establish themselves it began to become apparent that the curriculum, the vehicle for educational progress, needed to be reorganised also.

Too often the curriculum of the comprehensive school was that of the grammar, high status academic subjects were on offer to the academically able child and the rest suffered a watered down version of 'studies': European for those judged not capable of sustaining a foreign language, classical for those not taking Latin and Greek, social for the non-geographers and historians, and rural for those not taking 'proper' science.

The curriculum in secondary schools also began to take a predictable shape, mathematics, English, RE and PE for all plus a 'choice' from six option columns. As Cicourel and Kitsuse demonstrated many years ago (1963), the choice was in fact more illusory than real. In their study at Lakeshore High School in the USA they showed that the actual performance of students was interpreted by the school staff in terms of the expectations held for a particular student.

Thus two students could attain the same marks, but the way in which the marks were interpreted depended on the perception held for each student. Those perceived to be 'university material' were directed to high status choices, academic subjects, and those not seen as having the potential for higher education, despite having the same raw marks, were encouraged to opt for a more 'realistic' course.

One of the ways in which schools reorganised as comprehensive began to change the curriculum so that it would promote the struggle for equality of outcomes is the development of modular patterns (Moon, 1988, Warwick, 1987). These take the curriculum and re-present it in 'bite-sized pieces', usually in courses of between 20 and 30 hours, which may be put together for an award like GCSE or which can be taken as free-standing units.

As Moon points out, one of the major advantages of organising the curriculum in a modular framework is that it can avoid stereotyping. Each module has a set of learning outcomes and encompasses a span of time that is meaningful to a 13 to 14 year old. Girls can be encouraged to take modules in technology without feeling they are committing themselves to two years' or more work; low achieving pupils can take a range of modules without suffering the indignity of following a programme that marks them out as 'different'. Greater coherence can be effected in the curriculum through a clear understanding of what is intended and how students may demonstrate what they know, understand and can do. This is not the place to discuss in full the nature of the modular approaches nor to detail the achievements of those schools in the forefront of this curriculum initiative.

Will the success that has been developed in these areas be supported or impeded by the 1988 Education Reform Act? The Act represents a particular view both of the nature of learning and schools as organisations. Learning is seen primarily as the acquisition of knowledge rather than the development of understanding. Consequently the curriculum is divided into 'base', 'core' and 'foundation' units of RE, mathematics, English and science, together with history, geography, technology, music, art and physical education and, for secondary aged pupils, a modern foreign language 'specified in an order of the Secretary of State' (clause 3).

The list is that proposed by Robert Morant for the Board of Education in 1904, save that 'drawing' is now art, 'singing' now labelled music and what was 'manual instruction' (for boys) and 'domestic subjects' (for girls) now appears as technology. This content has to be packaged to identify the 'knowledge, skills and understanding which pupils of different abilities and maturities' are to attain at ages seven, 11, 14 and 16; that is the objectives, means and evaluation of each.

The working group on mathematics deliberated whether there was a risk that the existence of national targets would inhibit the development of the low achieving child. The conclusion reached was 'probably not' and, having affirmed a principle that 'as far as possible children should remain within the mainstream framework of attainment targets and programmes of study' (1988, para 10.31), acknowledges that much will rest with the teacher's skill in developing appropriate pedagogical styles and, as ever, that more research is needed.

The Mathematics Working Group has proposed 15 broad attainment targets in mathematics and the science group 22 for secondary pupils and 17 for primary with a further four for primary technology. When the full set of proposals is available there could be a total of 150/200 attainment targets with the authority of law behind them.

The danger, as ever, is that of trivialisation of the curriculum as received by pupils. In the anxiety to ensure that a legally enforceable 'balanced and broadly based curriculum' is delivered at the level of specificity indicated in the reports of the early working parties lies the danger that the mere acquisition of facts will prevent the growth of understanding. In the urge to achieve coverage those who find little comfort in academic work may be given an arid diet of superficiality which neither 'promotes' their 'spiritual, moral, cultural development' nor 'prepares' them for the opportunities, responsibilities and experiences of adult life.

It may have been preferable to issue the national curriculum documents as guidelines, templates of good practice against which schools could evaluate their extant curriculum rather than requirements that have to be met. It is essential, as HMI argued in 1983, 'that all pupils should be guaranteed a curriculum of distinctive breadth and depth to which they should be entitled irrespective of the type of school they attended or their level of ability'. In the headlong rush to articulate what an 'entitlement curriculum' ought to be we could destroy the essential quality of all curricula, the engagement in a dialogue by teacher and learner, a dialogue whose ends are diverse, whose pathways various but whose aim is constant – the enhancement of the quality of understanding.

The curriculum that is enshrined within the Education Act seems more to serve the interests of the Department of Education and Science to effect greater control and accountability within the system than to promote the concerns of the disadvantaged and dispossessed. A more serious criticism is that the Act undermines the organisational framework within which the comprehensive secondary system was set. Section 52 allows for the creation of grant-maintained schools and Section 105 for the creation of city technology colleges (CTCs); the ending of planned admission limits and the devolution of financial management onto secondary and larger primary schools increases organisational diversity.

The question can be fairly put as to who benefits from this diversity. It is the intention of the Secretary of State that a school that opts out of local authority control will not be allowed to change its character, similarly, a CTC must provide education for pupils of different abilities drawn mainly from the area in which the school is situated (clause 105 subsection 2).

This promotion of diversity, defence of the consumer, assumes a perfect bureaucratic world where individuals act rationally, where supply meets demand and where the equilibrium of the market is attained. In reality, the increased diversity of schools will exacerbate the differences between them, creating a pool of 'residual schools' unpopular with ambitious parents and the refuge of those too preoccupied with their own difficulties to ponder much over the quality of education provided for their children. A system that forces some into the worst schools is hardly one that meets the canons of social justice with which we began this article.

It is naïve to assume that the existence of city technology colleges or grant maintained schools will act as a stimulus to the rest. As schools increase in their heterogeneity, those that serve areas where there is a concentration of disadvantage will watch helpless as the more motivated, more able, more ambitious children move to the favoured schools, leaving them to cope with the rest, and worse, suffer the ignominy of having their results on national tests published, protected only by a general statement from the local authority, indicating 'the nature of socio-economic and other influences which are known to affect schools' (Task Group on Assessment and Testing, para 134).

The sadness of what is in effect the breakup of the comprehensive system is that it occurs at the point when the system was reaching a confidence and maturity which demonstrated that it could meet the demands of the late twentieth century. In 1965 members of parliament regretted that the separation of children into different types of secondary schools impeded the raising of standards. The Education Reform Act of 1988 in promoting that separation will undoubtedly contribute to the raising of educational standards for some. As ever these will be the children from advantaged homes, middle class and what was once patronisingly known as 'the respectable working classes'. The children of the poor, from ethnic minority groups, one parent families and those bearing the costs of industrial decline and renewal have little to gain from this legislation. The sadness is the greater as the Act comes at a time when the accumulated wisdom from attempts to improve schools was establishing a consensus on how schools might more effectively meet the needs of all pupils. The creation of an effective school depends not on the application of some well-honed formulae nor on the opportunities provided by legislation. Both formulae and legislation may influence the conditions within which members of the professional community seek to enhance the effectiveness of their schools. In the end what is important is the quality of the teaching profession: schools depend on the commitment of individual teachers often working alone and without the possibility of close supervision. This has been recognised in the rhetoric of government:

> The full force of teachers' professionalism will need to be put behind the national curriculum and assessment if both are to be beneficial to pupil and other 'customers' of the education service.
>
> (*The National Curriculum: A Consultation Document*, para 67)

A profession of high morale and self confidence that has earned the esteem of those its serves, primarily parents and their children, will create schools that are effective. The task is on-going; just as education ought not to have an end, in the sense that an individual could claim to be 'fully educated', so schools are in the process of becoming effective. Signposts are available, what is now needed are the stories of those who follow their direction, and accounts of their perception of the terrain covered and problems encountered. The journey is of utmost importance as it is about the enhancement of excellence in what we provide for our children. In serving the interest of some rather than all, the 1988 Education Reform Act may come to be judged as an impediment to the creation of that equality of outcomes so long seen as an essential right of all citizens.

3 Pre-school age children with special educational needs

Sheila Wolfendale

Introduction

For this chapter the author has drawn on some of the substance contained in a paper published in *Children and Society* (Wolfendale 1987). The particular relevance of that paper is that it provides a multi-disciplinary perspective on special needs and the under-fives, and a major theme pervading the NARE conference talk was the need to evolve policies of collective responsibility in the development of services to meet special needs of children under five, given the context that pre-school education is not statutory.

Educationists working with under-fives and in nursery settings find themselves regularly in contact with other professionals from health, social services, voluntary agencies. This chapter aims to reflect the reality of interdisciplinary contacts while maintaining that the pivot for the development of early learning opportunities for all children is educational and that, therefore, the 'lead department' in local authorities as far as under-fives (including of course special needs) is, or ought legitimately to be, education. The chapter concludes by considering the implications of the Education Reform Act for under-fives and special educational needs.

The Continuing Debate

All under-fives workers are well acquainted with the debates and controversies surrounding pre-school provision in the UK. These, unresolved, provided a backdrop to the themes of the talk. We are familiar with these continuing major issues:

- the relative contribution of home as a determinant of learning as against nursery (Tizard and Hughes 1984, Davie *et al* 1984)
- the necessity for and quality of child minding (Moss 1987)

- lack of unified services and the consequent need for service co-ordination (Bradley 1982)
- what are 'best buys' in and effects of pre-school provision (Osborn and Milbank 1987, Jowett and Sylva 1986)
- effects of day care (Calder in New and David 1985, Tizard 1986)
- consequences of pre-school intervention (Woodhead 1985)
- continuity between pre-school and school (Cleave and Jowett 1982)
- the unevenness and disparity of provision (Gilkes 1987)
- incompatibility between and confusion of aims and criteria for pre-school experience between establishments funded by different agencies
- underfunding for pre-school, nationally and locally.

Irrespective of differing views and attitudes towards any one or more of these issues, we would nevertheless acknowledge a number of overriding principles that are rooted within a humanitarian philosophy which concerns protection of children's rights; granting of equal opportunities; and acknowledging the universality of children's needs in relation to the individuality of their needs.

Professionals engaged in pre-school and early childhood education are likely to come from separate traditions and may have different perceptions as well as common goals. Some will have come through mainstream nursery experience with its honourable history of innovation; others by way of special/remedial education routes. How these experiences can be reconciled in order to provide equality of opportunity to all under-fives is a fundamental theme which is reflected in this article.

Reconciling traditions

Consideration of the growth of provision, in historical terms, reveals some commonality of principle, an inter-connectedness which will be exemplified here. The point is that this kind of overview is rarely possible by busy practitioners on the ground, working in parallel grooves but seldom in tandem, in social services, education, voluntary nurseries, playgroups, special needs assessment centres, units, nurseries. Thus a nursery nurse will confess to being ignorant and fearful of a certain handicap while demonstrating competence and confidence in dealing with a child who has tantrums or is language-delayed. Similarly, teachers who have specialised in the education of children with disabilities can feel daunted at the prospect of handling and coping with young children. By tracing these separately evolving traditions chronologically we can discern their major messages.

Early childhood education

The pioneers of early education, while differing from each other in methods and materials, essentially took what has come to be known as a 'child-centred' approach, wherein it was paramount to base education on a child's 'nature and needs' rather than on some preconceived theory. In their writing, Froebel, Pestalozzi, Edgeworth, the Macmillans and Susan Isaacs reiterate basic principles for effective learning, all of which involve the child as an active learner not just as a passive receptacle (Curtis 1986, Ch. 2).

Landmarks in the development of special education in Britain

The past two centuries have seen the gradual evolution of separate educational establishments catering from their time of inception for identifiable disabilities and categories of handicap (Warnock Report 1978). The original justification for separate education, while untenable, even anachronistic nowadays, provided for the education and protection of countless specially vulnerable children, and gave many teachers opportunities to develop understanding and expertise in an area of handicap and special educational provision. We are therefore the inheritors of this tradition whereby expertise, being concentrated, has accrued to the point now where technology allied with pedagogy can provide quite powerfully for children in need, in whatever their setting.

Compensatory education for 'disadvantaged' children

This 'tradition' is much more recent, yet the ideas have been pervasive: that organised, structured opportunities for 'disadvantaged' children in their early years can combat or offset the allegedly depriving effects of a poor (and therefore, by definition, unstimulating!) home. There are whole bibliographies on the American experience of Head Start, Follow-through, and the British initiatives of the EPA. These initiatives have been characterised by curriculum innovation, home–school links, parents as educators, and although results are equivocal (interpretation depends upon criteria, on assessment and evaluation measures, etc), much has been learnt about curriculum design and evaluation. A number of powerful techniques were tried out, such as behavioural approaches to learning and other coherent learning programmes. Their legacy is apparent today, such as the application of High/Scope in the UK (VOLCUF/High Scope).

Common to each tradition is the principle of meeting children's learning and other needs, even though differing emphases are evident. A final example of this inter-linking of ideology is the work of Maria Montessori. She began working with 'handicapped' children and concluded that the methods which she had found most successful in dealing with feeble-minded children would be quite applicable to those who were normal and that ordinary schools needed the sort of transformation she had accomplished at her own 'special' school. Her approach, in common with other innovators, was to get the very best from each and every child, using methods she had devised to achieve this goal.

The bedrock aspirations these educators have had in common, as far as early childhood educational opportunities are concerned, are expressed in a recently-published book which is based on contemporary research and which shows the continuing aspiration for a comprehensive preschool service:

> . . . our assertion is that adequate preschool provision can improve the quality of life of young children and their families; this conviction is given further support by the evidence we have presented in this book that pre-school education will in most circumstances aid the child's development, increase his educational potential and in the long run his overall performance. Thus investment in preschool provision and the improved quality of life it bestows may pay good dividends in the shape of calculable beneficial effects on the child's educational attainments five years hence and perhaps into the longer future.
>
> (Osborn and Milbank 1987, p 242)

Bringing special needs into pre-school services and developing pre-school services to meet special needs

The effects of reports and legislation

The Warnock Report (1978) put under-fives high on the educational agenda and set out a blueprint for assessment of needs; notification by one statutory service to others (in particular an obligation on DHAs to notify to LEAs, cf 1981 Education Act, Section 10); liaison between services and with parents; key personnel (e.g. its recommendations for 'named person').

Initiatives in under-fives and special needs in recent years have stemmed in part from these recommendations, some of which, of course, formed the basis of the 1981 Education Act. Circular 1/83 accompanying the Act devotes a section to under-fives and reiterates a commitment to integrating children with 'significant learning difficulties' or disabilities into mainstream pre-school provision (p 13). This presupposes co-operation between services (p 15), yet workers in all but a handful of local authorities could attest to resources and personnel not being made available to effect the good working links advocated in official reports.

Despite restrictions of finance and lack of initial endorsement often from higher echelons of management, the amount of innovative work in under-fives and special needs areas has been significant. Some of it has been established 'good practice' for several years, such as Portage, singled out for mention in the Warnock Report. Other work is still recent enough to warrant being described at present as 'emerging good practice'.

'Bringing the best together' – a summary of some of the initiatives

A number of developments are singled out for brief reference. For knowledgeable readers this part can serve as a reminder; for those who wish to read further key references are given.

Parental and family involvement

Developments of the last few years within mainstream nursery settings as well as within 'special needs' contexts demonstrate a commitment to dealing with the whole child, taking into account major influences on his/her life and progress. A key tenet is that of 'parents as educators' (Topping 1986) within broader ecological perspectives (Apter 1982, Wolfendale 1987a). A whole range of initiatives in pre-school settings has been described (Smith 1981, Tizard *et al* 1981, Raven 1980, Wolfendale 1983) with attempts made by these writers and others to put observed practice into theoretical and conceptual frameworks.

In a DHSS-funded, National Children's Bureau-based study, Gillian Pugh and Erica De'Ath surveyed pre-school schemes and centres in which parental/family participation was an integral feature. Materials have been developed from this study and two books describe 12 pre-school schemes and centres which are attempting to develop relationships between parents and workers (Pugh *et al* 1987).

One of the most advanced initiatives in the area of pre-school and special needs is Portage which has spread dramatically throughout the UK in the past 12 years. Portage as a comprehensive teaching/learning programme involves 'parents as partners' and is therefore a prime example of 'equivalent expertise' (Wolfendale 1983) wherein professionals and parents work together, sharing and pooling their experience and skills on behalf of the child.

The classic Portage model extends to the organisation and management of the programme at all levels and stages of operation. It provides a convincing demonstration of inter- and multi-disciplinary co-operation as well as effective parental involvement, thus giving evidence that, given a number of identifiable requisites, personnel from different disciplines can work together productively. There are now a number of books and articles on Portage – the National Foundation for Educational Research (NFER) publishes Portage books and materials.

The area of involving parents in assessment of the development and progress of their young children is a growing one. A number of instruments have been developed (Wolfendale 1988) including *All About Me*, a parent-completed pre-school schedule (Wolfendale 1987b).

Working for parents

This section describes the growth of self-help parents' groups and services for parents developed by several voluntary associations.

The 1981 Education Act (implemented 1 April 1983) has provided a powerful spur to the formation of such groups and services. While the Act reiterates a commitment to parental involvement (Sandow, Stafford and Stafford 1987) nevertheless many parents have felt excluded from decision-making processes and have formed alliances to challenge local authorities and to press for change.

Examples include the Parents' Campaign for Integrated Education in London; the Campaign for Choice in Special Education, also based in the Inner London

Education Authority; LINC in Rugby. In some of these, initial confrontation is now leading to constructive dialogue with local authority officials. The national umbrella organisation for these local and regional groups is 81 ACTION which was formed during 1986, has an agreed set of aims and publishes a newsletter. The groups exist for the whole age range, from pre-school upwards.

A number of voluntary associations have become committed to the idea of 'empowering' parents to speak for and represent themselves, and see their role as providing training, support and an expert voice as and when required.

Curriculum innovation
The question of the appropriateness of nursery curricula in particular and other pre-school opportunities in general has been a matter for debate for a number of years (Tizard 1974). Descriptive studies of pre-school education (Parry and Archer 1974, Gilkes 1987) have illuminated the debate to some extent and aims and objectives approaches to curriculum design can serve as pragmatic guidelines in the absence of a consensus about short and longer term criteria for early childhood education. Research and development into compensatory educational programmes, referred to earlier, have focused much attention on the issues without necessarily resolving them.

A major stumbling-block to consensus is the fact that 'curriculum' is an educational term, deployed by educationists. But there are anomalies within education, too. In 61 education nurseries catering for children with special needs surveyed by the Department of Education and Science (1983) less than one-third were working to a statement of intent about the curriculum.

Growth in provision for pre-school children with special needs
A number of significant developments were anticipated and advocated in two books published before the implementation of the 1981 Education Act. Chazan *et al* (1980) and Chazan and Laing (1982) herald growth in 'special' provision, increased parental involvement, the need for team work, planned intervention programmes, the advent of specialist support staff. That these developments have implications for initial and inservice training of staff is addressed by Chazan *et al*. The Warnock Report has remained influential in staking out certain philosophical ground rules, to which an increasing number of people are drawn, namely, integration.

Although few local authorities have written special needs policies and written commitment to integration, nevertheless 'on the ground' practitioners test out its viability by placing pre-schoolers with assessed special needs in education and social service nurseries, and in playgroups. The obligation upon LEAs to meet a child's special educational needs as set out in his/her statement of needs has led to an increase in specialist staff, visiting, or based in these centres and working with and supporting regular staff. Some teachers have a liaison brief that brings them into contact with other services and parents.

Despite these encouraging developments (see Potts 1987 for a brief overview) most of the aspirations of the Warnock committee in recommending the under-fives as a priority area remain unfulfilled, and there is a dearth of data on the effectiveness of integrating children with special educational needs in the pre-school years (McGlynn and Phillips 1987). The Select Committee (1987) examining the working of the 1981 Education Act has this to say about the under-fives and special educational needs:

> . . . the Act has facilitated progress and there has been some encouragement of home teaching programmes through educational support grants. However, the Department (of Education and Science) had little information about the working of the Act in this phase of education and offered no information about the numbers of children who may be receiving special education under the age of five nor of the number of children who might be the subject of statements below school age. In view of the evidence of the importance of early identification and intervention the Committee believes that a study by the Department in collaboration with LEAs and the DHSS of the Act's procedures in the preschool period is now necessary. (p xvi, para 40)

Implications of emerging practice for collective responsibility

There is evidence that policy for children with special educational needs under five varies between and among statutory services and local authorities. In the few examples of written policies on special needs and/or integration, the under-fives may be tacked on, or tagged alongside a general commitment to all children with special needs. Less tenable even than that situation are those in which no policy exists and well-intentioned initiatives such as those described above or smoothly functioning inter-disciplinary networks succeed because of personnel rather than the execution of a statement of intent.

It may be apposite to consider that a corporate stand on under-fives and special needs is now a moral imperative and that we should take seriously the clarion calls of Warnock and the Select Committee, not only because we owe it to children and their families, but also because

- good practice must not go to waste without the proper commitment and backing
- there is a danger of poorly utilising available resources due to lack of forward planning and co-ordination between services.

A small clutch of local authorities have evolved coherent and articulated policies for under-fives that automatically include special needs, as an integral part of a shared philosophy. For example, the written policy of one large northern metropolitan area stated 'It is important to protect children's rights'. The following is an extract from a shire county area development plan:

> Ideally there would be no institutional separation of children and families with special needs. Universal services would be available with a level of resourcing that would permit them to give appropriate support to individuals within a common overall structure. Specialist treatment bases might continue to exist where intensive work could be done on particular problems, but their aim would be to ensure that children could take advantage of mainstream services.

Collective responsibility; sharing responsibility; and accountability

A warning note is sounded in the Fish Report (on special education in the Inner London Education Authority 1985) for local authorities, voluntary associations and parents' groups to move towards stated, written policies on an integrated nursery and pre-school service:

> We found that the large range of professionals involved in provision and services for young children with special educational needs were often confused about how such needs could be predicted and what assessment procedures should be used. (p 46)

Collective responsibility operating within broader social and political contexts

Equal opportunities and children's rights are the bedrock principles of unified pre-school services. Special needs, disability and handicap are perceived to be part of a list of rights for so-called minority groups.

Yet the under-fives area has tended to be somewhat ignored when anti-racist, anti-sexist policies are developed. The Swann Report (1985, p 393) devotes half a page (out of 800 pages) to this age group and recommends extension of nursery facilities for ethnic minority children and greater numbers of staff from the ethnic minorities. Nothing is said to make it clear that 'education for all' extends to under-fives. It does, and Nicole Celestin's booklet (1986) shows how it can and should be applicable.

The political ramifications of resourcing and decision-making likewise cannot be ignored. Under-fives workers cannot afford to be concerned solely with so-called 'professional' issues. They need to stay vigilant against: erosion of pre-school provision; the disadvantaging (removal of rights) of women who are mothers; lack of funding of pre-school and special needs services; continued fragmentation of services. Fighting against threats to young children's rights to early childhood opportunities could be seen as an expression of legitimate collective responsibility.

Prospects for special educational needs in the early years

Thus far, the chapter has aimed to provide a review of developments, to identify emerging as well as established practice, and to demonstrate inter-connectedness of service provision. A number of principles, notably that of collective responsibility, have been set out as signposts for the continuing evaluation of services for the under-fives. But what of immediate realities and possible action for the present back in the workplace? There are a number of issues that already have and will continue to have direct bearing on day to day practice of which the major one will be the reverberating effects upon pre-school education of the Education Reform Act 1988.

The closing part of this chapter will raise a number of these issues with a view to alerting us all to the realities against which aspirations have to be aligned, if not reconciled.

Issues of daily practice: the educational perspective

While the government of the day is committed in principle and in law to extension of rights and access to education and other services for under-fives with special needs, the provision lags behind. In lieu of an overarching policy of universal nursery education, within which special needs would have an acknowledged place, we have the hotchpotch of provision with which practitioners are only too familiar, and which mostly reflects local and regional idiosyncrasies rather than a planned and coherent structure based on policy. Translation of policy into practice would mean acting upon specifics, such as the recommendations made in the recently-issued NUT *Guidelines on Negotiating for Special Needs* (1988):

> The early assessment of under-fives, home visiting, Portage schemes and nursery provision should be a priority time for the assessment process and additional support for the care of very young children with special needs attending nursery classes. (p 7)

Perhaps we can discern positive moves in respect of the government's intentions towards under-fives generally by some developments during 1988, as follows.

The setting up of the Select Committee to look at the whole under-fives area
A great deal of evidence has been given by all the associations concerned, and the Select Committee report was published in January 1989.

There was speculation about how seriously the committee would heed and take account of the overwhelming consensus that the early years are the seedcorn of the future, and that, commensurately, investment of the proper magnitude would have to be made to reflect that, and, also, to bring the UK in line with a number of other European countries, as far as provision is concerned (Moss 1988). One way of providing an integrated service, and one which is advocated by the National Association of Inspectors and Advisers (expressed in the NAIEA evidence to the Select Committee) is to develop combined centres, which offer education and day care. HMI sees mileage in this model, too (DES 1988).

Representation on special needs was also made to the Select Committee, by teachers' associations and others, making the point that early identification of delay difficulties is facilitated when the provisions and structures are in place. It is to be hoped that the evidence provided by Margaret Clark (1988) will be seen to be a vital concomitant to the evidence considered by the Select Committee.

Inclusion of pre-school in the grant-related in-service training programme (GRIST) for 1988–89

For the first time, monies are earmarked for training in the teaching of four-year-old children in primary classes, the specific purpose being to update and improve the knowledge and understanding of teachers and non-specialist advisers with responsibility for young children.

One of the liveliest issues of contemporary education is that of four year olds in school. Concern was expressed to the Under Fives Select Committee from all quarters about the inappropriateness of curricula and care for young children who are in effect 'pre-school' but not, in the main, receiving appropriate pre-school learning experiences, and who sometimes are in classes with children up to seven years of age.

There is evidence of sensitivity to the issues at local planning level and empirical evidence as to the differential needs of four year olds in primary schools (NFER/SCDC 1987), so the government is in no doubt about the seriousness of a situation which will be aggravated by the advent of the Education Reform Act.

The GRIST funding represents a timely response to addressing these issues, although a cautionary note has to be sounded – if the curriculum is not considered satisfactory for four years olds in general, what of its relevance for four year olds with special needs? Some may already be placed, with a statement of needs which 'protects' via the additional provision of a special programme, extra specialist teaching and/or welfare assistance.

There will be other four year olds, however, whose needs will go undetected or unmet by virtue of numbers, inadequate teacher recognition, and a myriad of other 'pre-referral' features of learning difficulty which accrue over time, even in infant school (Wolfendale and Bryans 1980). This is a critical problem for teachers, advisory teachers, advisers and educational psychologists to resolve.

Education Reform Act 1988 (ERA)

The ERA became law on 29 July 1988, though each of its many provisions will come into force at different times over the next few years. It is beyond the scope of this chapter to grapple with the full implications of the whole ERA for pre-school education, particularly with regard to 'opting out', financial delegation, especially as, at the time of writing, vesting days for each of these major elements have yet to be announced, and discussion would be speculative.

In the shorter term, it is possible to raise several issues that are of concern to those working with pre-school and special needs.

1 Parents and professionals will welcome the amendment to the 1981 Education Act which comes into force at once, to the effect that parents have the right of appeal where statements have been rewritten for any reason and must be informed in writing of this right.

2 LEAs will have the right (though not the duty) to employ such 'outside' specialists as speech therapists. This will be an important and helpful clarification of what has recently been a vexed issue, and will undoubtedly have a bearing on pre-school provision.

3 The national curriculum:
There are two relevant aspects to consider.

a For children in primary and secondary schools, the issue has been how to make the national curriculum sufficiently flexible to accommodate children with special educational needs, while safeguarding their rights not to be excluded from mainstream education. The legislation now allows for the temporary or permanent modification of statements (and in the case of non-statemented special needs pupils, to make temporary exceptions). Thus a pupil may be exempted from the national curriculum in the short or longer term; what exactly he or she will then 'receive' (i.e. the relationship of an individualised curriculum to the national curriculum) is of course a crucial issue.

b Implications of the national curriculum 'downwards' to four year olds in primary schools (see 'Issues of daily practice' above) as well as a possible consequential 'knock-on' effect on the education of three to five year olds in nursery schools and classes. There is a legitimate fear of 'straitjacketing' the nursery/early years curriculum to fit what some see as the constraints of a national curriculum and the requirements of the testing programme.

4 The testing arrangements: The national curriculum will be intimately connected to the assessment and testing schedule at years seven, 11, 14 and 16 and the same concerns expressed in 3 a and b apply. The programmes of study will apply from five years of age, likewise the attainment targets, although not in operation formally until the age of seven years, will of course be drawn from the study programmes in the first two years of statutory schooling.

The concept of 'teaching by objectives', and regular progress monitoring, can be regarded as offering a system whereby no child slips through the net. But the concern, in respect of the early years, is that we have never achieved consensus over what an appropriate early years curriculum should be;

besides which, provision is so varied nationally that some children are evidently disadvantaged from an early age.

In his evidence to the Select Committee on Under-Fives, the Secretary of State for Education, Kenneth Baker, said he appreciated the different starting points (into education) and said that schools could publish in their results a clear indication of the starting age of children in order to indicate those who are disadvantaged (unpublished evidence). This suggestion begs many issues.

Are these various 'reality indices' positive and constructive in sum for pre-school children with special educational needs? If we go only by the legislation and other portents, then the outlook is overcast at present and we are not sure how it will clear; if commitment and current initiatives are anything to go by, then the prospects are brighter.

4 Support for special needs in the primary school

Peter Smith

I will attempt to address this theme in the context of the current situation and to make suggestions about the future of support for special needs in the primary school based on experience of good practice in the past and present.

It is not surprising that many professionals involved in education are rather dispirited and disillusioned at this time. The rate of change and the lack of sincere consultation have led to an air of defeatism and concern which is frequently summed up in the analogy that they (the government) keep moving the goalposts.

Although there has been a recent escalation in the introduction of legislation we are all aware that the educational climate has gradually changed ever since former Prime Minister Jim Callaghan's historic speech at Ruskin College in 1976 when he instituted the Great Debate. Readers of this paper will need no reminding of the way in which the important recommendations of the Warnock committee were encapsulated in the 1981 Act but accompanied by a clear negative statement: 'There will be no additional funds'. Frankly, I find it amazing that so much progress has already been made in support of special needs and integration into normal schools without resources from central government. Following realistic appraisal of the current situation and the provisions of the GERBIL, I am convinced that we must respond to the government legislation. Of course we must, but at the same time we must endeavour to retain the practices and methods we know are right for our children.

Do we need to be reminded of the current legislation? Probably not, but I will make brief reference to what I sometimes think of as 'The Odds'. There are two items already with us that are symptomatic of the reduced trust and respect in which some ministers hold teachers. These are the pay and conditions which were imposed following the long spell of industrial action. As well as removing the salary negotiating machinery, they introduced the concept of GRIST days and the 1265 hours. As we all know, the 1265 hours represent a reduction of hours worked by most teachers. I think we must recognise that the five GRIST days have proved to be very useful and much appreciated by all. Those responsible must ensure, however, that the quality of programmes on those days remains high or disillusionment will come when the novelty goes.

The other new GERBIL clauses concern the national curriculum, age-related tests, local financial management, opting out, city technical colleges, open enrolment and open records. Some of these are very political and outside my brief, but there are those on which I want to comment.

The national curriculum will clarify the entitlement of every pupil and will therefore be helpful for those with concern for children with special needs. Although there is in effect already a common basic curriculum in our primary schools it will help to have an agreed statement. Personally, I am much encouraged that in response to pressure the Bill was amended to make it flexible enough to accommodate pupils' special educational needs. The government also accepted a Lords' amendment specifying special needs as a factor that may be taken into account in the resource allocation formula.

Open records should lead to better record keeping in the primary sector and will give further support to the general practice of consulting parents early about learning or behavioural problems.

The third provision I want to discuss is that of age-related testing. I was heartened to note that a new clause was inserted during the Bill's progress through Parliament, stipulating that the results of a pupil's assessment should be made available only to the pupil's parents, the governors or the LEA. This is better news, but I suggest that the utmost vigilance will still be needed by teachers and associations such as NARE and UKRA to ensure that assessment and testing are not allowed to exercise a deleterious effect on schools. Few teachers will disagree with the need for diagnostic testing of individuals or even with sensible assessment for monitoring of standards. Dangers exist, however, that tests could both dominate and limit the curriculum as well as reinforcing a sense of failure for children with special needs.

A recent pronouncement by a former Education Minister serves to remind us of the kind of thinking we must guard against. The ex-minister proposed that action should be taken against parents of disruptive five year olds who are unable to pass a test of 20 items. The test items range from the ability to dress themselves, to the ability to count from one to five and to recognise their own names in print. If this attitude is allowed to prevail there will be no room for different rates of development in our children. We now know too much about child development to allow this kind of testing to be inflicted on our schools, so we must co-operate in developing and using appropriate tests while, at the same time, resisting inappropriate proposals.

Having established my personal feelings about the current political situation and the changes resulting from the GERBIL, it is now necessary to pay attention to present practice with regard to special needs in the primary school. Perhaps the starting point for this discussion should be a historical one.

When I started teaching a junior class in 1947 in a London County Council school there was no provision at all. The school was a JMI school with over 400 pupils in ten classes, ten teachers plus a head teacher, a part-time secretary and a milk lady who came into school for one and a half hours a day to distribute milk. With over 40 in each class and no supernumary staff, the children with special learning needs were thought of as being dull and backward.

They were offered the same curriculum as the rest of the unstreamed class, i.e. they were on course to fail the 11 plus. Any extra help they received was through the dedication of any class teacher who had enough energy left over from dealing with the demands of the class as a whole. They were also subjected to the same monthly attainment tests through which the headmaster monitored the effectiveness of his teachers. I remember a lad named Alfie who was in the junior school for three years. The monthly tests were designed with the demands of the scholarship exam in mind but Alfie, with his severe special needs, did not achieve a single mark in any test during the three years. The only expertise available in connection with special needs in the 1940s resided in the divisional educational psychologist and, as there were over 80 schools in division one of the LCC, we neither expected nor received much help from that source.

During the 1960s, class numbers dropped sharply and concern for children with learning difficulties began to increase. This was the era of opportunity classes. Children with considerable learning problems were removed from mainstream classes for a few months and taught by a specially appointed additional teacher. The opportunity class teachers I knew either had some extra training and/or some special quality or flair.

Unfortunately, neither their teacher colleagues nor the parents understood the teaching techniques utilised. They assumed that pupils, mostly boys, of course, who were failing on the school reading scheme simply needed more and more opportunity to slog away at the phonics and sight vocabulary while under tight supervision. They failed to realise that the excursions, the painting, the model making and the drama were all necessary to generate interest and to build relationships and confidence. This was an approach to literacy learning that is now recognised and valued as the language experience approach. Still, most of us were glad to be relieved of responsibility for our failing learners for a few months. Alongside the occasional opportunity classes in the 1960s came a little funding for extra staff. Part-time teachers could be found working in odd corners with small groups of children needing extra help. These teachers, usually female, were recruited in response to advertisements that usually stipulated needlework plus some remedial reading.

The 1970s saw the beginning of serious attempts to develop remedial services in local authorities. People were appointed to co-ordinate the work of remedial teachers in schools. In-service courses proliferated, resource centres were established, publishers began to produce materials and a whole range of diagnostic tests was made available. The word dyslexia became a familiar label even though it did not in itself provide miraculous remedies for learning difficulties. Many advisory teachers and others who at present hold leadership posts in special education needs support services were seconded during the 1970s and 1980s to take one-year full-time diploma courses at institutes of higher education.

During the 1980s we have witnessed further development of provision in special needs. The Warnock Report and the 1981 Act which followed have drawn attention to the special needs of 20 per cent of the population. Steady progress has been made in many authorities in integrating some of the statemented children (the two per cent) into mainstream primary schools. I am sure this is a trend we all applaud providing the necessary staffing and facilities are made available. The benefit to the children with special needs and also to the mainstream pupils is plain for all to see.

It would appear, however, that the needs of some statemented children are such that they continue to require special provision in special schools. There have been several imaginative schemes where special schools or units have been placed alongside mainstream schools. This allows for special needs children to continue to receive specialist medical and/or educational help while also enabling them to integrate with mainstream children at an appropriate level.

I have made this broad but brief review of the development of provision for special needs partly to remind us of how much improvement has been achieved and also as a background to the rest of the paper. I intend to concentrate on provision for the 18 per cent unstatemented pupils who remain in mainstream schools but who, as Warnock reminded us, have special needs. I want to pay particular attention to present practice and to what may perhaps happen in the years ahead.

While I was preparing this paper the *Times Educational Supplement* of 5 August 1988 published a comment on the HMI report on secondary education. In the section on special needs the report notes that in 45 per cent of schools pupils are withdrawn for group lessons concentrating on basic language and numeracy, while in the other 55 per cent of schools special needs teachers work alongside the subject teachers in the normal classroom setting. HMI also commented that in general 'too little attention is given to the diagnosis of need before attempting to meet it'. I quote from this report on secondary education because I find the debate about whether or not to withdraw pupils with special needs is one which occupies the minds of primary teachers as well.

The debate is an example of unnecessary polarisation. I do not believe that it has to be a question of either/or. Both strategies have their place and it should be for teachers to determine the balance appropriate to their situation and the needs of their pupils. Later in this paper I intend to outline the curriculum and teaching strategies I hope will be retained within the national curriculum.

As it is vital that all children have access to the rich curriculum and to the kind of experiences that involve pupils with purpose it must be desirable that, at times, the special needs teachers work alongside mainstream class teachers. At such times the special needs teacher will be mediating the tasks, helping the pupils to benefit from the experience and at the same time observing their performance. At other times it may be beneficial to withdraw children with special needs individually or in groups for concentrated attention on an aspect of learning which has been diagnosed as necessary.

The role of special educational needs support teachers has become more complex and clearly defined in recent years. The special educational needs support service (SENSS) that I know well now has a structured hierarchy to ensure that available staffing resources are distributed through the borough according to needs. They also provide advice and inservice training for the SENSS team and for mainstream teachers. Thus the role of SENSS teachers is increasingly an advisory one. In addition to working directly with pupils with special needs they advise mainstream teachers about programmes of work and they carry out detailed diagnostic assessment as necessary.

The interaction between SENSS teachers and class teachers as they work together with the class and as they exchange information is a great improvement on the situation which pertained in the days when remedial groups were withdrawn and then returned to class with a total absence of communication.

Although I have stressed the importance of all children having access to the full primary curriculum, it must be recognised that some children do need special provision, more time, and/or extra help if they are to profit from the opportunity. The importance of incremental learning in some aspects of the curriculum is now widely accepted.

> It is now recognised that the tasks and skills to be learned by children with severe learning difficulties have to be analysed precisely and that the setting of small, clearly defined incremental objectives for individual pupils is a necessary part of programme planning.
>
> (Warnock, para 11.57)

Or as Ainscow and Tweddle emphasise in their important book, *Preventing Classroom Failure:*

> An objective based approach to teaching children with severe learning difficulties is needed. First ascertain what the learner already knows and teach from that point.

The tenets expressed in these two quotations have greatly influenced attitudes and the context of in-service courses, giving rise to such approaches as the special needs action programme.

Both the above quotations refer to severe learning difficulties but of course severe is a term open to varying interpretations. The incremental approach is often appropriate for any child with considerable learning difficulties. It is perhaps fair to say that experience of the kind of thinking involved also results in more perceptive provision for those children whose learning difficulties are less pronounced.

At this point there is need for me to give some detail about the shape and nature of the primary curriculum to which all children should have access. I am convinced that current practice in the best of our primary schools is second to none and I know this view is also held by educators in other parts of the world. This is not to suggest that our primary schools are perfect; perfection in something as complex and variable as education would be very hard to achieve. My belief is that our good practice has evolved over a period of more than 50 years and that it has developed in classrooms through the dedicated expertise of British teachers enjoying the relative freedom traditionally allowed within our education system. My concern is that increased external influence with accompanying loss of autonomy could lead to the demise of all that has been gained. I repeat, however, my conviction that primary teachers can adapt to the new legislation without abandoning the good practice which they know is right for children.

The remainder of this paper will be devoted to a description of that good practice.

A discussion of primary practice should, perhaps, begin with a definition of aims. Volumes have been written on this subject but I will offer a succinct aim that sums up, for me, the essence of good practice:

To provide experiences and activities through which all children may learn to:

observe reflectively
think effectively
discuss confidently
study efficiently
respond creatively
concentrate and persevere
work harmoniously in groups
read and comprehend independently
express themselves in speech and writing.

The emphasis on language development in this succinct aim is obvious but so, I hope, is the emphasis on learning through activity and with a sense of purpose. Equally important is the teacher's interventionist role in creating the learning environment, initiating the experiences and providing skills teaching as appropriate in accordance with the stage of development of the individual.

The organisation of a classroom to bring about the acquisition of concepts and the learning of skills requires considerable thought. The classroom environment needs to be a stimulating workshop yet requires provision of opportunities for listening carefully, paying attention and sustaining concentration. In presenting learning tasks and information to pupils a flexible organisation is required and children need training to be as independent as possible when working without direct supervision. Figure 4.1 provides a framework within which a teacher might plan.

ORGANISATION

		INDIVIDUAL	GROUP	CLASS
DEGREE OF CONTROL	FREE			
	CONTROLLED			
	DIRECTED			

Figure 4.1

The ILEA Report on Junior Schools 1985 listed factors contributing to 'good' schools. High on the list were:

1 Involvement of the teachers:

In successful schools, the teachers were involved in curriculum planning and played a major role in developing their own curriculum guidelines.

2 Consistency among teachers:

Pupils performed better when the approach to teaching was consistent. For example, in schools where all the teachers followed guidelines in the same way, the impact was positive.

My experience of successful schools certainly supports these two recommendations and I would suggest there are clear implications for SENSS Teachers and advisory teachers to be involved in school policy making to ensure that all children have access to the full curriculum. There is a need to influence thinking in staff rooms towards a balanced but flexible approach which avoids unnecessary polarisation.

Space allows me to discuss only a few aspects of the curriculum in any detail. Literacy and numeracy remain priorities for all children in the primary school. I will also devote some time to topic work because of the importance I attach to integrated approaches to learning.

Literacy remains the number one curriculum priority. It can be confidently stated that every experience and activity in the primary school uses language but also serves to develop it.

Reading has historically been viewed as being synonymous with the term remedial and still today it is a priority for attention by members of SENSS teams. As a past president of the United Kingdom Reading Association I wish to establish that while my association is concerned with reading it is also concerned with the full range of language arts and skills. Figure 4.2 summarises the nature of our concern and the way in which we view the interrelation of the four modes of language. Is is now customary to consider reading in this context.

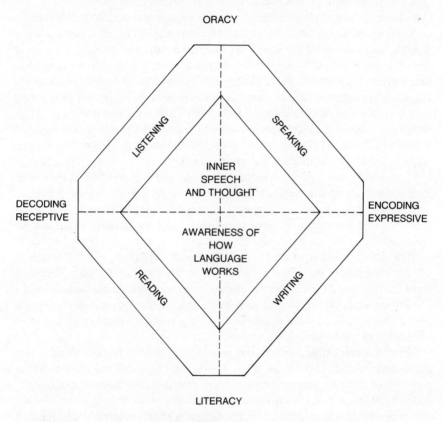

Figure 4.2

For a long time reading has been subject to a variety of fads and fashions. The current debate centres on whether children should learn to read through reading schemes or through 'real' books only. The trend to polarise in reading theory and practice is both unnecessary and unfortunate. The important thing is that children learn to read with confidence, understanding and pleasure. To ensure that this happens teachers need the resources to motivate and interest children and to structure the development of their ability to read for meaning independently.

Bearing in mind the different learning styles of children, all schools surely need a range of the best of reading schemes together with a multitude of real books. It is for the teachers, drawing on their professional knowledge and expertise, to use the materials appropriate for their pupils. The energy currently expended on this pointless debate would be better directed towards a concerted effort to persuade the government and local education authorities to fund a better teacher–pupil ratio in the early years. More opportunities for individual and small group work in the infant schools would make it more likely that children will achieve fluency in reading early enough to prevent the rejection of learning which so often accompanies failure as children move on into the older primary classes.

An important aspect of reading which must recieve attention is the relationship between sound and symbol. Most teachers encourage children to make use of a range of clues including picture clues, contextual clues and syntactical clues but there are also occasions when phonic skills are needed. This is also true in connection with spelling, and so phonic knowledge remains an essential element in the language learning programme. I was pleased to note in the conference programme that Lyn Wendon is conducting a workshop, 'Talking about Language'. Lyn Wendon has devised a Pictogram system which she calls Letterland. Through the Letterland characters children come to understand about sound/symbol relationships in a way which interests and excites them.

As children with special educational needs grow in reading competence, increasing demands are made on their skills because they are expected to learn through reading. Unless we continue to support these children in the upper primary and lower secondary classes their confidence can be undermined and the frustration/failure cycle re-established. Research has shown that many text books written in the subject areas for 11- and 12-year-old pupils have readability ages of 14. Such sentences as 'Climatic conditions deteriorate rapidly with increasing elevation' are not difficult because of the concepts embodied but because of the vocabulary used and the way the sentence is structured. A special needs support teacher working alongside a mainstream teacher is able to mediate such printed statements to pupils with special needs.

Sensitive intervention of this kind is greatly facilitated in classrooms where group discussion approaches are used. The Schools Council project, 'The Effective Use of Reading', recommends several strategies that involve group interaction as children work together to reach decisions or conclusions about information presented in written prose. SENSS teachers who are involved in school policy discussions should seek opportunities to influence teaching approaches in this direction.

The other side of the literacy coin – writing – is increasingly coming into focus. The schools curriculum development council's project 'About Writing' is fostering interest through working groups around the country. The growing trend to adopt the Graves approach, as explained in his book *Writing: Teachers and Children at Work* (Heinemann 1983) is particularly helpful for those children who find writing difficult. Graves divides the writing process into stages and, through the encouragement of conferencing, facilitates intervention without loss of face for the pupil. Acceptance of the separate stages of rehearsal, drafting, revision, editing and publishing as normal practice for writers encourages children with special needs to express their ideas in writing more confidently than was possible when children were expected to get everything right at the first attempt. Related ideas like shared writing, dictated writing and invented spelling together with the introduction of new technology including the word processor should all contribute to an easing of the tension associated with traditional attitudes to spelling and handwriting.

It must be remembered, however, that for all children the ultimate aim is still maximum competence in the conventional skills involved in writing. It follows, therefore, that alongside the encouraging innovations briefly mentioned, there must be school policies for achieving satisfactory standards of handwriting, spelling, grammar and punctuation, etc.

During the last few years an increasing number of schools have adopted agreed policies for handwriting. This is a welcome development since children need the support of consistent teaching and sensible attitudes if they are to acquire the fluent and legible hand they need for communication. My views on this subject are fully documented in *Developing Handwriting* (Macmillan 1977); *The Teacher's Manual for New Nelson Handwriting* (Nelson 1984; revised 1989) and *Holmes McDougall Handwriting* (Holmes McDougall 1988).

SENSS teachers are all too well aware of the difficulty of remedying handwriting problems once they have become deep-rooted. It behoves these teachers, in their advisory roles, to try to influence school policies and to encourage some form of monitoring accompanied by the diagnosis of significant faults.

Numeracy is the other major curriculum concern of SENSS teachers although, all too often, only a very small percentage of available resources is devoted to this subject.

All children need a degree of competence in mathematics and some facility with numbers is essential for successful living in present day society. The media and the community in general focus concern on number bonds and tables. There is no doubt that quick recall of number facts is still an advantage even in the era of calculators and computers. It is equally important, however, that children understand mathematical concepts and processes and that they see some purpose in learning the subject.

The Cockroft Report (1984) gave a most encouraging survey of good practice and advocated an approach which can be summed up through the mnemonic SPIDER:

Solving problems
Practical work
Investigation
Discussion
Exposition
Routine skills.

This approach is a balanced one, the teacher's role in promoting active searching for pattern and purpose being nicely balanced by the more conventional role of presenting information and setting tasks that practise algorithms and basic facts. The inclusion of discussion is also interesting and contrasts with traditional approaches which demanded silence in arithmetic lessons.

I refer back to my earlier remarks about classroom organisation. In a class which is accustomed to working in groups it is possible for a SENSS teacher to work alongside a group of children which includes one or more pupils with special needs. In that situation a child with learning difficulties has access to the full curriculum with his peers but also has the benefit of the SENSS teacher sensitively supporting and encouraging.

I conclude this paper with a brief statement about thematic work. Although topic work is sometimes justifiably criticised for being shallow and unstructured, I believe it to be one of the most valuable aspects of the primary school curriculum. During the last ten years there has been considerable progress towards ensuring that thematic work is incremental, that undue repetition is avoided and that the skills, attitudes, concepts and knowledge of the integrated subjects are taught sequentially. Good practice in topic work is complex and there is not space to describe it in detail here. A detailed account is to be found in Chapter 7, 'Reading Development Through Topic Work in the Middle Years', in *Teaching Reading: The Key Issues* (Heinemann 1982).

George Brown in *Human Teaching for Human Learning* describes a project based on what he calls Confluent Education. Figure 4.3 sets out a range of terms to show the relationship between the cognitive and affective aspects of learning. The labels employed all apply to well structured integrated thematic work and, I think, fully support my plea for its retention.

In conclusion I would suggest that the thrust of this paper can be summarised as follows:

Steady progress over the last four decades has brought us to a point where much of what happens in primary education is a source of pride. There has also been a steady growth in the number and quality of teachers engaged in special educational needs support. Our knowledge about how children acquire literacy and numeracy is now considerable. Our understanding of the ways in which children learn confirms the appropriateness of group work and of integrated studies which involve pupils with a sense of purpose. All of this suggests that, in responding to the new legislation and in adapting to meet its demands, we must not lose what has been so painstakingly developed. Above all, there must be extreme vigilance to ensure that testing is not allowed to become a retrogressive influence.

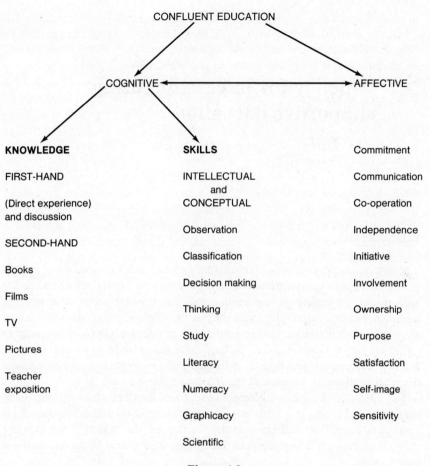

Figure 4.3

5   A policy for integration using supportive education

Phil Bell

Introduction

The aim of this paper is to consider a strategy which schools could adopt to help introduce a policy for integration. The paper draws on a model which, while not held up as the definitive approach, could nevertheless serve as a working document for schools wrestling with the realities of moving towards an integrated structure. NARE's silver jubilee conference provided a platform not only to reflect on past achievements but, perhaps more importantly, to set new goals for future developments. It is time to review the wider concept of needs and consider their implications in the wake of the Education Reform Act.

The 1988 Act offers an entitlement curriculum for all children encompassing nine areas of learning and experience – surely a step in the right direction. Built into the fabric of this entitlement is the requirement that it should embrace five curriculum characteristics, the first three being that it must be broad, balanced and relevant.

On the surface this structure would seem to have much to commend it, guaranteeing, as it does, every child a right to an educational curriculum of distinctive breadth and depth irrespective of the type of school he or she attends and irrespective of the talents the child possesses. However, as usual there is a sting in the tail and in this case it is the fourth characteristic, that of differentiation, which gives cause for concern. There are many ways of building differentiation into the curriculum and the Act is not prescriptive of any particular approach, but as Lady Warnock (1988) pointed out:

> the philosophy and objectives of the 1981 Education Act, which went some way to implementing the Warnock recommendations, are not much in evidence in the latest legislation.

In fact, they are conspicuous by their absence. The most far-reaching omission was the lack of any firm commitment to a policy for integration.

While no one would deny the requirement for progression and continuity, the fifth characteristics of Baker's curriculum package, I would argue that one essential characteristic has been omitted. This sixth characteristic is that of accessibility, for it is around this concept that the nature and fairness of differentiation could be decided.

Implicit in some definitions for differentiated learning is the assumption that it is the child who has the 'problem' when there is a breakdown in learning. If we accept, however, that as teachers it is our professional duty to bring about learning, then we are beholden to examine our methods regularly and to consider what constitutes effective teaching and learning styles.

The need for this regular review is pin-pointed in the Fish Report (1984) which states that 'the relative nature of the majority of special educational needs means that schools determine the extent and nature of the needs which arise'.

In secondary schools, in particular, this statement should be aired frequently to focus attention on the processes and practices adopted in the name of education.

If the stepping stones laid down by previous legislation and publications are to be extended, it is important to review initiatives which are attempting to implement a policy for integration. Integration is still very much in its infancy and working examples of its practice need to be documented, not only for the school's own evaluation purposes, but also to provide discussion documents to encourage other schools to take a careful and considered look at their own provision.

In helping schools to take a more considered look at their own structures the framework outlined in figure 5.1 may prove useful. This framework identifies five elements for consideration when reviewing a whole-school response to meeting children's needs, and will be used in this paper to raise key issues.

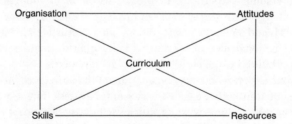

Figure 5.1

The framework can offer the opportunity, not only to raise the staff's awareness of the issues which surround the concept of meeting needs, but hopefully to challenge some of the traditional dogmas which beset it. For schools looking to develop a whole-school approach this diagram can provide a starting point for each department to articulate its position and, from these deliberations, find and build common bridges across subject departments to meet individual needs.

A primary goal in establishing some common ground must be to agree each teacher's role and responsibility for meeting children's needs. This will be achieved only if all staff contribute to the formulation of the whole-school policy.

The reward for encouraging all members of staff to be active participants in the decision-making process, so helping them to develop an ownership of the final policy, is that it gives the policy a greater chance of being fully implemented across the curriculum.

The framework in figure 5.1 does have limitations, particularly when attempting to treat each element in isolation. In any discussion it will soon become apparent that there is a considerable degree of overlap and intercorrelation which can not and should not be avoided. The fact that none of the elements are mutually exclusive can also be viewed as a strength, for this reinforces the important point that ideals, as well as children, do not fit neatly into narrowly defined and constructed categories.

Attitudes

A pivotal point for determining the effectiveness of a whole-school approach for meeting children's needs will be the extent to which the staff's awareness of their own prejudices, bias and misunderstandings is challenged. It is easy to see how these misconceptions have been formed, since the majority of teachers were educated and steeped in a system that perpetuated the concept of 'the remedial child', and was buttressed by policies and practices which continually reinforced the idea of a different child aligned with the need for segregation. It is vital, therefore, to recognise the difficulty many staff experience when faced with an alternative view which may contradict and threaten the very philosophy around which their thoughts and teaching style has developed.

It is of paramount importance to break this chain of thought dictated by concepts of 'ability' and 'segregation' and in its place to introduce a concept of individual needs and a policy for integration. This alternative model moves away from the conventional idea of a child with learning difficulties to one which recognises and builds on the child's learning achievements.

Like everyone else, teachers may be unaware of the prejudiced views they hold and admitting their prejudice can be a very painful process. The responsibility for challenging the conventional wisdom which surrounds the concept of needs rests heavily on the shoulders of those teachers aware of the injustice in the present system. Introducing change, however, calls for patience, sensitivity and consideration for others who may not have had the opportunity to move on in their thinking. The process of encouraging staff collectively to analyse and share their own concepts of 'remedial' and 'need' can bring to the surface the anomalies, inconsistencies and injustice which at present cloud the vision of some teachers.

Skills

In the enthusiasm to challenge the injustice in the system it is important not to overlook the needs of the teachers. Consequently, to prepare for integration, the existing structure may need a thorough overhaul achieved by a comprehensive programme of planned staff and curriculum development. The myth that certain teachers have 'special' or extraordinary 'expertise' needs to be dispelled and replaced with the realisation that the skills needed to meet individual needs are those associated with effective techniques for teaching and learning.

Courses, including GRIST, have traditionally tended to bring together individual teachers from different schools to consider current educational issues. For the member of staff concerned, the course may be most enlightening and motivating, but back in the reality of school this enthusiasm may be negated by a less than receptive staff. The introduction of the cascade model, in which the member of staff reports back to colleagues, has been introduced to alleviate this reaction, but this too has met with three fairly substantial problems: first, the idea of cascading presumes that the teachers will return from the course keen and willing to share their experience; second, that the teachers will have the expertise to allow them to cascade the experience effectively; and third, that group dynamics between course members in which security, confidence and understanding can develop from the shared experience is frequently dissipated when the groups disperse.

While GRIST courses can help to raise awareness of particular issues, the benefits of providing a programme of in-house courses addressed to a particular school's needs may have much more relevance for the staff.

If a school can tailor its in-house courses and make them relevant to the needs of the whole school staff, then the dynamics of that collective and shared experience may provide greater rewards. School led (be it school based or off-site) INSET has much to commend it and would appear to be a very productive and effective means of meeting the development needs of both the school and the staff.

The impact of such an approach was emphasised recently in a mainstream secondary school wishing to introduce a child from a special school who suffered from cerebral palsy. To begin the integration process a video showing the child's classroom behaviour was produced.

With the child's consent the video was shown to the secondary school's staff to raise awareness of the child's needs and at the same time to identify the staff's anxieties and areas for future staff development. The video provided a realistic and immediate means of conveying the child's needs to a teaching staff who had little previous knowledge of this condition, apart from sub-conscious 'prejudice'. The response from the staff was overwhelming. The video showed everyday situations which the staff could relate to, and enabled them to make very constructive comments.

A similar video was made showing the physical environment of the mainstream school and the tutor group of which the child would become a member if she came to the school. This second video was shown and discussed with the staff and child at the special school. This reciprocal arrangement allowed the secondary school to benefit from the professional advice of the staff at the special school and to respond to any concerns or reservations raised by the child.

Having gained the support of the staff, attention then focused on the children. A planned tutorial programme was prepared by the senior mistress, head of house and the child's tutor to raise the awareness of the children in the tutor group. As with the staff, the children were shown the video and their comments and concerns were counselled. It was found that although a four-week tutorial programme had been prepared, the children in the mainstream school were far more receptive and accepting of the situation and could not see any reason for delaying the child's integration. In response to the children's far more advanced views on integration the tutorial programme was revised and within two weeks the child was a member of the mainstream school.

This preparation eased the way for further integration of physically handicapped children into the mixed ability secondary school.

The integration of children with physical handicaps into secondary schools may not be new, but the issue being considered here is the process of whole school staff development.

Resources

Resources can essentially be divided into two components: primary and secondary.

The primary resource, the most precious and valuable of all, is, of course, the teacher. The excitement, entitlement and enabling aspects of the curriculum lie solely in this professional's hands. It is the teacher's management of the learning environment that will determine effective learning for all, a point brought out by Ainscow and Tweddle (1988). Without the vision, understanding and enthusiasm of this professional even the very best of secondary resources will fall far short of their educational potential.

The secondary resources are the tools the teacher brings to the learning environment in terms of equipment, ideas and materials. These tools should enable all children, not only to gain access to the curriculum but also to allow and encourage them to respond to it in a way which clearly expresses their understanding. The demand for these tools was recently illustrated in Ann FitzGerald's article (TES 1988) where she records Betsy Langford's poignant words:

> . . . children are used to feeling dissatisfied with their work, to expect chiding from the teacher and often mockery from their friends and to find that even when they've tried their hardest, the results don't reflect the amount of effort expended.

The secondary resource should provide a means or a vehicle for driving through this pain barrier experienced by many children, but apparently not recognised by many teachers. The skilled teacher who welcomes and values the child's contribution can do much to enhance the learning environment. If this enhancement is then linked with a resource which acts as a facilitator and so allows the child to record his or her thoughts in a form which reflects the hard work, the child's self-image, self-esteem and self-confidence can be further enhanced.

Inevitably, as time goes by, the necessity to record one's ideas and thoughts in a more concrete form tends to increase, so creating greater demands for productive skills. These skills have the effect of laying children open to closer inspection and increase their vulnerability through peer appraisal and criticism. The effect of peer recognition should never be underestimated, and as teachers we should find ways for all children to be able to enjoy the rewards of their endeavours. Teachers must value the child's contribution and through anticipation of his or her needs provide the necessary tools for the child to exhibit the work in the best possible light.

To this end, it is important to build up an impressive arsenal of resources to meet individual needs. These resources should be open ended and act as a facilitator to support the child's efforts, similar to those described by Bell and Best (1986), which are content free and can be applied in many contexts. It is often quite surprising to discover just how aware children are of their own needs and how they can frequently articulate the type of resource they need. Taking account of the way in which these needs are perceived, both from the teacher's standpoint and the child's, can be an illuminating experience. In discussions with the child it is often possible to plan a course of work to meet the individual's needs so that the learning process is negotiated rather than dictated.

If carefully planned, resources can help turn the curriculum into an integrative force rather than a competitive one. In such an environment the curriculum would welcome, celebrate and build on all the talents children bring to the lessons. By matching resources to the child's needs they become self evaluating, since, if they do meet the child's needs, they will enable the child to become an independent learner and not teacher dependent.

Organisation

A powerful factor which influences the effectiveness of learning is the structural organisation of the school. The school's structure can operate systems which either enhance or restrict the child's education. There is often a fatalistic predictability about a child's future achievements in certain structures which, while helping some, can unwittingly limit the progress of others. In these organisations there is a high risk that the self-fulfilling prophecy and expectation syndrome will dominate both the teacher's and the child's view.

In very simplistic terms the organisational structure would seem to dictate four views:

1 The school's view of the child, in which concepts such as sociological views (EPA areas), psychological views (schools for maladjusted), intellectual

views (grammar schools) and finally the new hybrid, the technological (CTCs), may affect the education a child receives.

2 The staff's view of the child. In certain organisational grouping there is the increased risk of self-fulfilling prophecies and expectation syndrome. Where the school legitimates the claim of ability groups by streaming, setting or banding, it can blinker the staff's view. Equally, the pupil's value to the organisation can also be implied in this hidden way and either overtly or covertly alter the teachers' actions. Unfortunately, it is rare for either the staff or the child to question the validity or wisdom of these structures.

3 The way in which the pupils view their peers has powerful overtones. In certain structures a child can be labelled by his peers and the labels are endorsed by the organisational structure. Pupil/peer recognition can hit at the very heart of the learning system and either inhibit or encourage progress.

4 The way in which the child views himself can also affect the learning environment by establishing different sub-cultures or affecting self-image, self-confidence and self-esteem.

These thumb-nail sketches show four components which contribute to the child's 'success' in the educational system. When seeking ways to integrate children certain prerequisites are necessary which will affect the school's organisational structure. One such requirement is the need for a mixed ability philosophy which actively encourages integration in all its forms. The adoption of a mixed ability philosophy does not, however, of itself necessarily guarantee that the individual's needs will be met.

Dessent (1987) argues that the differentiated curriculum within a school will always be limited if it does not recognise, reward and value diversity among pupils. Furthermore, simply valuing the pupils equally is not enough. There has to be the desire to produce a curriculum which is responsive to individual needs. If the structure pays greater attention to what the children achieve, rather than values them for what they are, its philosophy will be seriously flawed.

It is no accident that this paper has in its title 'supportive education' and not 'the supportive education department'. The difference is central to the case being presented. Schools which create a department or give teachers specific responsibilities for meeting individual needs can, inadvertently, reduce the responsibility of all teachers. We have only to look back to the debates about language across the curriculum to remember the puerile arguments over whose responsibility it was to teach language skills. The consternation this single idea provoked will be nothing compared with the new breed of whole-school responsibilities which are now beginning to emerge: technology across the curriculum, IT across the curriculum, and economic awareness for all being just the start.

For too long secondary schools have found it organisationally convenient to compartmentalise subjects. These functionally convenient but artifical demarcation lines have made the timetable easier to handle and have provided security for teachers who knew that for a single or double period their task was to concentrate on a specific subject. One problem which this structure often creates, however, is that the skills gained in one curriculum area are rarely applied in another context. There seems little transference of application from one subject to another.

This problem is even more pronounced when labels are applied to children or staff, particularly in relation to perceived needs. To nominate a teacher 'head of special needs' can confine the responsibility for meeting children's needs to a mere handful of staff. Even the innocent term 'support teacher' has the potential to lead into the same trap. This leaves secondary schools with the question of what options are left open. Could one answer be to call all teachers support teachers or is this too simplistic a response? Primary schools seem to manage with the term 'classroom teacher' and their cross-curricular approach may have much to offer the secondary curriculum. At present, however, such a concept is probably beyond the reach of all secondary schools.

Perhaps an interim step would be to develop the concept of co-operative or team teaching with the class teacher and support teacher working as a team, each sharing the responsibility for the education of all children, similar to the model described by Bell and Best (1986).

In this model individual teachers were given labels like 'support teacher', but their role was seen as an advisory or service position. The support teacher was there to support

1 The child
2 The teacher
3 The curriculum

This label was further obscured by the fact that the person so designated was a support teacher for one year group and was then timetabled as a subject teacher for another year group.

Curriculum

Just as it is counter-productive to separate education into individual subject areas, so too is the act of considering in isolation the four areas discussed. Each is inter-active, being an integral part of the others, and together they complement and extend the contribution to meeting the needs of all children. The interaction of the elements in figure 5.1 will determine the outcomes of both the stated and the hidden curriculum. The curriculum guide-lines outlined in the 1988 Act offer an entitlement for all children, but the quality of these experiences will be subject to the way schools interpret and act on these four important elements. If education is to be responsive and supportive to all children's needs then schools must provide two things:

1 A quality of education for ALL
2 An equality of educational opportunity for ALL children

The equality that is claimed is one of rights and they can be summarised as:

- the right to be educated with one's peers
- the right of education to adjust to meet individual needs
- the right to have one's contribution regarded on an equal basis with others'.

There is little point in making light of the enormity of the task ahead, but this should not discourage those teachers with the vision and determination to continue the fight for a structure that encourages integration.

6 Young people with special needs in the further education context

Richard Stowell

Students with special educational needs are to be found at every level of post-school education and training – in further education colleges, universities and polytechnics, and in adult education institutes and training schemes. Their numbers in further and higher education colleges in the UK alone were estimated in 1985 to be more than 55,000, representing remarkable progress even by comparison with the situation 15 years earlier when none but a few pioneering colleges made any special effort to accommodate students with disabilities or learning difficulties.

The special school sector was built up over a century or more. The first school for the blind was established in 1791 and there were a dozen or more such institutions by 1870. The 1850s also saw the establishment of schools for the physically handicapped and the 'mentally defective'. The picture was completed only in 1971 when children with severe learning difficulties, hitherto provided for by the health authorities, were brought into the education service. By contrast, and despite there being a duty on local education authorities since 1944 to provide for all up to the age of 19, significant numbers of young people with special educational needs began to enter colleges only in the mid-to-late 1970s. Yet by 1985 more than two-thirds of further education colleges, for example, ran special courses for such students.

It is not possible to talk of a 'further education special needs sector' as it is of a 'special school sector'. One reason for this may be that post-school provision is still very much in its infancy. Almost certainly more important are the forces that moulded provision and continue to give impetus to further development.

Provision for students with special needs can be viewed as analogous to a small ship on the ocean waves. Even to the extent that they represent a homogeneous group, people with disabilities and learning difficulties represent less than 0.8 per cent of all those enrolled in colleges of further and higher education. The 'ship' is therefore dwarfed by the size of the ocean which is post-school education and training; moreover it is an ocean which over the last ten or so years has been in unprecedented turmoil culminating in the hurricane represented by the 1988 Education Reform Act.

Not all the winds of the last decade have, by any means, been unfavourable, nor has the ship been entirely rudderless and without power.

Direction was first given to the work by the publication in 1978 of the Warnock Report, the results of a committee of inquiry into the education of handicapped children and young people. Two surveys conducted for the committee were of particular relevance to post-school provision: one, of young people, carried out by the National Children's Bureau (of which more later) and a survey by Her Majesty's Inspectorate. Although never published, the HMI survey is thought to have shown only isolated examples of special consideration afforded students with special educational needs.

The Warnock Report, by its detailed recommendations, and not least by nominating it as one of its three 'areas of first priority', put post-school provision on the agenda, even if the subsequent legislation to implement the Report (the 1981 Education Act), ignored post-school education and training.

Since Warnock, some sense of national direction has been given by the work of a number of agencies, not least Her Majesty's Inspectorate, which has played a very important role, instilling confidence in college staff and promoting good quality provision.

The Department of Education and Science in England has funded staff training materials, published recommendations for staff training (a 'special' professionalism), and administered an educational support grant to provide micro-computing equipment for students with physical disabilities and in-service training grant schemes which have promoted staff development for college staff. In Scotland, the Scottish Education Department has given similar encouragement, notably in its recognition of special educational needs considerations in the 'Scottish action plan' which has transformed Scottish further education.

The Further Education Unit, a curriculum review and development unit established in 1977 to make possible a more co-ordinated and cohesive approach to curriculum development in further education, has given a commendable priority to special educational needs. A series of 'mapping exercises' have reviewed the current state of provision, before the development of a number of curriculum frameworks. The first of these was 'From Coping to Confidence', published in 1985 and intended as guidance for staff working with students who have moderate learning difficulties. It was followed in 1987, by 'New Directions' and 'A Transition to Adulthood', in recognition of the increasing number of students with severe learning difficulties in the former case, and of students with considerable physical disabilities in the latter.

The National Bureau for Handicapped Students (NBHS) was formed in 1984 principally among college staff who themselves had disabilities. It has provided an advice service to staff and students, conducted research and published information, but perhaps most of all has provided through its regional and local groups, and national conferences, an opportunity for teaching staff and others to meet together on a regular basis to share ideas and experience. It too has published a number of staff training packages.

A feature of recent years has been the degree to which the differing agencies – HMI, the DES, Further Education Unit, and NBHS (now renamed Skill: National Bureau for Students with Disabilities) have worked together. More recently the Manpower Services Commission has strengthened links, as recognition grows that the division between 'education' and 'training' makes little sense in terms of meeting the needs of 16 to 19 year olds with disabilities and learning difficulties. Current collaboration in the development of staff training materials may augur well for further co-operation and joint training opportunities.

Each in turn has been influenced by involvement in the major OECD/CERI 'Transition to Adulthood' project, although to date the UK contribution to the project has been very limited. This could be an indication of a continuing unwillingness to recognise how much further advanced are many EEC and OECD centres in their education and training provision for people with disabilities.

Of all the agencies, only the Manpower Services Commission has had the control of the purse strings that allows positive steering; with the exception of educational support and in-service training grants administered by the DES, the other agencies' role has been confined to offering advice and expertise. Further education is a service delivered at local level by education authorities and colleges, who have often had room for independent action but little commitment to a coherent policy.

The area of special needs in further education/training has had to contend with the fact that it is but a very small part of a very much larger whole, and that the FE college and the training schemes are subject to the vagaries and constraints of the external environment. The 'ship' sails on a very large ocean. Steering without an effective rudder would have been difficult even with calm waters; in the last decade the waters have been anything but calm.

The most important contextual change has been in the labour market. The survey undertaken by the National Children's Bureau, when the Warnock committee was deliberating, showed that some 27 per cent of 18 year olds considered handicapped were currently unemployed, with 19 per cent seeking work. Although this is almost five times the proportion of non-handicapped who were unemployed, the figures also show that almost half of 'handicapped' 18 year olds were in employment, even if most of the jobs were repetitive, unrewarding and insecure. In the mid-1970s this picture was about to change, as economic crisis produced widespread unemployment, and particularly high youth unemployment.

The large-scale youth unemployment coincided with a collapse in apprenticeship schemes as industry, in recession, withdrew its support for the part-time vocational courses that were the stock-in-trade of the further education colleges, many of whom had evolved from the old mechanics institutes. Faced with the demise of their traditional courses, and with a government anxious both to increase the skills of the new unemployed young, and to be seen as doing something for the unemployed, colleges responded by mounting a programme of full-time non-vocational, or pre-vocational, courses. The new client group included many disadvantaged young people whose needs, it soon became apparent, were very little different from those traditionally thought of as having learning difficulties or behaviour problems. It was then but a short – though for many an agonising – step to provide special courses for those coming out of special schools and the remedial classes of comprehensives.

Thus it was that youth unemployment brought about, or at the very least greatly hastened, 'the new FE', and with it the spread of courses for students with moderate learning difficulties. Alongside college provision, training schemes under the youth opportunities programmes, particularly those run by the Elfrida Rathbone Society, catered for greater and greater numbers of 16 and 17 year olds with learning difficulties.

Progress in further education has been rapid, to the extent that a 1985 national survey undertaken by the National Bureau for Handicapped Students for the DES, and published as *Catching Up?*, showed that more than half the colleges in England ran special courses for 16 to 19 year olds with moderate learning difficulties. The survey also showed that 69 colleges provided full-time courses for students with severe learning difficulties, when barely a handful had done so five years before. Almost half the colleges made at least some form of provision for a group of young people who up until 1971 had been considered 'ineducable'.

The next decade will see a somewhat different trend emerging as demographic changes result in the number of school leavers declining by more than one-third. Young people will be at a premium, wanted by colleges and employers alike, and for this reason, young people with disabilities may find more doors opening to them. On the other hand the tide of youth unemployment that brought people with special needs into college along with pre-vocational education, YTS etc, will recede. It remains to be seen whether the special provision built up over the last decade will survive what may be the collapse of pre-vocational college-based education.

The second major contextual change has been shifts in government policy, operating in the context of large scale youth unemployment. The last ten years have seen reforms in the education system greater than probably ever before, culminating in the Education Reform Act 1988.

Pre-dating the Act, and in some respects in contradiction to the aims of the national curriculum that forms the core of the legislation, were the government's attempts to improve the structure and quality of vocational and technological education. The belief that many 'non-academic' 14 to 16 year olds were 'turned off' school because of the lack of relevance to the world of work, coupled with a desire to raise vocational standards, was given by government as reasons for the introduction of new pre-vocational courses in schools and colleges. Others have expressed the changes in terms of the need to produce a more compliant and disciplined youth work force. Whatever the reasons, new courses were established, prime examples being the certificate of pre-vocational education (CPVE) and the technical and vocational initiatives (TVEI). Outside school, the youth training scheme (YTS) replaced a largely discredited youth opportunities programme (YOPS).

From the point of view of young people with special needs, many of the new courses have the virtue of being flexible, student-centred, and of incorporating a good deal of individual programming. YTS has been a major provider of new opportunities and through its funding mechanism, its special assessment and age exclusions, and its provision of special equipment and services, it has shown itself to be responsive to the needs of very many young people with disabilities and learning difficulties. TVEI schemes were slow at incorporating special schools but their numbers are increasing, with the active encouragement of the training agency which, with Skill, has produced a number of information and training packages. Similarly, CPVE is proving to be a useful vehicle for delivering the mainstream curriculum to students with special needs.

The next decade presents many challenges. Building in opportunities for student progression is one of these, so that special courses, very necessarily built up over the last 15 years, do not become an end in themselves but rather a means towards mainstream education and training. Pre-vocational education initiatives are beginning to provide one progression route, but may not survive the rapid reduction in the number of school leavers.

The absence of a coherent national policy on the post-school education and training of people with disabilities continues to inhibit its development. This is particularly so in relation to the complex levels of benefits, grants and training allowances which distort people's choice of course and too often act as a disincentive to any form of education or training. The absence of an 'aids to study' scheme, whereby students might acquire essential communication and study aids, is also an important inhibiting factor. Information technology is playing, and will increasingly continue to play, a major role in opening up the curriculum to people with disabilities.

Above all, the challenge of the next decade is to improve the quality of post-school provision. *Catching Up?* showed there to be some 43,500 students with disabilities in public sector further and higher education in England. There is widespread geographical variation – provision is much stronger in the North-West and the East Midlands for example, compared with the South and South-East – and the number in higher education has not expanded to nearly the same extent. People with disabilities are still heavily under-represented in further education, and training and imaginative efforts are required to correct this.

The question of quality now needs to be addressed. Are we content with the quality of college provision, which in some instances has appeared to be close to a 'care and containment' policy, or are we going to ensure that students with disabilities receive the maximum opportunity to realise their potential?

7 Special educational needs: an adult education response

Sue Abell

Introduction

Educational resources in Britain are very much concentrated in the statutory sectors and many schools and colleges have made fine provision for those with special educational needs. But they tend to offer full-time courses aimed at students under 19 and many adults continue to have special educational needs long after they leave full-time education. Indeed, with the rapidity of change in modern Britain, the need for continuing educational opportunities is on the increase for all adults.

During the 1970s it became clear that adult education was mainly serving the needs of well educated and socially advantaged members of our society. The Russell Report, *Adult Education – A Plan for Development* (1973), suggested that a comprehensive adult education service should be 'readily accessible to all who need it'. The Report pointed out that disadvantaged groups were grossly under-represented in adult education and suggested steps that might be taken to remedy that situation.

Vigorous efforts were made to tip the balance more in favour of those with greater needs. These moves have had some success and adult education is probably now more open, more flexible and more responsive to the needs of the whole community than it was then.

Essex has an equal opportunities policy which should mean that adults with special educational needs are well represented among its students and this is, indeed, the case. In fact, out of a total of more than 60,000 students enrolled for adult education in 1988 probably 3,000 have special educational needs. 'Probably', because they are not categorised that way and may simply enrol for classes along with other students. A limited number attend clubs (such as Gateway, sports, orchestra, for the deaf) but the majority attend classes, about 50 per cent of them within the adult basic education framework.

Community education organises two large camps each year for special needs students in addition to class provision which it arranges for a number of specific groups of adults:

- with moderate and severe learning difficulties
- recovering from mental illness
- with an inherited or acquired hearing impairment
- with visual impairment
- who are asthmatic
- who are cerebrally palsied
- recovering from strokes or head injuries
- with a combination of the above disabilities or impairments.

Some swimming, movement and sports groups cater for a wide range of disabilities including impaired limbs, spina bifida, multiple sclerosis, epilepsy, cystic fibrosis, Down's syndrome, myelomeningocele, arthritis and accident injuries.

Subjects offered

Within adult education there are three main groups of students:

- those within the basic adult education framework who usually study literacy, numeracy, coping/life/social/home skills, communication, sign language, lip-reading, Braille, typing
- those who are part of the general arts programme and who learn handicrafts, music and movement, dance, drama, orchestral playing, cookery, photography
- those who are involved in developing physical skills such as swimming, movement, yoga, body-awareness.

But the group most demanding of provision is that of adults with severe learning difficulties who are newly resident in the community.

They have usually taken part in a preparatory programme through social services or the health authority, but once out of institutional care, the fragile skills, sometimes learnt over a painfully slow time, can be lost through lack of use. These members of our society have difficulty with basic communication skills often because of the sheltered nature of their life and background.

The programme that is devised for them will usually be geared largely towards communication skills and will probably include craft, drama, and life skills which thus serve a dual function.

It is not always clear how far it is possible or desirable to integrate such students into the regular adult programme. Providing the classes at adult centres is a positive move towards integration, but the teaching required in the classroom is specialised and is generally done in separate classes.

Type of class

Provision available through community education includes classes, workshops, long courses, drop-in centres and residential summer schools, some of the latter specifically for students with severe learning difficulties. The need for these was identified when the regular programme of summer schools for ABE students began to attract students with severe learning difficulties who could not cope with the curriculum offered but seemed to gain great benefit from the opportunity for residential education.

Location

Activities take place in adult education centres, school-based centres, swimming pools (including some at special schools), hostels and homes. In a few instances, community education buildings have been adapted with deaf-loops, ramps, toilets, and stair lifts. Special transport arrangements are often necessary.

In addition to the specific programmes offered, adults with special needs are encouraged to join classes in any of the other subject areas offered by adult education and the community education service is able to offer support for such students through volunteers who are specially recruited, trained, and supported. Befriending schemes have been established so that, where it is desirable, students with special educational needs can be accompanied by a volunteer helper who will interpret or explain and assist as necessary.

Training of tutors

Tutors teaching specific classes or incorporating special needs students in their regular classes require good support, and regular training is offered to them. The county offers certificates in the teaching and learning of adult basic education and a particular option is available for tutors working with students with severe learning difficulties.

Adult education is part of the further education service and some adult education tutors take advantage of courses offered, such as City and Guilds 731.

Co-operation and partnership

Collaborative links have been set up with colleges, social services, the health authority and a wide range of voluntary organisations.

The programme offered by adult education for dysphasic adults illustrates this co-operation. Referrals come from the health authority whose speech therapists undertake assessments of students and often team-teach with adult education tutors. The regular training programme is jointly planned by adult education advisory tutors and senior speech therapists. The course team includes members from both disciplines. All agree that this has enormous advantages as they learn a great deal from one another and are better able to serve the needs of the group in other contexts as well as that of joint provision.

Individual help

Adult education in Essex thoroughly embraces the use of volunteers in its service. They are recruited regularly, trained and deployed. Their expenses are paid and they make a magnificent contribution to the service, enabling group tutors to increase the flexibility of their classes and ensuring individual help whenever it is needed.

Referrals

Offering the right kind of help where it is needed requires a comprehensive assessment scheme. Luckily, Essex has eight full-time advisory tutors for ABE and all have had training and considerable experience in assessing special educational needs. This means that wherever they live in the county, adults with special educational needs can ask for individual assessment, counselling and programme planning.

Advantages of adult education for students with special educational needs

With its comparatively meagre resources, adult education might be seen as being at a disadvantage when catering for adults with special educational needs but, in reality, it has some features which enhance its capacity to respond. Ironically, its part-time nature gives it its greatest flexibility. Tutors are appointed as and when required and this makes it possible to set up new classes without too much preamble. Provision for head injured adults is an example.

The health authority has been advocating adult education classes for discharged head injured patients, and community education appointed an experienced tutor to pilot a course. Her report resulted in

- the recruitment of volunteers
- the design of a training course
- identification of resources
- a plan for increased provision.

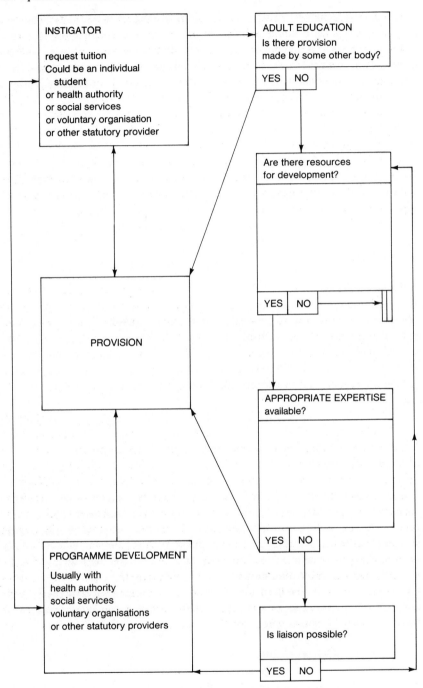

Figure 7.1

The lessons learnt will be disseminated through the county training programme and may well result in the establishment of provision in other parts of the area.

The use of volunteers constitutes another advantage for adult education. Volunteers bring skills that complement those of the tutor, lead to a better student/tutor ratio, and facilitate the teaching of individuals with idiosyncratic needs. Perhaps the most potent advantage for adult education is that it sees itself catering for developing learning needs over the whole adult age range. It can make provision to dovetail with schools or colleges for 16 to 19 year olds, but it also offers opportunities for students with special educational needs to continue their education when most schools and colleges no longer have courses for them. It offers continuing education not only in the continuous sense, but also continually, in response to changing needs that might emerge with a different life-style, increasing age or acquired disabilities.

The curriculum

Adult education provides a mixture of special classes and integrated provision. But the full integration of special needs students has a long way to go, and requires much more commitment to the adaptation and modification of plans and a further shift of resources to those whose need is greatest.

The future of special education needs for adult education

An awareness of the responsibility to respond to special educational needs permeates the whole of adult education, often starting on a small scale through the initiative of dedicated individuals. But success breeds replication and good examples of provision soon spread to other centres. There are 40 adult education centres in Essex and each is responsive to the special educational needs of adults.

But there are also major gaps. Building up relationships with other agencies is time consuming and not always productive, so the links tend to be forged one by one by the few full-time staff available for this important aspect of developing special needs work. Our adult education service does not have staff who are wholly responsible for special needs and is dependent upon generic full-timers and a few specialist part-timers. Although this leads to productive links with other agencies and services, it cannot be in the best interests of the students. A truly responsive adult education service can only exist when specialist staff are appointed or designated to take responsibility for this important area of work.

PART 2

Sharing Expertise

8   Sharing expertise: developing the consultative role

Gerda Hanko

Introduction: acting on recognition of the interactive nature of emotional, behavioural and learning difficulties

That schools differ widely in outlook, expertise and resources, and that such differences help to influence the degree to which individual pupils may find it difficult to progress has been one of seminal emphases of the Warnock Report (DES 1978). Recognition of the interactive nature of children's learning needs has spread since then, with the implications for mainstream schools

- that children with special needs have to be seen as being the responsibility of the school as a whole
- that this requires whole-school approaches to meeting them
- and that the learning situation itself needs to be examined for its possible contribution to children's learning difficulties, instead of merely looking in the child for causes.

Publications now abound which aim to develop 'ways of supporting the kind of school that', with Hegarty (1987), 'provides for each according to need as part of its normal provision, perceives special provision as an integral part of the whole', and aims to prevent learning difficulties (Booth *et al* 1987) instead of just reacting to them.

Incredibly, these developments appear to receive no recognition in the 1988 Education Reform Act, and could well be halted for want of explicit official support. I want to suggest that joint problem-solving consultancy approaches – developed to maximise existing expertise – can and need to be geared to prevent this from happening, and to consolidate and further such developments in aid of meeting the special educational needs of all children.

Although a number of surveys have shown that practice has been slow to change, the ground has at least been prepared for change. Fewer teachers have difficulties in responding to reminders that children share substantial common ground regardless of whatever special attention they may need at any one time. This has helped teachers to realise that what they offer specially to their neediest children may be of relevance to others. Schools seem less reluctant to accept that the difficulties some children experience may well point to a more general problem in school or classroom interaction; and teachers who have been helped to respond more appropriately to those pupils whom they had found most difficult to teach, have found that in the process they were becoming better teachers to their other pupils as well, with their job satisfaction rising accordingly. All teachers need now to be given this experience, and all those in a position to provide it – because of their own good experience and expertise in meeting children's special needs – have themselves to be enabled to share it effectively with fellow professionals.

Enabling all teachers to provide for each according to need: skill enhancement within a problem-solving framework – the shift in role for the specialist supporter

For teachers to meet the range of special needs of all their children is clearly a formidable task, and without effective support of all teachers many children's needs will remain unmet. In the face of even further diversion of financial resources for training away from special needs, can we build on what expertise we have to find economic and yet effective ways to overcome the present difficulties, to deepen all teachers' understanding of learning and behaviour problems and of the way in which they might be resolved *within the learning situation of the classroom*?

As my title suggests, one way forward can be seen to lie in developing the consultancy role of those in a position to help teachers meet their pupils' special needs. I want to focus here on an 'affordable' way of reaching a maximum number of teachers with this aim, i.e. the group consultative training approach. While most of what follows with regard to consultation skills will also be relevant for working with individual teachers, the focus will be on group consultation; not merely, however, as a numerically economic approach, but as one that can show how personal resources can be maximised through working in groups with colleagues, using skills which are also relevant to the group members as teachers.

Current support is insufficient both in quantity and quality. Support staff, numerically increased in some areas, but threatened with further reductions in others, are able to reach only a minority of the estimated number of children in need of special attention. They will continue to do so, whatever their number, while the problem is seen as mainly one of numbers, of needing more specialist staff to work individually with specific children, away from the learning situation where the difficulty occurs.

More people are now aware of the built-in hazards that go with attempting to deal with a difficulty away from the context in which it arises, of the illogicality of such endeavour, and the wastefulness of selective provision that fails to maximise the school's and school services' existing resources.

Current provision has been criticised for:

- relying on support staff as sole experts, bearers of remedies and answers (thereby implying that these are beyond classroom teachers' competence, 'deskilling' them by encouraging abdication of responsibility)
- ignoring the difficulties of following the advice of others from outside one's own work setting, especially if it seems to suggest that one's own expertise is to be supplanted by it
- the reinforcement of arbitrary distinctions
    a between pupils (those with and without 'special needs'; those with special 'educational' needs and those with behavioural and emotional ones) and
    b between support staff (such as expecting SEN staff to focus on methods of achieving 'educational results' without also attending to the interactional emotional and behavioural context of learning failure, seen as the remit of pastoral care, counselling and the psychological services)
- and for altogether offering an unco-ordinated and overlapping, segregated and selective, conflicting and even rivalrous service.

Demands to redress such insufficiencies have led to calls for school-based staff development schemes for all serving teachers as an integral part of a special needs related properly co-ordinated unified in-service structure (cf Hegarty 1987, Sayer 1987, Wolfendale 1987); and for staffs within and across schools and the school services to meet and pool their expertise, share and deepen their understanding systematically in school-based discussion and workshops. Furthermore, such a structure should also cater for the need for ongoing support of special needs postholders, to deepen their awareness of existing expectations and evolving needs of the fellow professionals with whom they are working – expectations and anxieties both voiced and unvoiced (cf Laslett and Smith 1984). They also require continuing support in those inter-professional consultation skills which can preserve them from being left 'stranded, resented and counter-productively (deemed to be) bearers of answers to problems which the rest of the staff could be helped to resolve for themselves' (Sayer 1987).

All this implies, as has been pointed out in the collected evidence presented to the 1987 Select Committee inquiry into the implementation of the 1981 Education Act (cf vol 2 of the evidence), and to many others since then involved in attempts at educational reform:

- a shift in the role of former 'remedial' teachers, of pastoral care and special needs post-holders, and of school-attached educational psychologists; and
- an extension of their remit to 'initiate and facilitate staff development programmes' (NARE 1985); i.e. of crossing boundaries into other colleagues' territory.

Both should receive official sanction and both require in-service training opportunities to acquire the necessary skills. In the absence of official sanction, however, the ground already covered in the development of school-based consultative in-service programmes may itself offer the wanted training opportunities for special needs post-holders and those who could give them support in their turn.

The training needs of special needs support staff as 'initiators and facilitators of staff development programmes' have been shown (cf Lloyd-Smith and Taylor 1988; Sayer 1987.; Hanko 1985, 1986, 1987) to centre on the development of interprofessional skills of

- understanding the professional needs of the classroom teachers with whom they are to work
- learning ways of pooling expertise rather than one-sidedly attempting to impart it
- redeploying some of their skills – over and above applying them in work with failing, disheartened or work-refusing children – for working with fellow professionals whose expectations may likewise be in conflict with those of the would-be supporter, just as those of work-refusing children tend to be in conflict with those of their teachers.

The magnitude of the special needs post-holder's task becomes clear if one considers that these skills are to be geared to assisting classroom teachers of varying lengths of career experience (often considerably longer than that of the 'qualified' supporter) and range of subject specialities (beyond the supporter's expertise) – teachers already under pressure from many directions and with ambivalent feelings about 'having problems' and 'being seen as in need of help'; and if one considers that the supporter's extended task is to deepen these colleagues' understanding of 'special' learning needs, to enhance their skills, discover and develop their strengths and the confidence that the professional know-how they possess can be summoned for responding more appropriately to most of the behavioural, emotional and learning difficulties they encounter.

Ambivalent feelings, mixtures of resentment, disbelief, hope, disappointment with remedies that 'didn't work', and demands for answers counter-productive to the task at hand have to be understood and dealt with constructively, and reasons for them appreciated. On the one hand, the supporters need to learn how not to collude with any counterproductive dynamics of the institution they are trying to serve (such as the expectation of direct advice, collusion with which would further heighten the expert image of the 'deskilling' specialist come to deliver solutions); on the other hand, since their primary task is augmenting the teachers' own skills, they must be able to cope with attributed evasion of responsibility, with not knowing their job, with letting people down. One teacher's despair may tempt them to fall into the 'rescuer' role; other teachers may strike them as ineffective so that the supporters become judgmentally prescriptive with those 'why don't you

. . .' bits of advice that can make things worse by letting the teacher feel how others can handle them better.

Let us now look at the primary task of enhancing classroom teachers' understanding and skills through a joint problem-solving approach; then study an example of group consultation in practice; and finally consider the utilisation of sessions for basic training in consultation skills for designated specialists.

Consultative case discussion as a school-based joint problem-solving staff development approach

A growing number of staffs within and across schools and the specialist services are now engaged in developing such joint approaches, meeting as teams in school-based discussions and workshops, with the explicit aims of pooling their expertise, sharing and increasing their understanding of the factors that may lead or contribute to children's learning difficulties, and finding their own most appropriate solutions to them.

One such approach in particular, the case discussion model (cf Daines 1981, Hanko 1985/7), has met with considerable interest, and continues to be found helpful by primary and secondary teachers of all lengths of career experience as they work with their consultant supporters in clearly defined ways.

A support and training technique has been developed, based on the Caplan model of inter-professional process consultation (Caplan 1970), a technique of regular group sessions where consultant and colleagues pool their equal but differing expertise in a process of joint exploration of a difficulty experienced in a group member's work setting, such as, for instance, the context of a pupil's learning difficulty. In the process of exploration the consultees' expertise is supplemented by one another's and the consultant's, and in this way professional understanding and skills are extended. It is the consultant's task to assist the exploration and the finding of alternative workable solutions to the problem, *within a problem-solving framework*. He or she attempts this by

- asking answerable insight-generating questions and promoting this skill in the group
- supplementing the teacher's expertise with that of others
- and generating information that can help to highlight the issues underlying the problem that is being explored, so that new solutions are found.

The problem-solving framework distinguishes the case discussion model from *ad hoc* case conferences, lunch-time 'surgeries' run by educational psychologists where teachers can discuss the difficulties they experience with specific pupils, or meetings arranged to deal with crisis situations. In all these the discussion remains specific to the difficulty that brought it about.

The problem-solving framework, in contrast, ensures that the information that emerges regarding a specific pupil's difficulty in its context is generated in such a way that it also helps teachers in general – whether or not they know the pupil under discussion – to learn to ask themselves the kinds of questions that are helpful whenever problems arise in any pupil's learning situation. As a staff development activity it is designed to be of both *immediate and long-term use* in the classroom and school setting, and thus meets an important stipulation for effective in-service work.

Group consultation in practice

The aims of the consultative exploration are thus:

- to deepen teachers' understanding of individual needs
- to become aware of obstacles to the learning task
- to develop their abilities to meet these needs by adaptations within the context in which they occur,

within the remit of an ordinary teaching day: that is to say, through

- the day-to-day learning programme (analysing it to discover its remedial/ therapeutic potential)
- therapeutic-educative relationship experiences between teacher, pupil and other classmates (activating the educational potential inherent in daily classroom interactions)
- developing teachers' skills in consultation and negotiation, on behalf of the pupil, with colleagues across departmental and managerial boundaries; with parents as partners in their children's learning; and, where indicated, with members of other professions across institutional and professional boundaries (cf DHSS guidelines 1988, which, ironically, suggest more awareness of what may be achieved through the personal and social education aspects of the school curriculum than their DES counterparts with regard to the forthcoming national curriculum).

The following example of a joint problem-solving session, discussed in greater detail elsewhere in a different context (Hanko 1985/7), illustrates both the range of issues that can arise for exploration, and the processes which can be activated in group consultation to contribute to insight and solution. In particular, it demonstrates the constant simultaneous focus on the twin concerns of the approach, the special needs of children as learners, and the professional needs of teachers in relation to them.

Attention is paid to the negative effects which some children have on teachers when, for various reasons, they seem to be 'unteachable' and to reject what their teachers are trying to offer. One of these effects can be what Britton (1981) refers to as the phenomenon of re-enactment as an unwitting professional response to the dynamics of a child's situation, the difficulty that exists for professionals not to re-enact – and thereby aggravate – what the child already experiences, and the ease with which they may collude with his sense of hopelessness and negative feelings.

The case shows how failure to resist such re-enactment increases the teacher's difficulty, as it is detrimental to the help he might otherwise have been able to offer. The question was whether supporting the teacher on this basis might lead to the required change in his attitude, help him to see the situation in a new light, and thus affect his perception of the problem. The presentation of Dave's case has been chosen to highlight the core consultation skills it called into action.

The staff group concerned (composed of teachers from a middle and a first school sharing a site) had met weekly for a number of times, when one of them, Mr E, presented eight-year-old Dave, 'an infuriating boy, who never listens and who can't even copy from the board; there is nothing one can do with him'.

In previous sessions, Mr E had already shown himself, through his constant 'yes, but . . .' interjections, as the group's resident 'butter-in', breezily polite but seemingly unable to accept that anything that was being suggested would work. With remarks like 'Ah well, that never did me any harm; I have gone through worse', he would brush aside his colleagues' explorations as irrelevant, yet hint at having himself suffered as a child. Such personal comments can however not be taken up in a professional staff support group, being outside its brief and scope which differ from those of a personal therapy group. Far from disregarding them, however, such comments need to be 'heard', since our personal experiences can affect our reactions to others in general and teachers' reactions to pupils and the demands they make on them.

Mr E described Dave, now in his second term at this school, as exasperatingly 'lazy', always talking to others, the only one in the class who will make a mess of things, who cannot even copy from the board, but who can sometimes surprise by good work. He never listens, just switches off, does the opposite of what he is told and underachieves in everything. Mr E finds it hard to understand, if he compares Dave with his 'hard-working, extremely bright sister', one year older, also at this school, how there can be two such different children in one family. He quotes the mother as confirming that Dave is an infuriating boy, and quite different from his clever and hard-working sister.

At this point, the group, already developing the skill of asking 'answerable questions' from a position of expertise to be shared, ask for further information on the basis of what Mr E had told them: 'You mentioned how he can surprise you by occasional good work. What was that about? In which way was it good?' But Mr E could at that moment not remember, and this lapse of memory made him rather thoughtful.

The group then recalled their own experiences with children who refused to work and how often there seemed to be another child in the family who 'cannot do anything wrong'. They gave examples of how some of their attempts at building up self-esteem seemed to have worked.

Mr E, however, countered each example with either 'it won't work with Dave' or 'I've tried all this', and switched off at any good idea offered, unable to listen, making himself, like Dave, the only one in the group so different and obstructive. He gradually induced in the group a feeling of hopelessness, which must have resembled what both Mr E and Dave were feeling in the classroom.

It seemed not to be a good idea, at this stage of the group's life, to comment on these similarities, which might have made Mr E even more conspicuously different from his colleagues, especially since, as well as asking insight-generating questions, they had told him how they had handled things better, which had moved Mr E to reject their suggestions as unworkable with somebody like Dave.

Could one instead help the group to become more supportive towards him? Could one, for instance, strengthen Mr E's own support potential by stressing the way he noted Dave's good work? Could one promote his buried awareness into a skill of giving matter-of-fact recognition to a child's potential, of giving a child hope about himself, instead of confirming his negative stance by showing surprise at occasional good work or using it to prove that Dave 'could do better if he tried' (as we so easily exhort when we are exasperated, and as the group seemed to be doing with Mr E)?

Questions like these in the consultant's mind led to fanning a small positive spark in seemingly totally negative behaviour, and this made a difference to Mr E both in relation to his colleagues in the group, and as Dave's teacher to whom a way out of a vicious circle of perpetual defeat could in this way be illustrated, again without explicitly referring to the analogy of the situation. This led the group to recall, towards the end of the meeting, how they, too, had got nowhere with work-refusing children while they constantly demanded better work from them (thus identifying with Mr E as having known failure instead of contrasting their own better results with his, as they had done earlier) but how they had been able to help them when they had worked on the relationship.

At the next meeting, Mr E almost casually mentioned that he had been trying out one or two of last week's ideas and that Dave seemed quite responsive to him this week. He was now showing his own responsiveness to Dave and Dave's response in return, which made Mr E more hopeful about him. A few weeks later, he also reported with some amusement how he had involved a colleague (not a member of the group) in discussion about another pupil when he had caught both himself and his colleague 'fixing' the child inadvertently in his bad behaviour.

Equally interestingly, Mr E felt he was managing to convey something of his greater hopefulness to Dave's mother, using insight-promoting questions when she kept praising her daughter and complaining about Dave, and asking, for instance: 'What are the things you can be nice to him about at home? Could we work together on these?' Dave's mother in turn seemed to be becoming more accepting.

While Dave was still a problem, it now seemed to Mr E remediable. It no longer aroused feelings of exasperation, as it had done when he failed to link what had amounted to a form of work paralysis with the hopelessness which Dave must have felt about himself both at home and at school.

This example of one case discussion, lifted out of a sequence of weekly meetings, may appear a laborious way of achieving small gains, consuming time which teachers, pressed as they are, can little afford. The cumulative effect, however, of attending to such questions consistently over a period of time is considerable and, as teachers agree, eventually time-saving. There is, after all, nothing more time-consuming than having to teach children whose needs one does not understand.

In addition, however, sessions like this, or sequences of them, can be used as a consultancy training ground by inviting from any of the school services those with specialist qualifications and good experience in meeting children's special needs, to attend such meetings as participant observers acting as co-consultants.

Special needs post-holders have in this way been able to develop their consultation skills with teachers, while educational psychologists who have begun to extend their remit in this way have found this to be a realistic way of meeting the supporters' own need for ongoing support.

Training opportunities for developing the consultative role

The above description of a session as an example of consultative joint problem-solving will have shown how it differs from other forms of support such as counselling, giving advice, or supervision. To achieve the twofold aims of consultation – deepening teachers' understanding of any pupil's special needs, and enhancing their ability to meet them – the consultative role has been geared as outlined to:

- supplementing the teacher's expertise with that of the group (instead of the group and consultant trying to supplant it by showing they can handle things better)
- generating information and experience that can highlight the problem and 'reframe' it by changing perceptions; and doing so by promoting the skill of asking answerable awareness-promoting questions.

The consultation skills employed in this session had been:

- the listening skill of noting – behind the teacher's breezy rejection of anything that looked to him like advice – his own sense of failure with a failing pupil; i.e. understanding how one difficult situation (failure for the pupil) may be 'mirrored' in another (failure for the teacher), with consequent reinforcement of the difficulty through re-enactment of the symptoms by the teacher

- the skill of communicating at different levels without necessarily articulating them. The consultative task was to keep the focus of discussion on the pupil, but simultaneously to deal with the teacher's perception of the problem (the reinforcing effect it was having on both pupil and teacher) by giving him through group support the kind of liberating learning experience which he could transfer into the teaching context with Dave
- diverting attention from his hopelessness, while helping the group to support him vis-a-vis the child to be helped – not by recounting their own success stories but by recognising what support potential he might already have, buried as it was but ready to be drawn out by support from others. This was geared to helping him to behave likewise with a failing pupil, so that both he and the child had less need to make others feel useless.

By understanding something of his own behaviour as self-defeating (an understanding that was achieved without loss of face since explicit comments were avoided), and respecting the feelings behind the pupil's refusal to work, the teacher could stop re-enacting and reinforcing the pupil's negative experience, could relax his pressure and abandon his preconceived ideas about Dave. His spontaneous reports in later sessions suggested that he had made a beginning in that direction, and had even begun to apply, with colleagues outside the group and with the boy's mother, the skills used in the group.

There had thus been a level of skill enhancement for work in the classroom, and of skills training and transfer to working with colleagues within the group and others on the staff, and for achieving a mutually educative partnership between teacher and parent.

What is being looked at in all case discussions is a sequence of focal points of which trainee consultants need to be made aware, to be able to highlight the interactional context of the difficulty. The starting point must be the teacher's current perception of the problem if there is to be a widening of awareness and reframing of it as the exploration proceeds.

The teacher's perception is likely to be affected by his feelings about the pupil, dented self-confidence through not being able to be a 'good enough' teacher to him, which a more objective analysis may help to restore. Dated, or even outdated knowledge about children and learning processes may need to be supplemented; and the teacher's own untapped resources may be tapped for effective use in promoting the pupil's progress.

As has been shown in detail elsewhere (Hanko 1986, 1987, 1989), knowledge that can highlight the underlying issues has to be supplemented, and skills have to be developed in the group, which the designated supporter will have been applying in his work with children, but now has to redeploy for work with fellow professionals. These are used to focus their awareness on the learner, the learning task, and the learning environment, on the interactive nature of learning difficulties and their behavioural and emotional concomitants. The knowledge supplemented and shared in the exploration will concern:

1 *The pupil* (how such emotional, behavioural and learning difficulties as are being discussed, may develop; how disturbance-producing experiences can affect behaviour and learning)

2 *The pupil's classroom and working groups* (how an individual's behaviour may have a function for the whole group who may then try and prevent him from changing it; how groups may be handled so as not to 'need' one child's particular behaviour and instead support his progress)

3 *Teacher and pupil in interaction* (awareness of different professionals' reactions to particular difficulties and behaviour patterns; their potential effect on pupils)

4 *The learning programme and learning tasks* (possibilities of adapting these to the needs gauged, so that learning can take place and the therapeutic potential of the curriculum be utilised (no matter how nationally prescribed).

The skills to be furthered in the exploration deal with:

- gauging needs underlying the overt behaviour
- making special bridging efforts to reach the child's 'teachable self'
- designing new learning experiences to meet the needs gauged (relating to 2, 3, 4 above)
- enlisting effectively, in support of the child's learning, his parents and others in the family, colleagues within and across feeder schools, and, where indicated, specialists from other services (development of negotiating skills across professional boundaries).

In short, teachers are helped to offer all children, as Quinton put it when reporting his and Rutter's findings (1988) on the healing effects of teachers on children in even severe adversity, 'good school experiences, such as some form of success, accomplishment, sense of self-esteem or just pleasure in school activities', with consequent better adjustment in adult life – even if they did not always seem to have an immediate effect(!).

Knowledge of findings like these are an example of the kind of insight-promoting information which often helps to give teachers new heart to proceed in spite of seemingly overwhelming obstacles.

Over and above the skills required to develop effective joint problem-solving groups, however, trainee consultants also need to become aware of what is involved in setting them up.

Setting up and developing joint problem-solving groups – experiential training of co-consultants

Mr E's group had been a two-term group of middle and first school teachers sharing a site, all members attending the weekly sessions for the two terms, with myself as a temporarily school-attached consultant. There are, however, no set rules for the composition of such staff groups within and across schools and school services, variations to the theme being as numerous as the institutions they are to serve.

Staff groups may be short-term or long-term, or a mixture of both, with a core of long-term members working with short-term participants who join for an agreed number of sessions in turn – this particular structure affords a good opportunity for a school to build up a core of its own consultant teachers.

Staff groups may be for one school only, or, as in the example above, meet across feeder schools (whose staffs may otherwise still work in splendid isolation from each other) to great mutual benefit. Any such group may be working with one consultant only. The consultant may, on the other hand, be able to suggest to the head teacher that an invitation be extended to other support staff with such specialist qualifications, from within the school or the school services, to act as co-consultants, with a view to developing their own consultative skills. A co-consultant already in touch with the school as part of his traditional remit may in this way be able to extend it through remaining in regular group consultative contact long after the initiating consultant's commitment has ended – and may of course himself become an initiating consultant with his other schools. Schools have welcomed such arrangements with open arms.

Thus, where a group is to be set up, the range of different structural possibilities needs to be outlined so that the school can decide on the structure that may best meet its needs.

Preparing the ground for setting up a group: a consultative training exercise in its own right

Much will depend on how the possibility of starting a staff development group is first raised. A group may be requested by the school itself – a more frequent occurrence now under the new GRIST and 'Baker day' arrangements – especially if the head, a persuasive special needs post-holder, pastoral care tutor, or other members of staff have heard of such groups working well elsewhere. Or the initiator may be a tutor from an in-service teacher training department, a member of a child guidance unit or related school services involved in consultancy training, the school's educational psychologist with good experience of working with teachers, interested staff from the local special needs or teachers' centre, special schools or units or the LEA advisory team. Whoever the initiator, he or she needs to know how to help create the conditions favourable to a good working group.

Trainee consultants need to appreciate that the procedure of informing an interested school of the different structures that have been found to work well in different settings, and of inviting the school to decide which they might wish to develop in the first instance, is in itself an important part of preparing a supportive climate. This will be needed – but should not be expected to exist from the outset – if the group is to become an effective working group. Much of the success of a joint problem-solving consultation group will depend on the way in which it is set up, and this is a consultative exercise on its own.

Space does not permit more than a summary of the aspects the would-be consultant needs to consider jointly to ensure both a good beginning and optimum development for such a group, and readers are therefore referred to the guidelines offered in detail elsewhere (cf Hanko 1985/7).

These include such essentials as a preliminary sounding meeting with the head and whoever else is part of the school's senior management (i.e. anyone in a position to further the aims of the group) to secure their sanction and support; and an introductory meeting with as many of the staff as possible and manageable, for instance over a working lunch, regardless of who will eventually join the group, so that everybody knows what it will be about and interest is generated even in those who may not wish to join it.

Issues that need to be raised, and ground rules to be agreed, will concern such matters as:

- confidentiality and functions of membership
- frequency of meetings, timing and venue (staff need to be safeguarded from competing commitments)
- length of course
- size and composition of the group.

Probable misconceptions about a consultant supporter's role have to be handled; credibility and relevance of one's own experience and expertise need to be established in a non-assertive but authoritative way; appreciation of the teachers' professional expertise needs to be conveyed, together with an awareness of the difficulties that can prevent them from exercising it to its fullest extent; and it needs to be spelt out clearly what such a group would be able to offer and what, together, one may reasonably hope to achieve – one must not raise hopes of cures for all ills. The emphasis is on staff development, not on deficits that need changing.

Conclusion

In conclusion, joint problem-solving and the consultative sharing of expertise can maximise scarce existing resources and increase the capacity of teachers to meet the individual needs of all children; stimulate teachers' personal judgment and initiative as to the best educational 'therapies' open to them, raise their sights as to how to help all children, whatever their difficulties, to learn and to cope, how to offer them those 'good school experiences such as some form of success, accomplishment, sense of self-esteem or just pleasure in school activities' found to be so valuable even in later life (cf Quinton and Rutter 1988).

It is now more important than ever, in an economic climate as unfavourable to education as the present, with attempts at major educational reconstruction in which the special needs of children may well be lost sight of, that developing the consultative role and process are seen as an important way forward.

9 Developing a whole-school approach to disruptive pupils

John Atkinson

Before attempting to set out an approach to disruptive pupils, I believe it is important to preface the debate with a general comment on education – first, because the nature of the topic can generate emotions that lead to a distortion of the author's overall perspective, and second, while I am critical of many educational responses to disruptive pupils I do not wish to add to teachers' feelings of being under siege.

It is my belief that teachers are doing remarkably well in an era of prolonged attack upon state education that has led many consumers to come to believe that schools and teachers have somehow failed, by producing children ill equipped for their roles in society. I would contend that the scapegoating of the education system, in general, and of certain local authorities, in particular, has acted as a diversionary tactic for the inadequacies of central government responses to the funding of the state education system, their failure to stem the spiralling decline in teachers' morale and the pitiful attempt to provide real job opportunities for school leavers.

The scale of the difficulties facing our schools goes unrecognised by too many in our society. The scale can be illustrated by the fact that 30 years ago our young people were maturing at a later stage than now, but in many cases were leaving school at an earlier age and taking up employment – the gap between adolescence and employment was perhaps only 12 months. Today many boys and girls at school are more confident, articulate, mature and consequently, in some cases, more threatening, yet the time lapse between adolescence and employment could be three to four years. It is the schools, and their teachers, who have had to shoulder this burden, increasingly so in a climate where opportunities are diminished and our pupils rightly feel let down, frustrated and alienated from a society that appears insensitive to their plight.

The vast majority of teachers recognise that the carrot and stick argument of 'work hard and you'll get a good job' is ridiculed by many youngsters, at an earlier and earlier age. Equally they recognise that their pupils are exposed to

sophisticated and easily accessible media which graphically, and at times gratu-
itously, portray the violence and disharmony that exists in society.

It is a fact that since 1976, when Jim Callaghan made his celebrated speech at
Ruskin, the education system has been subjected to an unprecedented flow of
Education Acts (1980, 1981, 1986, 1988), committees of inquiry (Warnock,
Taylor, Elton) and curriculum documents from HMI, DES, 'think tanks' and
academics. Schools have battled valiantly, however, to come to terms with the new
demands of curriculum and examination reform in a climate of industrial unrest
and limited resources.

Moreover it seems ironic that while the Secretary of State for Education attacks,
and rightly attacks, the appalling attendance rates at certain schools, and
apportions blame for this situation by claiming that children are bored, he offers a
solution, in the form of the national curriculum, of a diet of mathematics, English,
science, history, geography, a foreign language – all hamstrung with a pedestrian
approach to evaluation in the form of bench-marks.

As Ted Wragg says: 'this list of subjects I did when I was at school in the 1950s.
It is as if curriculum development in the past 30 years had never existed' (*Times
Educational Supplement*). Such an approach ignores the magnificent efforts of
many of our schools to create a vibrant learning environment encapsulating the
need for technological sophistication and real understanding as opposed to mere
accumulation of facts unrelated to their present and future worlds. It is to be
hoped that teachers respond to the positive utterances of David Hargreaves and
Keith Evans (director of education for Clwyd) and continue curriculum innovations within the confines of the national curriculum.

The importance of disruptive behaviour and its impact upon society, in general,
and schools, in particular, is highlighted by the current committee of inquiry into
school discipline chaired by Lord Elton. At this juncture I wish to make five
statements pertinent to the issue and then advance a framework of how schools
can respond positively to deal effectively with disruptive pupils.

1 It seems indisputable that there are a tiny minority of pupils whose
   behaviour is so disturbing that mainstream schools are unable to cope, in
   the present circumstances, with the manifestations of this behaviour.
2 It seems indisputable that in a minority of cases, the causes of the disturbing
   behaviour are located wholly outside the responsibilities of the school and
   that the school is impotent in what it can offer.
3 There is a much larger number of pupils who exhibit disruptive behaviour
   which can, should and must be dealt with by an effective school response.
4 The segregated forms of provision that exist to deal with disruptive pupils
   reflect a bias in terms of race, class and gender that is too conspicuous to go
   unchallenged (Coard 1971, Tomlinson 1981, Eggleston 1986).
5 Just as schools have been accused of creating pupils with learning difficulties, it is possible to argue that schools create disruptive pupils.

Whenever I ask teachers and trainee teachers to respond to two questions about disruptive behaviour:

- What did you feel?
- What did you want to do to the child?

I invariably receive responses such as 'anger', 'fear', 'frustration', 'inadequacy', 'failure', 'my ideals went out of the window', 'I wanted to throttle him/her'. While I accept that these may be legitimate responses to difficult circumstances, I also reflect that these responses are from mature, talented and committed teachers. The fact that disruptive behaviour often leads to considerable stress, anxiety and absenteeism suggests that it is all the more important that schools tackle the issue with more clarity and imagination. On the grounds of efficiency, alone, it is important that mature, talented and committed teachers are not demoralised by disruptive behaviour, and lost to the teaching profession.

Disruptive behaviour has a direct and, at times, devastating impact upon teachers, but it is important to establish that it is not a recent phenomenon. Galloway (1982) and Furlong (1985) present a body of evidence that disruptive behaviour has always existed among boys and girls, in state and public schools, across the age range but more prominently in the lower ability range. As Furlong (1985) says:

> . . . a golden age of pupil behaviour when children attended with regularity and did their teachers' bidding without question . . . may have existed. What is clear is that this golden age did not exist in the mid 1950s, in the first part of this century nor in the first half of the last century. (p 25)

Despite this reassuring message from history that disruptive behaviour is not an event peculiar to contemporary education and recent evidence that there has been no dramatic increase in such behaviour, it has to be acknowledged that anxiety about disruptive behaviour has increased.

Galloway (1982) identifies three reasons put forward for this increase. First, it is the manifestation of the violent society in which pupils live. Second, teacher unions and associations have highlighted the problem to inform and attract sympathy from the public. Third, the range of existing services seems unable to cope with the demand. This anxiety could be further compounded by the 1988 Education Act as competitiveness and accountability feature more prominently in the daily life of teachers. Finally, the media portrayal of political and educational events has presented an unsavoury image. From the William Tyndale affair, the Brent affair and Burnage affair interspersed with riots at Handsworth, Toxteth and at football matches, it is the levels of indiscipline in school that are featured prominently as the primary cause.

Naturally, the causes of disruptive behaviour are frequently debated but unfortunately sloganised. Reasons such as 'over-indulgence in the early years'

(NAS 1974) and the perennial 'parental attitudes' (PAT 1976) are typical examples. It is my contention that the response to causes of disruptive behaviour has focused too much on within-child factors. As Galloway (1982) states:

> Responses to disruptive behaviour must not only recognise the importance of factors in the pupil and his background, but also the relevance of factors in the school itself.

I believe that too many school responses to disruptive behaviour are negative. Frequently the strategies adopted are either to suspend or reject the disruptive pupil and, in certain cases, ignore the fact that disruptive behaviour has occurred. As Bird (1984) has pointed out, these schools perceived disruptiveness as arising from either the irrational behaviour of pupils or the limited educational expectations of working class pupils or the pupils' personal problems of adjustment to the school. Such explanations fail to acknowledge the possibility that schools may be responsible for creating and sustaining disruptiveness. I am arguing that schools must respond more positively; as Hargreaves (1984) states:

> The theme of our remarks on the severely disaffected and disruptive is this: First, seek to integrate and, when that fails, find a positive alternative.

When Reid (1986) identified seven causes of disruptive behaviour (under-achievement, the family, links between school and parents, peer group relationships, the gulf between the general public and teachers, schooling *per se* and teachers), I believe that he highlighted the very issues schools need to turn their attention to and over which they might have significant influence. Furthermore, the six categories identified by the Pack Committee (1977):

1 Pupil and authority
2 Pupil and work
3 Pupil and teacher
4 Pupil and pupil
5 Pupil and property
6 Pupil and public

indicate the possible interactions involved in disruptive behaviour and provide a framework in which schools can begin to formulate policies to resolve the problem.

To devise policies that directly lead to more positive and imaginative approaches, I am proposing that schools need to focus on two particular strands of educational research: first, the research that has been developed in relation to 'effective schools', and second, the principles that underpin 'The Whole-School Approach to Special Educational Needs'.

In the 1960s and 1970s a substantial body of evidence emerged which claimed that schools made little or no difference to pupils' outcomes. The Coleman Report (1966) and the Jencks Report (1972) from America accompanied British evidence, in the form of the Plowden Report and Bernstein (1970), to portray a pessimistic view of the influence of schools upon pupils. As Reynolds and Sullivan (1981) state, the evidence suggests

> that what a child takes from his or her school depends very little upon the quality of the school experience itself but very greatly on the nature of the pupil's intelligence and family and community background.

Such evidence encouraged and sustained the focus on within-child characteristics, illustrated by theories of cultural deprivation and linguistic deprivation.

A number of strong individual, but unrelated challenges were advanced. Counter arguments were put forward that schools and LEAs could influence attendance, intake ability, streaming, teaching styles, levels of classroom management and involvement of parents, all of which directly and indirectly influenced pupils' behaviour.

I believe, however, that over the past 20 years an important body of evidence has emerged which strongly suggests that schools do make a significant difference both to pupil attainment and pupil behaviour. Power (1967), in his research into 20 schools in Tower Hamlets, identified a variance in delinquency rate of 0.9 per cent in one school and, at the other extreme, 19 per cent.

As both schools had a similar catchment area, he postulated that it was the schools themselves that made the difference between their pupils' behaviour.

Reynolds (1976), in his study of nine schools in South Wales, identified considerable variance in measures of attendance, academic achievement and delinquency. Two types of school, 'incorporative' and 'coercive', were identified according to the way in which they tried to involve pupils in achieving their goals. It is possible to identify the characteristics of each school.

Coercive schools

- No attempt to involve pupils in school life
- No attempt to enlist support of parents
- High level of institutional control
- High rates of physical punishment
- Low tolerance of acting out

Incorporative schools

- Allow pupils to take part in lessons
- Allow and encourage work in groups
- Involve pupils in extra-curricular activities
- Pupils, across the range, act as perfects

- Good relationships between teachers and pupils
- Minimal institutional control
- No use of physical punishment
- Close relationship with parents

It is abundantly clear from Reynolds's findings that schools can adopt certain strategies that will have a positive influence on pupil behaviour. Hargreaves (1975) points out that Jordan (1974) has identified two types of teacher, which might well complement Reynolds's two types of school. By identifying the characteristics of each type, interesting information emerges about the ways in which different teachers can elicit different types of behaviour from similar pupils.

Deviance – provocative teachers

- Assumed children did not want to work
- Thought it unreasonable to provide alternative strategies
- Saw discipline as a contest teachers had to win
- Were unable to defuse tense situations
- Frequently issued ultimatums
- Believed in value of confrontations
- Considered pupils as anti-authority
- Punished inconsistently
- Neglected deviant children in interactions
- Made many negative evaluations
- Used sarcasm
- Believed children, generally, were not to be trusted
- Avoided informal contacts outside the classroom

Deviance – insulative teachers

- Assumed children want to work
- Had clear rules and made them explicit
- Were firm
- Did not have favourites
- Avoided confrontations
- Allowed opportunities to save face when they punished children
- Did not publicly denigrate children
- Were optimistic about children
- Perceived all children as contributors
- Liked and respected children
- Were good humoured and trusting
- Enjoyed meeting children outside the classroom

In 1977 HMI published a report *Ten Good Schools* which was followed by

Rutter *et al*'s (1979) celebrated work *Fifteen Thousand Hours*. Rutter *et al*, in a detailed analysis of 12 schools in an inner London borough, make bold statements about the influence that schools have upon pupil attainment and behaviour.

> Schools can do much to foster good behaviour and attainments and . . . even in a disadvantaged area schools can be a force for good.
>
> (Rutter *et al* 1979)

This predominantly optimistic view is further enhanced by Rutter *et al* who were prepared to identify five key areas which were associated with good schools and suggest ways in which each area can be developed to promote positive behaviour and improved attainment levels. The five areas are: schools as organisations, group management, the establishment of school values and norms, consistency, and pupils' acceptance of norms.

Despite criticism of these research findings, I remain convinced that they offer a framework for schools to investigate themselves as organisations and for teachers to analyse themselves as individuals when meeting disruptive behaviour. Furthermore, three other significant reports (Hargreaves 1984, Thomas 1985 and Mortimore 1988) continue to present evidence that schools have a significant influence on pupil behaviour.

As Reid *et al* (1988) state:

> Thus, the correlation between disaffection and bad schooling should never be treated lightly as the long term consequences in society could be devastating.

By paying attention to specific recommendations of Hargreaves (1984), Thomas (1985) and Mortimore (1988), schools and teachers can come to realise that the reduction of disruptive behaviour is likely to be achieved, not by behaviour modification techniques, punitive sanctions or by delving into alleged within-child factors, but by modifying those school structures, and their interaction with pupils, that have such a significant influence on pupil attainment and behaviour. In this way they will be able to meet the needs of individual pupils in a more effective manner. In short, I am stating unequivocally that effective schools exist. The factors that contribute to effective schools are well documented. Disruptive behaviour can be reduced dramatically by schools concentrating on those factors over which they have direct control. It is now firmly established that effective provision for children with special educational needs is achieved by paying attention to the curricular, pastoral and self-enhancing aspects of the school.

> If teachers are to tackle their school's problems realistically, they will need more and better courses on such issues as pastoral care; effective classroom and school management; coping with and overcoming disaffected and disruptive pupils through appropriate teaching and curriculum strategies, as

well as finding ways of undertaking constructive school and self-evaluation programmes . . .

(Reid 1988)

and

when normal individuals show an inability to learn in school, yet are perfectly capable of learning in other situations, one should be driven to consider what aspects of the society are creating negative attitudes to schools and whether changes are necessary in the schools themselves.

(Widlake 1984)

In *Improving Primary Schools* (Thomas Report 1985), there is a detailed analysis of the performance and experience of working class primary aged schoolchildren. In the report there is a wealth of clearly documented evidence highlighting the best practice in ILEA primary schools and providing evidence of contributory factors toward the creation of an effective primary school. In its concluding section, it pays particular attention to the very issues raised by Reid above and offers advice on the way forward. It makes specific points under the section on schools:

It is, in our view, more important to forge a whole school policy than to take on new practices piecemeal.

(Thomas 1985)

The report continues by making reference to the factors that might be instrumental in contributing to the development of a whole school policy: curriculum-general, language, mathematics, expressive subjects and physical education, science, social education; schemes of work, children's progress and school organisation.

The examination of a school's curriculum should take account of what children do and also of what they learn from what they do. Children should be happy at school and acquire positive attitudes to learning, developing new interests as well as pursuing old interests. Learning to read, write and do mathematics have high priority, and children should learn to apply these skills in a variety of ways.

(Thomas 1985)

In *Improving Secondary Schools* (Hargreaves Report ILEA 1984), specific recommendations, aimed at all involved in the delivery of the education service, are highlighted to reduce levels of underachievement and disaffection. The report makes recommendations on four areas which can only enhance the ability of schools and teachers to meet the needs of disruptive pupils.

First, attendance, which can be a prime factor in disruptiveness, is highlighted, and practices which will ensure each school has an effective policy are outlined:

- A senior teacher being charged with specific responsibility for pupil attendance
- A list of absentees being produced quickly, ideally by morning break, for use by appropriate teaching and office staff (see Reid, 1982d)
- Devising a sensitive scheme for the immediate follow-up of absentees, either, for example, by telephoning home or by sending out letters to parents/guardians
- Form tutors ensuring that records of attendance are as accurate as possible and explanations for absence produced when pupils return to school
- Heads of year/house monitoring the work of form tutors
- Heads of year/house and teachers with responsibility for pupil attendance having regular meetings with education welfare officers, perhaps once a month
- Regular spot checks for specific-lesson truancy and for pupils leaving school before the end of the school day
- Rewards in the form of praise or prizes for individual pupils or classes with an excellent attendance record
- Penalties for pupils who are persistently late
- Absentees and truants welcomed quietly back to school and efforts made to re-integrate them socially and academically.

Second, the report highlights the inadequacy of the curriculum in the fourth and fifth years and as Galloway (1982) discovered this was the age at which suspension rates accelerated. The source of much disruptiveness in many secondary schools is the boredom, frustration and sense of futility many pupils feel in relation to the curriculum. To counter this Hargreaves suggests that heads of departments should guarantee that

- Pupils exercise all communication skills – talking, listening, reading and writing – in equal amounts, with the same value ascribed to each
- Topics and relevant issues are raised in classes which stimulate pupils to express opinions, argue, explain and negotiate for a consensus
- The assessment of oral skills is considered as important as the assessment of other skills
- Teachers will ensure there is an oral component in any assessment procedure they devise, and will pressure external examination bodies to do the same.

Third, the report makes recommendations to deal with the concerns of study skills, homework and underachievement. If the issue of disruptiveness is to be met, then underachievement is a key issue and providing pupils with the opportunity to learn how to learn (study skills) and follow the routines of other pupils (homework) will be ways of reducing underachievement. The report recommends that

- Head teachers, in consultation with the whole teaching staff, instigate a clear homework policy and introduce measures by which its implementation is regularly monitored
- District inspectors/advisers provide headteachers with support and advice on the matter of homework policy and practice
- Head teachers ensure that the school informs parents fully about the homework policy and takes measures to enlist their support
- Head teachers seek to provide opportunities for pupils to complete their homework on the school premises
- The Authority, in the longer term, should investigate the extent to which additional resources are needed for supervised 'extended study' by pupils and meet these vital needs
- Head teachers and teachers ensure the school has a study skills policy and helps pupils both to acquire independent learning skills and to pass examinations. In this latter context, schools and districts within local authorities can make a major contribution by:

  a devising INSET programmes with the aim of creating a body of expertise within each subject area of the curriculum
  b preparing study skills booklets for pupils
  c introducing a teachers' guide which provides ideas and examples of good practice within schools
  d devising a booklet for teachers comprising supplementary papers on specific topics such as the ILEA (1983) package on 'Effective Learning Skills'.

Fourth, Hargreaves recommends that there are general school policies which can effectively improve performance. The policies require the support of the local authority and proper resourcing but they provide an ideal framework for schools seeking to become more responsive to their pupils and the communities they serve. The report recommends that:

- the authority should advise governors to take account of appropriate experience when considering staff for promotion
- induction and probationary year schemes be improved
- head teachers ensure that all heads of department have clear job specifications
- inspectors, when their help is sought by head teachers, give high priority to improving the effectiveness of heads of department

- the authority provide courses on basic classroom management and in dealing with disruptive pupils, especially for teachers in professional difficulties
- heads of department ensure that members of their subject teams participate in meaningful self-evaluation exercises
- heads of department adopt policies of using classroom observation and co-teaching methods to ensure and/or raise the quality of teaching as appropriate
- schools pioneer self-evaluation, quinquennial reviews and staff appraisal and course monitoring schemes (see ILEA, 1977; 1982)
- head teachers designate a deputy as staff tutor with overall responsibilities for staff development within the school
- head teachers establish a representative staff development committee to advise them and the staff tutor on the school's INSET programme
- the inspectorate include a component on staff development and INSET in all management courses for head teachers and senior staff
- the authority give greater priority to school-focused INSET to meet increasing demand
- the authority give higher priority and better financial allocation to the in-service education of teachers (INSET) which extends opportunities for teachers to observe and learn from the work of colleagues in other schools
- the authority make financial provision to enable teachers to visit schools outside the ILEA (perhaps along the lines of the West Glamorgan Teacher Fellowship Scheme – see Reid, 1985b)
- the inspector for pastoral care work co-ordinate with a committee the promotion and development of the pastoral curriculum through INSET
- the authority make provision for more local and central courses on the pastoral curriculum and make PSE a high INSET priority
- head teachers ensure all information about the school's INSET programme is on the innovation exchange information sheets
- divisional educational officers enable schools to replace satisfactorily teachers away on INSET courses
- the authority provide schools with substantially increased administrative assistance
- the authority grant head teachers a half-term sabbatical leave every five years.

Mortimore (1988) continues this approach of identifying factors that contribute to school effectiveness. Bayliss (1986) summarises the interim report of 1986 and outlines 12 'rungs' on the ladder of success. I am totally convinced that the solution to the search for ways to handle disruptive pupils lies in this impressive body of evidence and recommendations.

In turning to my second strand of educational research I am encouraged by Reid, Hopkins and Holly (1988):

One eventual measure of the success of the post-Warnock 1981 Education Act will be the extent to which schools are able to combat their non-attendance, disruptive and disadvantaged pupil problems through their special needs programmes.

Indeed.I believe that the effective delivery of such special needs programmes is very much dependent on the organisational structures and educational philosophy that underpins the approach to special educational needs in any school.

Traditionally children with special educational needs have been seen in terms of a deficit model – just as disruptive children have. All too often they have been segregated from their peers to form 'remedial' classes – just as disruptive children have. In these withdrawal classes they have frequently been offered an inappropriate, low-level curricular experience accompanied by low teacher expectation – just as many disruptive children have. Invariably children in such groups have demonstrated the cumulative effect of such approaches through poor levels of achievement, low self-esteem and deteriorating standards of educational attainment and behaviour – just as disruptive children have.

This deficit model which has so patently missed the needs of children with special educational needs is being supplanted, at an increasing pace, through a whole-school approach. By paying attention to this approach, I believe its central tenets can be adopted to provide a way forward for a more effective response to disruptive pupils.

I wish to tackle three major issues which have influenced this changing philosophy and relate it directly to disruptive pupils. First, a key factor in the move towards a whole-school approach is the evidence which highlights the necessity for the child with special educational needs to be provided with access to a broader curriculum (Warnock 1978, Widlake 1984, HMI 1984). It seems appropriate therefore that disruptive pupils have full access to the curriculum which requires that schools acknowledge this in their planning.

The second factor is the evidence which suggests that knowledge and skills acquired in the withdrawal approach do not necessarily transfer, and curriculum content is often divorced from the ordinary curriculum. (Gipps, Goldstein, Gross 1987). The move towards in-class support is equally valid for disruptive pupils. Indeed the evidence (Wilson 1980, Evans 1981) suggests that disruptive pupils are exposed to an inferior curriculum which may only add to their difficulties.

The third factor supporting the whole-school approach is the benefits of wider experiences and peer interactions derived from the involvement in the curriculum which are essential for the full development of the 'whole child'. It seems patently clear that disruptive pupils need more, not less, interaction with their peers and more, not less, involvement in the whole life of the school. The isolation or bunching together of such pupils only provides them with poor role models and intensive interaction with other disturbed children.

The whole-school approach means that every effort is made to 'normalise' pupils with special needs.

Pupils are included in school plays and productions, included in school teams and have their work displayed upon walls and in school magazines as often as other pupils. (N Butt 1986)

It is for schools to embrace the same approach for disruptive pupils. The whole-school approach implies that ALL staff will ensure that all pupils with special needs are identified and provided for. Hence, I am arguing that ALL staff accept similar responsibility for disruptive pupils.

The curriculum considerations of the whole-school approach imply that pupils will be in the mainstream classes and the responsibility of the class teacher. Support teaching will take place instead of withdrawal. Hence, subject and support teachers will need to develop expertise in modifying curriculum materials *and* managing behaviour problems.

In conclusion, I am advocating that, as the whole-school approach grows in popularity as a positive response to children with special educational needs, it is important that schools, as organisations, and teachers, as individuals, reject the segregationist policy towards disruptive pupils which might appeal to some teachers and government policy makers. By embracing the evidence from the 'effectiveness of schools' research and adopting a whole-school approach to special educational needs, we can create a truly comprehensive service of education in which it is accepted that ALL teachers have responsibility to meet the needs of ALL children. This will require a creative response to the curriculum, the pastoral service and the management structure.

It is important that the category of children with moderate learning difficulties, which has escalated to frightening proportions, is not replaced with a new category of disruptive pupils. Both categories are dangerous because of the subjective and inadequate forms of assessment which are used and the social, educational and economic effects on those labelled.

We need to offer disruptive children an education that does not limit them in a straitjacket designed to serve the political and economic needs of a society characterised by a culture of individualism. We need to provide an educational service that does not promote disruptive pupils nor reject disruptive pupils. We must not disable or marginalise them in a society that increasingly seems interested only in the successful. We need to offer an education that enables them to play a positive role in society by giving them the opportunity to use their talents. It is my firm view that the education service has a moral responsibility to address the issue of disruptive behaviour before a so-called solution is imposed on it.

10 The role of school governors in meeting special educational needs

John Harrington

The 1981 Education Act is still in force. It has not been repealed or superseded by more recent legislation. This point was emphasised by Professor Klaus Wedell in the keynote lecture of the conference. It is important to bear this in mind in any study of the role of school governors in meeting special educational needs.

However dramatically their powers and responsibilities may have been extended by the 1986 and 1988 Acts, their legal duties in this matter remain exactly as stated in section 2(5) of the 1981 Act.

> (5) It shall be the duty of the governors, in the case of a county or voluntary school, and of the local education authority by whom the school is maintained, in the case of a maintained nursery school
>
> (a) to use their best endeavours, in exercising their functions in relation to the school, to secure that if any registered pupil has special education needs the special educational provision that is required for him is made
>
> (b) to secure that, where the responsible person has been informed by the local education authority that a registered pupil has special needs these are made known to all who are likely to teach him; and
>
> (c) to secure that the teachers in the school are aware of the importance of identifying, and providing for, those registered pupils who have special educational needs.

The Act goes on to define 'the responsible person' as the head teacher or designated governor. In practice delegation to the head teacher is usually seen as the most reasonable and educationally sound arrangement. The legal process is similar to those by which head teachers exercise responsibility for health and safety and the prevention of nuisance or disturbance on school premises!

Nursery schools are mentioned separately because education acts do not automatically apply to them. They are, therefore, not required by law to have governing bodies although some LEAs, including Berkshire, established such bodies some years ago and have subsequently applied most of the requirements of legislation to the ways in which they conduct their affairs.

In areas with long nursery waiting lists it has been usual for governors to establish admission panels drawn from their own members. These panels meet termly with head teachers to decide whether priority should be given to the admission of certain individual pupils because of particular educational or social need. Consideration would be given to factors such as social deprivation, stresses in the family, difficulties with language or learning and substantiated medical problems. In this way the governors of nursery schools and primary schools with nursery units have been actively involved in decisions about special educational needs. They have valuable experience which could usefully be shared with governors of other types of school who are facing a similar challenge.

As a legal precedent section 2(5) of the 1981 Education Act was significant because it was addressed directly to governing bodies and assigned a primary role to them rather than the local authorities. This approach continued to gain impetus in subsequent consultation processes and legislation which emerged.

Through all this process, and partly because of the pressures created by it, the central role of governors has received little public attention. Few books dealing with education for special needs have referred to governors. In the case of one otherwise excellent book governors looking for reference to their own role in the index would have found nothing listed between 'Failure' and 'Handicap'! One of the exceptions was '*Management and the Special School*' edited by Tony Bowers which devoted 17 pages to the governor's function. The book predates the 1986 Act and concentrates explicitly on management issues but it still contains much useful and relevant advice.

Local authorities responded to the Act by concentrating more on special needs in their governor training programmes but produced relatively little written information for general distribution. This was understandable. Priority had to be given to the statutory duties of constructing and publishing procedures for the assessment of pupils with special needs and the monitoring of their progress. Now that the legal framework for the rest of the century appears to have been set attention can be given to the task of interpreting it for governors. In Berkshire a working group of advisers and head teachers has produced a draft document summarising the duties imposed by the 1981 Education Act, the help and resources available to enable governors to carry them out, and specimens of statutory returns.

If governors are to be helped to perform their duties under the 1981 Act effectively, these duties must be set into the context of the responsibilities imposed by the 1986 and 1988 Acts.

The first real impact of the 1986 Act came to governors with the requirements to produce a formal report to parents and hold an annual parents' meeting. Presenting a report before an audience in this way and making themselves vulnerable to questions and criticisms were new experiences which many governors continue to find unsettling. It was not easy to find a way of presenting prosaic information in a way which would attract parents. Some schools serving a clientele with reading difficulties selected a distinctly tabloid format. 'Did you know? Governors tell all!' was the headline chosen by Kennel Lane Special School in Bracknell. Some of the school's achievements were then listed followed by the invitation 'Want to know more? . . . then come along to our Annual Meeting for Parents on Tuesday 5 July.'

In all schools the governors' obligation to report on the discharge of their functions obviously includes their response to special educational needs, and in special schools is synonymous with it. The question which immediately arises is: 'how do we report on a function which is entirely concerned with the wellbeing of individual pupils without breaking confidence?'. There is no simple answer but it is generally advisable to describe the disappointments in broad terms as they affect the whole school ('the LEA has been unable to grant our request for extra welfare assistance') and present the successes individually but anonymously ('through the efforts of the governors a reading aid has been provided for a partially sighted pupil').

It would certainly be improper for the governors to go into the medical or educational case history on which the call for provision had been based. Their chairman would have the support of both the Secretary of State and the LEA in discouraging, and ultimately forbidding, discussion of the performance of an individual pupil or teacher at an annual parents' meeting. The usual advice would be to suggest a private meeting between the chairman, the head teacher and the parent who raised the issue.

In cases of noteworthy personal achievement such as the award of a swimming trophy to a disabled pupil the governors may consider it entirely fitting to mention the name, but care must be taken not to introduce an undesirable element of competition or rivalry. This danger exists also in secondary schools where the governors' report must include information in a prescribed form in relation to public examinations – in effect, a publication of results.

It will be important for governors to present their reports in such a way as to ensure that the quality of their schools is not judged solely by academic results but by success in meeting the educational needs of all pupils, including those whose progress can never be measured on an examination scale. They can only achieve this through a systematic analysis of their responsibilities towards the curriculum as a whole.

It always has been desirable for governors in special schools to have some knowledge of the curriculum in mainstream schools and for this awareness to be reciprocated. In the future this will be essential as the system moves towards an integrated structure. The government has reaffirmed its commitment to the principle of integration envisaged in the 1981 Education Act. Articles of government made under the 1986 Act gave control of the secular curriculum to governors of aided schools and required the governing bodies of other maintained schools to study the LEA curriculum statement and consider how it might be modified to meet the needs of their schools.

Within such a framework the duties imposed by the 1981 Act could be accommodated fairly easily, but another challenge was immediately presented by the introduction of the national curriculum with its mandatory package of core and foundation subjects. Although some adjustment would have to be made to new criteria for apportioning teaching time, these subjects were not new. Adapted in various ways, they formed part of the teaching programme for mainstream and special pupils for many years.

A more worrying element was the requirement to assess the progress of each pupil formally at the ages 7, 11, 14 and 16. The advocates of education for special needs were not reassured by the terms of reference of the task group established by the Secretary of State. This group was asked to advise on what forms of assessment, including testing, would be most appropriate at each age. Would this mean that children with special educational needs, whose chronological age had little relevance to their scholastic progress, would be publicly judged against certain criteria applied nationally to the whole ability range? What would be the position of children for whom the LEA had issued a statutory statement of special need? The Secretary of State replied that the national curriculum would apply to statemented children but the statement might set out any changes to meet need. Changes would also be permitted in attainment targets, programmes of study and assessment arrangements.

The parliamentary Select Committee on Education saw a need for clarification and a more analytical approach, but the call for a national advisory body was rejected by the government. Senior members of Her Majesty's Inspectorate who expressed similar anxieties have initiated an internal review of statutory procedures by DES officials. Governors will await with interest the outcome of this review and of the Secretary of State's consideration of the issue of new or revised circulars. In the meantime they have the immediate task of responding to special educational needs on the basis of the information which is available to date.

The national curriculum guidance which has been issued at the time of writing on the two core subjects of mathematics and science shows a welcome emphasis on statements of attainment rather than testing. Taking science as an example, the programme is divided into areas of study, one of which is 'The Variety of Life'. The first attainment target is that 'Pupils should develop their knowledge and understanding of the diversity and classification of living things and of the relationships, energy flow, cycles of matter and human influences within equal systems.' Brief summaries are then given of the relevant programme of study to be followed by pupils in the age groups 5 to 7, 7 to 11, 11 to 14 and 14 to 16. When pupils reach the upper limit of each age group their attainment would be measured by teachers against a series of nationally prescribed criteria. These range from level one, requiring a knowledge about the wide variety of living things, to level ten, which requires an understanding of cycling of the major elements and the role of microbes and other organisms in maintaining the cycles. Thus an able 11-year-old pupil might attain level 7 in a particular subject while a pupil of the same age in the same school who has learning difficulties might reach level 3. This information will be given only to the parents of the individual child. Governors who are attuned to education for special needs will be aware that 'Low' attainment level may represent greater progress and achievement on the part of pupil and teacher than a 'High' attainment level. It is an important part of their role to promote equal esteem in the community for every aspect of the work and activity carried out in the school.

Sensitivity to the feelings and perception of parents, individually and collectively, is an essential quality for all school governors. They will be asked to exercise it particularly where there is special need and in the other delicate area of sex education. Governors must decide whether this subject is to form part of the curriculum for their school. If it is included, they must also decide on how it is to be taught. The government's circular (8/87) which lays down the guidelines to be observed stresses the importance of a spirit of confidence between parents, governors and teachers in the approach to this question. It should be remembered that parents do not have a statutory right to withdraw their children but governors have a duty to make a decision on any application for withdrawal which is made to them. In the case of religious education the right of withdrawal is statutory and governors are recommended to make themselves familiar with the special status which is accorded to this subject in the national curriculum.

The emphasis which has been placed so far on the curriculum is intentional. Unless governors are thoroughly familiar with the task the community has entrusted to the school they will not be able to make informed decisions about the staff, educational resources, premises and money which are necessary to accomplish it.

The Articles of Government made under the 1986 Act gave to the governors of county and controlled schools the duty of devising arrangements for the appointment of staff, excluding head teachers and, in some authorities, deputy head teachers. Governors of aided schools, as the legal employers of the staff of their schools, have always had the right to make their own staffing arrangements subject to the establishment laid down by the authority. Although they were legally autonomous they usually followed guidelines issued by the LEA and, in the case of denominational schools, diocesan authorities. If governors of any maintained school wished to take formal action on the basis of a teacher's level of competence or suitability for continued employment at their school they would have to comply with LEA policies on redeployment and support for teachers experiencing professional difficulties. They would also have to observe the requirements of national employment legislation and this would always be the case whatever developments may occur on the education side.

The 1988 Education Reform Act extends this power to the point where governors can require the LEA to give notice to a teacher if this is their decision after passing through all due legal processes. The cost of this extended power is that governors will be liable to defend their decision before an industrial tribunal.

These processes have been described because they provide an active demonstration of the recent change in the balance of power between governors and local authorities. It is hoped that most governors would spend the whole of their service without having to face such an unwelcome decision as the dismissal of a member of staff and would be able to concentrate their efforts on engaging and supporting the best people to carry out the educational tasks for which they were responsible. In the context of special need this means selecting competent, adaptable and understanding staff who are sensitive to the needs which present themselves in the school and who are prepared to undertake the study and training required to keep pace with developments. This extends to the appointment of ancillary and technical staff, who would be expected to have the same sympathetic qualities, and to making a case for help from the authority's teaching and support services or for a welfare assistant to help with an individual pupil.

The governors' responsibility for school premises likewise has implications for their special needs role. If the school has on its site a special unit for pupils presenting particular medical, social or educational need, the governors should certainly be totally familiar with its purpose, sympathetic towards its aims and actively concerned with its work. If they are not, they should question their suitability to serve as governors of that school. The suitability of the premises, the need for improved access or relocation of equipment and the provision of items such as ramps, carpeting or acoustic tiles where appropriate are all matters which should concern governors if they are to 'use their best endeavours' to ensure that special needs are met – the duty which is binding on the governors of every school.

The evaluation of physical resources extends to items which are more obviously learning tools such as hearing or reading aids and books, audiovisual materials and project packs. For all these tasks governors will need the help of specialist staff such as advisers, advisory teachers, doctors, nurses, therapists, psychologists and, most importantly, classroom teachers. It will be impossible for all members of a governing body to absorb all that needs to be known about the vast subject of special needs and to be adequately informed at the same time about all the other endeavours which they have to promote. Delegation will be essential, either to an individual governor, as recommended in the Warnock Report, or to a sub-committee on duties relating to special needs.

The sub-committee pattern has several advantages. It divides the task into more manageable proportions, it increases the number of people available to visit the school during teaching hours (preferably to become actively involved in the work) and it gives an opportunity for shared membership with other sub-committees dealing with the curriculum, staffing and finance.

The devolution of financial management is one of the most important developments in recent legislation. By 1992 all secondary schools and primary schools with more than 200 pupils will have responsibility for their own budgets. The pattern of financial management for smaller primary schools and for special schools will be determined by the LEA after consultation with governors. By economic necessity this pattern will have to be accommodated within a structure which is attuned to decentralisation so there will inevitably be more delegation even to the governors of the smaller schools.

It will undoubtedly be an advantage to governing bodies to have more control over the resources of their schools and greater flexibility in the deployment and use of staff, premises and materials. This will include the power to reduce expenditure in any one of these areas in order to devote more funds to another, for example, by choosing to spend money released by a staff vacancy on educational equipment rather than on recruiting a replacement. This power brings with it the responsibility to ensure that decisions are made and priorities are set upon the basis of the best educational advice available. Governors who are committed to the cause of special education will have to bid for a share of resources in competition with the advocates of other areas of the curriculum who will be pressing their case with equal vigour.

This competitive element will be sharpened by the policy of open enrolment, introduced by the Education Reform Act, which gives parents the right to have their child admitted to any school which has a place. The parental vote will be even more powerful if it is proposed that a school should opt out of local authority control and transfer to grant maintained status. This is presented in legislation as an opportunity for parents and the local community to run their own schools with funding direct from central government. Such a decision, taken through the prescribed secret ballot procedures, could ultimately be imposed by parents on a governing body.

In discussing proposals with parents and the LEA the governors would need to be fully aware of the possible educational and financial consequences including the terms on which support services for special needs would still be available, and at what cost, from the LEA or elsewhere. It would not be lawful for a grant maintained school to reject children with special needs who were otherwise eligible for admission but it is impossible to legislate against the temptation to work towards greater academic activity or to concentrate on subjects which are regarded as prestigious by the potential client group.

In spite of all this complexity the focus of the governor's moral and legal duty remains the individual pupil. This is reflected in Articles of Government made under the 1986 Act in the procedures laid down for dealing with the exclusion of pupils from school and with the appeals which might arise from exclusion. The central feature is a case conference which brings together parents, governors, teachers and other professionals in a joint effort to resolve the problem presented by the case.

This procedure is by no means limited to exclusion. Head teachers frequently convene case conferences at an early stage in an effort to meet a pupil's needs before this crisis point is reached. Many governors are likely to preside over a case conference at some time during their term of office and for chairmen, particularly those serving large schools, it may become a regular and frequent experience. All the pupils concerned will have special needs in the sense that there is some defect in their response to the educational programme being offered by their present school. With advice from the head teacher and the LEA representative, when present, the governors presiding over a case conference will have to be able to evaluate the options put forward, including alternative education outside the mainstream school system, and make a recommendation.

Faced with a pressing requirement to absorb a great amount of educational, legal and procedural information, governors have an obvious and urgent need for training. This point is being stressed by many organisations representing the interests of people with physical, mental or educational disabilities.

Because of the scale of the need, the limitations of staff and resources and the pressure of other work it is unrealistic to expect that local authorities could provide a comprehensive training programme immediately. Governors will, therefore, depend heavily upon the guidance and information which can be provided for them within the school.

As in the past, the information for guidance will be conveyed mainly by the head teacher's report, which governors would come to regard rightly as a source of sound professional advice, subjects for discussion and a welcome touch of humour ('Mr C scored three goals for the staff against the pupils and also acted as referee'). As current legislation takes effect these will continue to be important elements but the style of presentation of the report can be expected to change as the governors receive greater control over school based resources and the power to make more executive decisions.

Head teachers may find it helpful to consider the format now being commended by some local authorities to the officers responsible for the preparation of the committee reports. This format comprises the following sequence of headings: purpose of report, decision requested, summary of supporting arguments, financial implications, comments of other professional officers and supporting documents.

In the context of a head's report dealing with special needs the decision required could relate to anything from the building of a new unit to the provision of additional welfare or teaching assistance for an individual pupil. In all cases, after stating the purpose of the report, the head teacher needs to set out clearly the decision he or she would advise the governors to take.

It is not a case of imposing a decision but of ensuring, through the presentation of supporting arguments, that the governors are aware of which of the options stated is the most educationally sound. If they take any other course of action they must be prepared to defend it. The case for setting out financial implications is obvious in a situation in which the school budget is controlled by the governors. The 'other professional officers' whose comments might be incorporated if appropriate would include not only the officers and advisers of the authority and centrally employed caring and counselling staff but also teaching and ancillary colleagues within the school. Discussion in the staff meeting should have taken place before any proposal affecting school policy is presented to the governors and a class teacher should certainly have been involved in any submission about an individual pupil. Any reports produced by these professional colleagues should take their place, with any relevant papers produced by the authority, as 'supporting documents'.

If governors are to make good decisions on meeting special needs their approach must be equally systematic. The following advice could serve as a framework.

First look at the membership of the governing body to discover what relevant expertise is available or might be made available by co-option. The myth that governors are all 'uninformed lay people' should be dispelled at an early stage.

Decide whether a governor or group of governors forming a sub-committee should be appointed to assist the chairman in dealing with urgent pupil matters and to assume responsibility in special needs. If a sub-committee is appointed, consider the advantages of some common membership with any other groups appointed to deal with staffing and resources, including finance. The sub-committee might then find it is helpful to note any immediately available information about good practice elsewhere and consider the questions which they propose to ask during their first consultation with the head teacher. If pursued effectively, this consultation could lead to a planned programme of visits to classrooms or units and periodic reports of governors' meetings by the sub-committee, the headteacher or teachers dealing with special needs in their daily work.

Concurrently with this programme the governors should be making themselves familiar with the roles of centrally based staff who could help them, such as special needs advisers, psychologists and support teachers, and seeking their help in interpreting the authority's statements on policy and procedures. They should also press for the training necessary to enable them to carry out their duties of securing provision for individual pupils and working to ensure that special education is esteemed as highly as any other form of education within a system in which schools will have greater control over resources and the setting of priorities for their use.

11 The role of welfare assistants in supporting children with special educational needs in ordinary primary schools

Terence Clayton

Introduction

The use of welfare assistants, non-teaching assistants, teachers' aides, auxiliary helpers and ancillary staff, which those who assist teachers with their non-professional duties are variously called, is not a recent innovation in either special or ordinary education. More than 20 years ago, the Plowden Report (1967) drew attention to such staff and made recommendations regarding their recruitment and career structure, numbers, role, and training requirements, emphasising, in particular, that, 'ancillary help should be used not simply to maintain, but to raise educational standards'.

Later, the Warnock Report (1978), in focusing attention on the integration of children with special educational needs, cited the committee's awareness of the important contribution made by non-teaching aides, as they were described. The report noted that they not only provided care for children but enabled teachers to attend to others and also that the aides themselves carried out important educational work under the teacher's direction.

Teachers themselves, despite some reservations, have also welcomed such assistance (NUT Report 1962, Clunies-Ross 1984) and certainly since the implementation of the Education Act 1981, numbers have increased considerably. In their recent survey, Goacher *et al* (1988) showed that 76 per cent of LEAs recorded a 'substantial increase' in the number of welfare assistants/non-teaching auxiliaries and 65 per cent indicated that this was an area attracting priority funding.

Welfare assistants and education

Given this welcomed increase, how can welfare assistance be best employed? Duthie (1970), in studying the teacher's day, estimated that about one-third of a teacher's time was taken up with duties of a non-professional nature which 'auxiliaries' could undertake. Duthie included 'housekeeping' activities, preparation of materials and supervision as legitimate duties. Duthie, and later Kennedy & Duthie (1975), were concerned with general rather than special education and authors who have focused on special needs have suggested a wider brief.

Hegarty *et al* (1981), for instance, identified four main roles which they described as care, educational, para-professional and general. Care, which was mainly to do with children's physical well-being, typically included help with dressing, toileting, feeding and mobility. The educational role usually amounted to freeing the teacher from mundane classroom activities or carrying out instruction under the teacher's guidance, whereas the para-professional role involved helping with physiotherapy and speech therapy exercises.

The general role was a mix of less tangible duties including acting as a mother figure, friend or confidante. A similar analysis was put forward by Hodgson *et al* (1984). Specialist roles have also been experimented with, for instance, by Kolvin *et al* (1981) who trained and used aides to provide nurturing treatment to pupils with emotional and behaviour difficulties.

Assistants and the curriculum

Brennan (1985) felt that classroom assistants as a resource were relatively little exploited in curriculum terms with most assistants in special education acting as facilitators by helping children with disabilities to do what other children can do for themselves, or relieving the teacher of classroom chores. Brennan felt that they could be used to enable teachers to individualise and extend the curriculum and suggested the following activities:

- Supervision of ongoing work to free teachers for individual or small-group work
- Supervision of repetitive work or practice
- Supervision of generalisation of established skill or knowledge
- Conversation with disadvantaged or other pupils who need extended conversational experience
- Supervision of small groups on out-of-school projects
- Contribution of local knowledge in environmental projects
- Point of contact with local people who may contribute to curriculum
- Assistance with pupils who have problems with mobility

- As a 'reinforcer' in behavioural learning
- As a recorder in experimental teaching or in establishing behavioural base lines
- As a contributor of any personal skill in practical or artistic activities
- As a potential contributor of additional local knowledge in any relevant aspect of curriculum development.

Recruitment and training

Anderson (1973) noted that great variety in the methods of recruitment of assistants, hours of work, and the amount of timetabled contact with special needs children. The situation was still much the same when Hegarty and his colleagues (1981) carried out their study of LEA integration schemes. They noted that one LEA employed only qualified personnel, whereas others were content to recruit mothers who had had first-hand experience of bringing up their own children.

The latter was particularly the case with assistants allocated to named children with special educational needs in mainstream classes. Hodgson *et al* (1984) also found that some schools required qualifications whereas others looked for personal qualities such as flexibility and good interpersonal skills.

Training following appointment is also evidently not universal, for Goacher *et al* (1988) recorded that only 28 per cent of LEAs were offering training to their assistants in order to implement the 1981 Education Act.

The literature on other aspects of the job is sparse and the field generally, as Dessent (1987) has noted, is poorly researched. Many of the studies that do exist have been small scale or have had some other issue, such as integration, as their key focus, referring to welfare assistance either in passing or as a subsidiary concern. Nevertheless, useful insights have been offered by such workers as Anderson, Hegarty and Hodgson.

The Wiltshire study

This study arose out of two concerns. The first was a local need for accurate information about current welfare assistant practice to enable the resource to be provided as effectively as possible and also to identify good and inappropriate practice, and adopt or remedy these as necessary; and to identify training needs. The second and wider intention was to start investigating some of the basic research issues.

The study focused on welfare assistants working with children with special educational needs in ordinary primary schools and aimed to identify background experience, previous training and qualifications; conditions of service and appointment procedures; general duties and specific activities undertaken; opinions about the usefulness of these activities to both pupils and teachers;

assistants' role preferences; and views regarding the kind of support and training required for effective service delivery.

The survey involved an analysis of all statutory assessment documentation as well as the administration of a detailed questionnaire to heads, class teachers and welfare assistants. Follow-up interviews, case studies and classroom observation are also planned. Returns were received from 100 welfare assistants working with 98 children in 72 schools. Preliminary findings are discussed below.

Results

Background experience, training and qualifications

The welfare assistants were asked about their experience before taking up their current post. Almost all had brought up children of their own and 80 per cent had had voluntary experience in schools. Approximately half had organised or helped with playgroups and a similar number had previously worked as welfare assistants. However, only one in five had had experience of handicapped or difficult children. It was interesting to note that 84 per cent had had three or more different types of experience.

As far as their training and qualifications were concerned, one-third had no qualifications at all and less than half had obtained basic school qualifications.

On the other hand, a quarter had received secretarial or office training and nearly one-fifth held first aid qualifications. At the other end of the scale, six were qualified teachers, three of them at graduate level.

Briefing, support and supervision

Once appointed, almost everyone was briefed, mainly by their head teacher but also in about half the cases by their class teacher. It is also worth noting that parents briefed the assistants more often than professionals such as educational psychologists, doctors, speech and physiotherapists.

The questionnaire did not ask about specific help to assistants from the LEA support services but, instead, looked at special needs support to the school as a whole. Materials and equipment were provided in nearly half of the cases, mainly by advisers; extra tuition, often on a weekly basis, was provided by specialist teachers; and there were many occasions when advice and support was made available, usually on an occasional basis, by educational psychologists and specialist teachers. Specific training was limited and occasional.

Role of welfare assistants

The assistants were questioned in detail about their duties and specific activities undertaken. Over 90 per cent stated that they frequently supervised and assisted small groups of children engaged in educational activities set by the teacher, and encouraged children by offering appropriate attention and by showing interest in their activities. Slightly fewer assisted individuals and related children's progress to their teacher. Half or more frequently also helped children with dressing, administered first aid, made and maintained teaching aids of various kinds and helped the class teacher with the general management of behaviourally difficult children.

In general, the assistants undertook a great variety of activities, many of them frequently. In terms of total expenditure of time, instructional and general care and supervisory activities were clearly the two main duties. These duties were also listed by the assistants as the ones which they felt were most helpful both to the child and the teacher and were also the ones which they enjoyed most and felt most competent in completing. Least time was spent on cleaning and administration and recording.

As far as the organisation of their work was concerned, only four said that they spent all their time with the 'named' child, half worked with other special needs children or undertook general duties and 92 per cent said they also worked with normal children. The assistants were in fact appointed by the LEA to work primarily with 'named' children.

Training and support requirements

The assistants were asked what help and training they needed in order to carry out their duties more effectively, and both head and class teacher were asked to comment on the same issues independently.

Substantial numbers of assistants wanted training in specific skills, particularly behaviour management and first aid, and about half regarded attendance at a training course on the general role of the assistant as important.

Nearly 40 per cent felt that they needed more information about the problems and background of individual children and about one-quarter would have liked more general information about the child as well as more advice about how they could help to meet the child's needs.

Head teachers felt that their assistants' main needs were knowledge and training about classroom teaching, routines and methods as well as first aid and behaviour management skills. They also felt that a general induction course focusing on special educational needs would be helpful. The class teachers identified knowledge of classroom strategies and routines including small-group work, speech and communication skills and special educational needs generally as important considerations for training.

Discussion and conclusions

From the results of the survey it can be seen that many of the welfare assistants had varied and substantial experience of children and schools. Nevertheless, only about one in five had experience of handicapped or difficult children. However, one might expect such opportunities to become more widespread as the number of such children supported in mainstream continues to grow. The assistants were also not a very well qualified group either in terms of formal school qualifications or further training. Thus, if their role is to develop beyond the 'house-keeping' duties described by Duthie, further training will be essential.

The picture with regard to briefing and preparation was encouraging with only one assistant reporting that she had not been briefed. Head teachers took the main responsibility for this but class teachers also made an important contribution. The extent and quality of briefing possibly accounts for the overwhelming view of the assistants that their duties were ones which they had expected to be doing when appointed. Support to schools in terms of materials and equipment, extra tuition and advice and assessment, all seemed at least adequate whereas in-service opportunities were limited. Heads and class teachers were particularly keen that the assistants should have a working knowledge of classroom practice and assistants and teachers wanted specific training, especially in relation to behaviour problems and first aid. Approximately half of the assistants also wished to attend an induction course on the general role of a welfare assistant.

The welfare assistants' duties were wide-ranging with face-to-face instruction (under the teacher's direction) and general care and supervision taking up most time. Irrespective of the type of difficulties presented by the children, there was a substantial core of activities which more than 70 per cent of the assistants engaged in. This suggests that one priority is a general initial training supplemented by training in more specific skills relating to the presenting difficulties of the children being supported.

Over 90 per cent of the assistants frequently supervised and assisted small groups of children engaged in educational activities set by the teacher, and slightly fewer worked with individuals and related their progress to the teacher. The assistants not only preferred these sorts of activities but also felt that they were the ones most helpful to both child and teacher.

Not uncommonly, studies of this kind which relate to relatively uncharted areas raise more issues than they solve. One feels, however, that a systematic start has now been made in the identification of current welfare assistant practice from which specific issues can be highlighted and followed up. Among these must surely be more explicit job descriptions coupled with suitable role titles, and a general recognition of the need for training.

12 Issues of multiprofessional co-operation

Eva Gregory

Working collaboratively with other professionals in relation to children, whatever the setting, is a must, although we are not necessarily very good at it, nor do we know very clearly how to achieve it.

> Improvements in professional practice and inter-agency co-operation are still necessary and procedures still need to be further developed.
>
> The thrust now must be to ensure that professionals in individual agencies work together on a multi-disciplinary basis.
>
> If co-operation between agencies in providing protection to children is to be effective it must be underpinned by a shared understanding of the handling of individual cases.
>
> This Circular provides advice on action which should be taken within the Education Service to enable cases of suspected abuse to be properly considered and pursued. It emphasises the importance of co-operation between agencies concerned with the probation of children.
>
> The development of inter-agency co-operation acknowledges that:
> careful consideration must be given to the details of works arrangements between doctors, nurses, social workers, police, teachers, staff of voluntary organisations and others responsible for the care of children.
>
> (DES Circular 4/88)

The above statements are taken from recent publications which have emerged as a result of the Cleveland inquiry.

Not that the events of the Cleveland inquiry are necessarily typical of the events in the educational field; nonetheless, this was a situation which called for multi-professional co-operation, and the inquiry investigated some of the difficulties in achieving this.

The language of these reports is one of exhortation and of encouragement to the wide range of professionals concerned with the protection of children. It differs little from the language of other inquiries which have been held regarding tragedies which have affected a number of children in the last 15 years; in fact it is interesting that there is considerable similarity in the themes which form the basis of conclusions of many of the earlier reports.

Major concerns are invariably expressed about the difficulties experienced by a number of professionals having to work together with a common aim. There are also other assumptions. These include a belief that working together in a collaborative way is merely a matter of communicating the right things to the right people at the right time. Furthermore, it is suggested that things often go wrong because there has not been an adequate transfer of information between the professionals involved in situations which have led to tragedies.

Although I have referred in an oblique way to the inquiries and reports which have been made in relation to child abuse and the tragedies relating to a number of children, the intention is not to concentrate on this topic but to consider issues which arise in multiprofessional collaboration in general and those specifically relating to education. This is particularly relevant as many of the earlier recommendations are full of good intentions, but little attempt is made to explore why there are difficulties when different professionals are expected to work together and make decisions together.

There is little in the literature concerning education which concentrates to the same extent on professionals collaborating in order to achieve some outcome or goal as there is in the health and social work fields. This leads one to think that the expectation of collaboration among a spectrum of professionals is more characteristic of health and social services than of the education field. One suspects that there are a number of reasons for this, including less acceptance by educationists in allowing non-teachers to make decisions on a joint basis. This may appear as a somewhat generalised and sweeping statement; nonetheless, as a comparative newcomer, the practice and acknowledgement of multi-disciplinary working in education is less well established. Perhaps an exception to this is the mode of operation in some special schools, particularly those for emotional behavioural difficulties (EBD) and for 'delicate' children. In these schools various multiprofessionals are involved, so that co-operation and joint decision making is a more acceptable and standard practice. The work of EBD schools, in particular, has been based on a historical model of treatment, largely influenced by the ethos of medicine and psychiatry, where different disciplines are expected to contribute.

Nonetheless, even in these so-called therapeutic settings, all has not been sunshine and light. In hospitals, the word of the doctor carries more weight than anyone else's, regardless of whether the ward sister has had 20 years' experience and he or she two. Inevitably, this ethos has been transferred to psychiatry, where the word of the psychiatrist has tended to predominate, but probably less so than in general medicine. It goes without saying that this pattern was repeated in EBD schools where the multidisciplinary approach prevailed to some extent. In fact some colleagues have argued about the success of this mode of operating. There is clearly an advantage in sharing information about children and families; in an EBD school setting the situation is made more complex by the presence of the head and the psychiatrist and their status.

In trying to analyse why difficulties arise when various professionals try to collaborate, a large number of factors have to be considered. These relate not only to the personalities concerned – and this aspect should not be underestimated – but also to a variety of concepts and aspects which are frequently associated. Thus power status, knowledge and expertise are as relevant as the ethos and rules of an agency, or the perception and values of various individuals.

One way of exploring the complexity of these issues is to borrow from a systems approach, which relates and considers the behaviour of an individual in the context of the system in which he operates. This means that the behaviour of one component is seen as affecting and being affected by the behaviour of others.

All professionals work in systems. These have boundaries, hierarchies and boundaries between sub-systems. Furthermore, all social systems have rules governing the way people should behave towards one another, what is acceptable in terms of behaviour and tasks and how the rules are made. Another characteristic of a system is the existence of an ethos or culture which is closely related to their characteristic as a social organisation.

It is with this approach in mind that it would be useful to highlight and explore the most pertinent issues in relation to multiprofessional co-operation.

Power and authority

There is an assumption, illustrated by the way multiprofessional collaboration is exhorted, that the various professionals who are involved in the personal social services have an equal voice and influence. In practice, this is far from the case. For instance, in a medical situation, the status of the doctor will in most cases influence and outweigh the decisions of other professionals, no matter how democratic the intention of all. It is difficult for others to challenge the views of a doctor; similarly in a school, the head's authority, status, autonomy and responsibility outweigh that of other professionals, whether they are subservient to him or of collegiate status. In fact different systems give varied credence to the hierarchy which exists. The point to note is that some individuals have more power than others and the way they are able to exert this authority depends to some extent on the system in which they function and on the way they are viewed by others.

Society gives considerable authority to doctors and sees them somewhere near the top of the pecking order because of the mystique medicine holds for most people. Doctors in turn behave in a certain way in order to conform to society's expectations and reluctance to challenge 'clinical' decisions. Doctors, in fact, take on the characteristic of the system they function in.

In this connection, it is relevant to mention the role and status of the education social worker (or education welfare officer). From personal knowledge and from publications it is clear that in some situations the education social worker is seen as equal with other professionals with whom he has to collaborate. In others, the school staff, psychologists, inspectors, accord him a much lower status than their own. In practice, this implies less weight is given to the education social worker's views, rather than a collaborative approach to resolving the problem. Undeniably, there are still heads of schools who expect the education social worker to comply unquestioningly with their directives. Depending, of course, on the way the education social worker sees himself within the education system, his own perception of his role and expertise will influence collaboration between himself, teaching staff and other professionals.

One point requiring further exploration concerns the extent of a professional's influence and the authority from which this is derived.

Society accords specific powers to certain individuals. There is an unwritten 'pecking order', which means that decisions made by those with higher status are difficult to challenge by others whose role is considered lower down the professional hierarchy. One way of overriding decisions of those seen in the more influential strata of authority is for the others to collude or combine their opinions and thus challenge these views and so affect the decision-making. A recent event concerning a case illustrates the hierarchy of multiprofessionals and the difficulties of co-operation and decision making.

The meeting in a social service department was called to discuss the future of a child who had been in the care of a local authority for some time. The multiprofessionals who met included the nursery teacher. Out of eight professionals who attended the meeting only three actually knew the child and family – the teacher, the health visitor and the social worker. The departmental managers' knowledge of the case had been gleaned only from the records and what they had been told. In spite of the views of the three professionals who knew the family and who felt that this child should eventually be reunited with his mother, the views of the managers predominated so that the outcome was quite different from the expectations of the 'grass-roots workers'. The latter found it difficult to challenge openly the views and decisions of those who had been accorded greater status and authority, in spite of a tacit assumption that decisions were made on a multiprofessional basis where all individuals were accorded an equal status.

Knowledge and expertise

Allied to status and authority are specific knowledge and expertise. The fact that an individual has authority does not mean that his knowledge and expertise are of a higher order than other professionals concerned with a particular issue. Although specific knowledge, whether it relates to the law, or to the policies of the education authorities, or to child development, will no doubt influence the way professionals from various disciplines consider an issue, such knowledge in itself accords power to an individual. Similarly, the extent to which a professional is seen to have exclusive knowledge affects how much influence s/he will have in making decisions. One of the difficulties about ascribing specific knowledge to a profession is that none of the professions who are likely to be concerned with a child at school will have expertise which is exclusive to them.

It is for these reasons that teaching, social work and nursing are seen as belonging to a semi-profession as each discipline borrows from others so that in terms of expertise there is considerable overlap (Goffman 1962). This is particularly true of professionals who work within the education system and those who are directly involved, such as social workers.

Because the boundaries of knowledge of education professionals are permeable, such knowledge is likely to be challenged and questioned. The expertise is not discrete and this in itself can affect the way collaboration is achieved. It is quite probable that the teacher, the doctor, the psychologist and the social worker all consider themselves expert and able in assessing family relationships of a child experiencing learning difficulties at school. The difficulty then arises about whose perception and assessment to accept as the most accurate one.

Values and perceptions

There is current awareness and recognition that different professions exhibit different values and have different perceptions about situations and problems. The difference in values and perceptions is often attributed to social class and occupational influence and the system within which individuals operate. In fact, it is suggested that the historical emergence of professions reflects the multiplicity of values in society. Furthermore, the nature of work setting produces value differences. For example, teachers usually deal with groups, whereas social workers tend to deal directly with single individuals; teachers are concerned with the transmission of information, while the social worker is involved in trying to change interpersonal relations and living conditions.

A vivid example of different perceptions can be found in the views of the police who may at times be involved in multiprofessional collaboration. They, too, are influenced by the system in which they function – a system concerned with enforcing the law and bringing the miscreants to justice.

These differences in goals and premises invariably affect the way different professions collaborate, or not, as the case may be. It seems that too little recognition has been accorded these differences in perception and in values in co-operative working, especially when things go wrong. Blame is then apportioned to one simplistic cause, for instance, poor communication. This oversimplification discourages understanding of the reasons for different perceptions.

A further aspect of different value systems is the question of confidentiality. Professions concerned with children and families take a variety of stances on this issue. Quite often confidentiality can be seen as an overriding obstacle to successful communication between professions. It is not necessarily the principle itself, but the way it is used by professionals, which creates a barrier. Pleading that information sharing breaks some ethical code, as sometimes occurs between professions, can be misguided and not in the interests of the child concerned. In this respect, problems have been experienced with doctors, although this is improving where child protection is concerned. But heads of mainstream and special schools are still confronted by the locked medical cupboard where children's records are kept, because these are considered 'confidential' by the health authority employing school doctors and nurses.

Information gathering and transmission

When Dr Johnson was asked whether he found it difficult to share information, he replied: 'Difficult do you call it Sir. I wish it were impossible.' Clearly, he stated what some of us must wish at times: that life would be simpler if we were not obliged to share information with others. Having to transmit information places an obligation and a burden. It expects individuals to take a pro-active stance, to make decisions as to the kind of information which must be shared and with whom.

Because of differences in values and perceptions, professions involved in work with children and families do not always recognise the appropriate cue to when information should be passed on, when it is meaningful and is so important that others should know about it. The timing in relation to the sharing of information is just as important, although often not recognised.

There is evidence that both the education system and the social service system will fail some families because neither knows about the particular family members in the other milieu, whether at home or school. This reciprocal ignorance, based on inadequate information exchange, provides a fair breeding ground for the development of ignorance and stereotyping.

This was one of the findings of the Maria Colwell inquiry, the first in a series of similar inquiries. Information about the foster family was available to some professions but not to the social services department. This breakdown in communication was not deliberate, but occurred because one group of professionals did not appreciate the importance of the information they possessed and its relevance to the care of Maria Colwell. Similarly, Maria's teacher became much more ineffective because she was not given vital information which would have alerted her more to the situation the child found herself in.

Being able to transmit information depends partly on satisfactory record-keeping. Not only must the information be reliable and factual, but it must indicate a source and whether the child and his family are aware of it. It is also difficult to transmit information which is not a re-statement of others' opinions or distortions. Recipients of information need to be objective and evaluate its reliability.

One of the difficulties confronting many professions, especially those working in personal social service, is the danger of misinformation being perpetuated.

There are many instances when incorrect factual information was handed on from one social worker to another and in the past there has been little or no opportunity to challenge this.

With increasing rights of the public to have access to their records held by the education and social services, some of this misinformation has a better chance of being challenged and corrected.

Training

It is interesting to see that one of the main remedies recommended by central government to overcome some of the problems of multiprofessional co-operation is the creation of inter-agency training schemes to provide individuals from different disciplines with a common core training. At the same time, the Cleveland inquiry found that one of the reasons why things went wrong was inadequate training in child protection of all the professions involved. Although no one would quarrel with such recommendations, especially the proposals that there should be multidisciplinary training, it should be acknowledged that multi-professional co-operation is a complex activity which is not going to be resolved by exhortation, improved communication and training alone.

Some new thinking is needed about which knowledge and skills are best learnt within separate professions and which are most usefully addressed in cross-professional groups. What is important is that multidisciplinary training is not a substitute for basic professional competence. At present, one of the options is that all basic training should follow a multidisciplinary model. Another option is for all professions to be taught about other agencies during their basic course, and only later go on an interdisciplinary training course at a local level. For most professions, the latter option is used sporadically. In social work, for example, considerable emphasis is placed on collaboration with others, but there is little information about what others are taught in their training.

One suspects that teachers are taught little about the functions of other agencies and there is little emphasis on the need to work with other professionals in the pursuit of providing education and services for children. Similarly, social workers and other professionals such as doctors and health visitors probably have only the roughest idea of what teachers are taught and how they are trained.

What does seem to be clear is the need to improve the basic knowledge and skill of many of the individuals who work in education and social work and to emphasise the need for multidisciplinary working; such an emphasis could well be a new and different approach for colleagues in the education services.

One of the main conclusions is that if we want professionals to collaborate and work together, we have to devote resources to teach people to do this early on in a professional training. We also need to experiment and learn what is the most successful approach.

13 Social skills training – a relevant skill for support services?

Bernard Levey and Susan Miller

Introduction

The recent government initiative on the question of discipline in schools is responding to increasing concern long felt by teachers (Lloyd-Smith 1985) that disruptive pupils are becoming a matter of paramount urgency as, indeed, is the need to find a solution to the problems they present to teachers and other students.

In contrast there is a sentiment abroad that behaviourally disordered pupils profit little by being *excluded* from mainstream since their chances of reintegration are decidedly poor (Topping 1983) and the argument necessarily follows that efforts would be better directed at dealing with such children in the regular school setting.

In order to resolve the somewhat irreconcilable nature of these two problems (i.e. to deal with disruptive pupils while endeavouring to mainstream them) many LEAs, post Warnock and the 1981 Education Act, have begun using staff from either special schools or units to support mainstream schools in their work with difficult children (Ellis 1985). INSET, co-teaching, counselling, withdrawal programmes, behavioural contracts are all currently in evidence (Ellis 1985, Wheldall *et al* 1985) but to date group work which is either directed at *developing* social skills or *remediating* inappropriate social behaviour has not been promoted by mainstream support services to the same extent as in the USA (Weissberg and Gesten 1982).

It is not clear to the authors why this should be the case – many teachers have commented to them that the development of appropriate socially skilled behaviour is crucial for children, be they withdrawn, hyperactive, isolated or aggressive. The same authors have witnessed a growth in personal and social development programmes, in health and hygiene programmes and multicultural work, but they have also noted that these tend to be aimed at all children and do not set out specifically to enhance socially skilled behaviour. The tendency, in such programmes, is to focus on raising levels of awareness either didactically or through discussion as opposed to permitting the practice of social skills, for example, through the medium of role-play.

The aim of this article is to direct the attention of those connected or directly involved with the support services to the area of social skills training by way of examining the issues surrounding this work and discussing the problems of carrying it out with certain groups.

Definition of social skills

Most definitions of socially skilled behaviour are in terms of a deficit model, e.g. the

> socially competent individual is able to recognise appropriate modes of behaviour, have the necessary actions within his or her repertoire, and possess sufficient confidence to carry out the required activity . . .
>
> (Davis 1983)

or

> a useful working definition is to view social skills as those components of behaviour that are important for a person to be successful in their inter-action, in a manner which does not cause physical or psychological harm to others.
>
> (Spence 1983)

These definitions assume that pupils would use appropriate social skills, in their day-to-day interactions, if only they had them, in much the same way that they would use basic phonic skills in their reading, if only they had them. This is not true for some children, however, and in an article entitled 'Verbal Mediation in Young Aggressive Boys', Camp argues, citing research by Flavell, Beech, and Chinsky (1966) that there is a failure by aggressive as opposed to impulsive and phobic types of children to produce appropriate social skills even though these skills are within their repertoire of behaviours.

With respect to the definition of social skills offered by Spence (1983) one wonders how a person can 'be successful' without making others seem 'unsuccess-ful'. Moreover, one is forced to ask what in fact constitutes appropriate socially skilled behaviour especially when the norms for such behaviour can justifiably vary across settings and social groups.

Socially skilled behaviour must, therefore, remain a concept which emphasises propriety while taking account of the interactional nature of an individual's social behaviour and his or her environment.

Unique features of SST

The essential content of SST work with children is to develop social skills, both specific (e.g. eye contact) *'microskills'*, and general (e.g. interpersonal problem solving strategies). This training can be conducted with those whom we perceive as *lacking* them or with those who may not exhibit any problems but whom we feel could benefit either because they are deemed at risk or because their general development might be enhanced by exposure to such training.

SST training distinguishes itself from other more didactic methods of teaching personal and social skills by virtue of its emphasis on a planned sequence of learning steps. These are intended not only to raise an individual's awareness of what is or is not appropriate socially skilled behaviour but also how to put it into effect both in a mock role-play situation and in real life. Thus, the most common format for an SST training session begins with a discussion of the problems inherent in a social situation, followed by modelling of appropriate skills, controlled role-play, feedback of role-play performance (perhaps with the use of video) and finally and most importantly a 'homework' assignment intended to allow the opportunity to generalise and practise rehearsed skills in everyday situations.

Starting an SST group – issues to consider

The order in which the following issues are treated in this paper is not prescriptive but pragmatic. Thus, type, size and method of selection of group, setting, programme type and the method of skills transfer are to be viewed as interdependent and the resolution of one will determine the outcome of another.

Type, size, method of selection of group

At-risk or symptomatic group
An at-risk group can be considered to be any group of students felt to be in need of social skills training either because of age, immaturity or vulnerability, e.g. nursery children (Chazan, Laing, Jones, Harper and Bolton 1983), those in mainstream class with no apparent problems (Weissberg and Gesten 1982), students with moderate learning difficulties in special school (Aware programme [Elardo and Caldwell 1979], as utilised by Carnforth School, Humberside LEA since 1981). The type of programme selected when working with this type of group will be directed at making the members more socially aware rather than remediating known social skill deficiencies.

A symptomatic group, in contrast, is one which is already presenting problematic behaviour indicative of inappropriate/deficient interpersonal skills.

Members of such a group could be non-assertive, social isolates, have poor impulsive control (Meichenbaum 1985) or be conduct disordered of the over-reactive type (Stott 1974). If the group is already symptomatic the content of the social skills programme followed will reflect their presenting problems. It is not necessarily the case that each type of group requires a singularly different social skills programme nor is it the case that members of the same SST group need exhibit identical or indeed similar social skills deficits.

Homogenous or heterogeneous groups
In contrast to the previous statement regarding the desirability or otherwise of group homogeneity, several studies in the domain of SST have been carried out with homogenous groups. For example, Camp (1987) dealt with aggressive boys, Brown, Wynne and Medenis (1985) dealt with hyperactive/impulsive children, Bornstein, Bellack and Hersen (1977) dealt with non-assertive children.

It must be remembered, however, that these studies were conducted in order to research the effect of different types of intervention with clinically homogenous samples, whereas teachers and educationists, whose primary concern is not research, may not have the time or the interest to conduct well controlled documented studies with this type of group. Indeed, when support work is conducted in a specific school it is often difficult to find sufficient numbers of children who are aggressive or hyperactive or non-assertive etc to form a homogenous group (Levey and Becker, 1988, in a study still in progress, had to draw a quorum of non-assertive children from two comprehensive schools).

Moreover, it should not be considered a problem if an SST group contains a mixture of non-assertive, impulsive and aggressive types, since the latter may often exhibit similar social skills deficiencies. For example, Spence (1980) describes a microskills training programme used with delinquent adolescents that is not unlike a programme used by Bornstein *et al* (1977) for withdrawn children.

Finally, with respect to the question of whether one should work with an homogenous or heterogeneous group, Cross and Goddard (1988) state that it is useful to include non-symptomatic adolescents in a group to act as positive role models, thus improving the group's balance and, the authors would argue, making it easier to manage.

Cognitive maturity level of the group
Cognitive and emotional maturity levels are important factors for consideration when planning a curriculum; the assumption being that unless children can comprehend the content of the curriculum they will be unable to assimilate it. This also holds true for SST programmes because the skills we as educationists are aiming to develop are predicated upon complex social and moral concepts.

Of course, it is possible to promote the use of a social skill without the child understanding why it is necessary to behave in a particular way but, as Cross and Goddard (1988) point out, 'usable social skills are always complex; complex in the sense that they are composed of interdependent cognitive, behavioural and affective dimensions'. It follows that an individual child is more likely to acquire and practise a learnt social skill if all three of these dimensions are targeted by the SST programme.

Choosing group members and group size
The question of whether or not a child should be included in a group will be determined partly by some of the issues already discussed and partly by the group complexion and its size. Not every child wants to join a group whether for remedial reading or social skills training and it is necessary to take into account children's opinions even if the ultimate intention on the part of the teacher is to alter that opinion.

Effective methods for both authors have been to ask group members if they wish to join or to build up the group gradually by asking initial members to select other future members who are in turn 'offered' the opportunity to join the group. These two methods of selection aim to avoid the problem of group members feeling from the outset that they have been obligated to join the group by teachers who find them troublesome.

Group size can be affected by the number of adults involved, the nature of the children involved and the methods used for developing appropriate social skills. For example, a lesson taken from the programme 'Active Tutorial Work' which involves no role-play and is delivered as a lecture, though promoting social skills will not be as demanding of teacher time as a programme which involves role-play, discussion, video feedback and the setting of individualised homework assignments.

This latter type of programme requires at least one adult for five children and, if the teaching of microskills is involved, possibly two adults for five children. Programmes such as Aware (Elardo and Caldwell 1979), Getting Along with Others (Jackson *et al* 1983) can be led by one adult working with the children, though two adults present means that there is more opportunity for guided role-play and discussion.

Choosing an appropriate work setting

The authors envisage that most support teachers using SST programmes are likely to work with groups in a school setting. The advantages of working in schools (as opposed to hospitals or clinics, etc) are that staff involvement can be promoted, children can be dealt with in the setting where they may have most difficulties, and skills can be transferred more readily. The disadvantages are that consideration might not be given to psychological and physical space, factors which can jeopardise a programme.

Psychological space for teachers to be therapists
In a recent exercise conducted in a junior school with aggressive/impulsive children the authors elected to involve regular school staff (both key staff members) in the programme. The staff reported that often in the SST sessions

they felt obliged to allow certain (undesirable) behaviours to pass without comment, whereas, if these behaviours had been exhibited in their classes, the children would have been disciplined.

Difficult or undesirable behaviours are to be anticipated in SST sessions and the authors concluded that the problem of reconciling the conflicting demands of being an SST therapist on one or two days of the week and a teacher for the remaining time was difficult for these particular teachers to resolve. One suspects that most mainstream teachers would find this role change difficult to master. This assumption clearly has implications for those support teachers wanting to deliver SST programmes in mainstream schools though close collaboration between school staff and the support teacher on issues such as discipline in the SST session, selection of students (i.e. exclusion of those children in an involved teacher's class) and content of the programme can help resolve role conflict problems.

Physical space to conduct the programme
Outside agencies working in a school invariably need to secure a place in which to work, and appropriate resources. For SST programmes it is important to have a regular room with appropriate facilities, e.g. space, socket for video, materials and resources (especially teacher time), and regular pupil attendance. (The authors have had experience of staff forgetting to release the children for the SST group.) In short, SST programmes which are not allocated space on the timetable and space in the school are less likely to succeed.

Type of SST programmes

SST programmes may usefully be categorised in four ways:

1 Programmes aimed at developing problem-solving skills
2 Programmes aimed at developing specific interpersonal behaviours
3 Programmes aimed at developing impulse control
4 Programmes aimed at developing appropriate social behaviour by manipulating environmental antecedants and consequences.

Problem-solving SST programmes
The work of Spivak and Shure (1976) exemplifies the problem solving approach to social skills training. Their early work, capitalised upon by Elardo and Caldwell (1979), Chazan *et al* (1983) and the Rochester School Programme (Weissberg and Gesten 1982) starts from the premise that those who demonstrate inappropriate social skills or lack social skills do so because they do not know how to

• read the thoughts and feelings of others as revealed to them through behaviour

- express their own feelings through their own behaviour
- empathise with others
- read social situations and work out a response from a range of alternatives.

The goal of the above approach is to enable the socially inept to learn these skills through role-play and discussion and then attempt to employ them in real life settings.

Microskills programmes
A great deal of research (Van Hasselt *et al* 1978) has gone into analysing the strictly behavioural components of socially skilled behaviour. Spence (1980) in a manual of social skills training, has produced a chart for assessing interpersonal skills. She lists 24, ranging from facial expressions, posture, social distance, to the amount of speech hesitation and personal self disclosures an individual makes while interacting with others. How many of these micro-skills are essential or relevant to competent social interaction is uncertain, and Spence (1983) argues that further research is needed to clarify this issue.

The authors recognise that teachers interested in SST work may not have the expertise or knowledge base to conduct micro-skills programmes. It is arguable, however, that there is inevitably a need to focus on the minutiae of children's behaviour when trying to improve their social competency.

Impulse-control programmes
Although these programmes are similar to problem-solving approaches in that they aim to encourage children to think about social situations and generate alternative solutions, they tend to focus more closely on encouraging participants to inhibit their automatic response to a situation by initially practising 'stop and think' strategies in less demanding non-social situations.

This approach was promoted by Meichenbaum and Goodman (1971), and Levey and Miller adapted its use with a junior school population (unpublished study 1988). Such programmes require the child to overtly talk himself through his impulse control, then move on to covert self talk while engaging in more and more complex social situations. Such an approach, referred to as cognitive behaviour modification (CBM), assumes that one of the problems socially unskilled children have is that of not controlling their impulsive behaviour at a conscious level.

By having children talk themselves through situations where they are likely to be impulsive, the aim is to raise their level of awareness of their difficulties and failings. As Meichenbaum (1985) points out, however, in citing a study by Brown *et al* (1985), a network of approaches involving all concerned individuals (adults and children) and encompassing problem solving, applied behavioural strategies and CBM techniques needs to be used.

Applied behavioural strategies

The manipulation of antecedent and consequent events to promote or discourage behaviour as exemplified in Wheldall and Merritt's BATPACK (Wheldall and Merritt 1987) has long been promoted by psychologists as a way of dealing with inept, socially unskilled, problematic children from a general classroom management perspective.

Its limitation is that it tends to play down the contribution the individual child could make to his or her improvement because the onus is placed on the adult to manipulate the antecedent and consequent variables rather than to encourage the child to examine how he or she can read social situations more effectively (antecedent variables) and by astute problem solving produce more desirable consequences (consequent variables). Despite these limitations the applied behavioural approach is often the most direct and least time consuming of all approaches cited.

Transfer of skills

It is necessary to plan for and build into any SST programme procedures by which skills acquired in the session can be transferred to the real life context. This inevitably requires the support of staff not directly involved in the programme as well as the co-operation of the group members.

Thus homework assignments based upon the work covered in an SST session are more likely to be carried out if non-involved staff provide the necessary supervision and encouragement to group members to complete them. Staff co-operation of this kind is more likely to occur if they perceive the programme positively and realistically. It follows that anyone proposing to set up an SST group should make staff aware both of its limitations and benefits and stress that because group members are being confronted with precisely those social situations they have been unable to cope with in the past, not all their attempts at behaving in a socially competent fashion will succeed either within the context of the group or outside the group. It needs to be stressed, however, that if the goal of generalisation is to be realised group members need to be exposed to demanding social situations albeit within the confines of a well and individually planned homework assignment.

In addition, the completion of homework assignments by group members needs to be perceived by them as an essential exercise. In some respects this can be achieved by the manipulation of consequences (undesirable or desirable), but as Cross and Goddard (1988) argue, the use of self and group generated assignments which are received by these same persons can help improve the latter's commitment to homework.

Conclusion

The complexity of the myriad issues which require consideration before embarking on SST work will probably deter many support teachers, not least because its efficacy is not as yet proven (Spence 1985), whereas the demands it makes on teacher time and resources has been clearly detailed in this article.

It may, therefore, seem more appropriate, at least in a school setting, to teach pupils appropriate social behaviour not as a separate entity, as is the case with full-blown SST work, but in the context of all curricular activities. At an informal level many schools, as part of their overall ethos, attempt to impart to children the social attitudes and behaviours the school considers desirable and in some authorities (Humberside LEA) the cross-curriculum approach to the development of personal and social skills has been formalised. It remains the case, however, that some pupils appear to require a more intensive and specialised type of help if they are to acquire these personal and social skills, and inevitably outside agencies, whether they be support services, psychological services or social services, are called upon to provide this help.

The authors would conclude, therefore, that support services, in order to extend their armoury of possible interventions, need to be able not only to run SST groups but to develop an awareness in their colleagues of the nature of such work, perhaps with a view to training them in its use. This is not to say that SST work is a panacea for the growing concern among teachers about disruptive pupils, since many other factors have a bearing on discipline problems (Rutter *et al* 1979). It follows, therefore, that a well conducted SST programme should be perceived as an adjunct to other approaches which aspire to develop in pupils the kinds of behaviours and attitudes which will enable them to live more harmoniously with others.

14 Sharing information concerning LEAs' organisation of educational support services and developing the role of the support teacher

Lois Hockley

The title, composition and function of the LEA's educational support services for children with special educational needs

Although Warnock recommended the title 'special education advisory and support service', titles in operation include learning difficulties support service, special education support service, support service for pupils with special educational needs, advisory teacher service, special education support team, and teaching and support service.

Concern has been expressed about the use of the word 'support' which could imply a less than equal relationship between support ancillary and real specialists (Hart 1986), but perhaps this reflects lack of understanding about the various teacher roles.

A change in title and function from peripatetic remedial service was probably easier for everyone concerned when either a service was disbanded and the new service created, with those staff eligible and interested joining the new service; or a time lapse was built in and clear notification given to schools as to the function of the service in the future.

It is interesting that Moses *et al* (1987) found that services predominantly concerned with advising teachers tended to be smaller than those that spent most of their time teaching pupils. This presumably depends on the particular specialism/s within the service. Some teachers in small services have been known to spend most of their time assessing individual children!

Warnock recommended that unified services be established to provide effective advice and support, even if this entailed restructuring existing advisory staff and resources. Confusion can easily occur because different LEAs have very different roles for support teachers, advisory teachers and, owing to the different line management structures, advisers.

To be able to provide effective and quick support to mainstream teachers, a service that caters for various specialisms under one umbrella has many advantages. It enables the support teachers to verify their views, and if appropriate, determine who is to be the key support teacher, and offer suitable and immediate assistance to the child and the mainstream teacher with the minimum of red tape, and hopefully without conflicting emphases and approaches.

Moses *et al* (1987) found that progress toward unified services has been slow, with only one out of five authorities surveyed combining existing support services to form a generic one.

The function of a support service is to assist the school in its task of catering for all pupils, not to act in its place. The size of the service therefore requires consideration so that the availability of support does not increase the likelihood of segregated provision. The function of the support service needs to be understood clearly by all if it is to operate successfully and to the benefit of all those working in the classroom. In every case, the support and involvement of the head teacher is a key factor in ensuring the success of new initiatives of services. How many services have a short document outlining the intended partnership between the school and the service? This would be helpful for people joining a school or service and would prevent some of the difficulties support teachers face.

Some support services are disappointed that their contribution can commence only at the junior phase, because the county council has not seen fit to provide more staff so that the service can cover the younger ages, or to grant the service greater flexibility.

It is possible that the function of support services may be confused or threatened by the links developing between some special and ordinary schools. Support may, however, be provided by the special school at the outset, but in the long run any necessary support must be established within the ordinary school, as an integral part of it.

The roles of all concerned with the education of children with special educational needs

It is a sorry state of affairs when children with special educational needs are used in power struggles between professionals, both within the education circle and between differing professionals.

Interprofessional collaboration can be very rewarding when it works well, but competition sometimes replaces co-operation. Specialisation can fix territorial boundaries and make attempts towards a sharing of responsibility for all pupils very difficult.

Support can be provided by different kinds of teachers, by personnel from medical, social, psychological and other services, by parents and other members of the community and by pupils. The support of governors in the future is going to be extremely important. Also, as Sayer (1985) indicates, if all teachers are to feel responsibility to all children then all officers and advisers should have their brief extended too.

School-focused policies for supporting these pupils

How many schools have a policy for supporting these children, and the resources needed throughout the curriculum – or is there a tendency to rely on the external services for both? To a degree this will depend upon what the service has available to it, but even more perhaps on the support teacher. It is understandable that support teachers want to feel valued, but consideration needs to be given to the long-term effects of the action. It can be distressing to learn that a school or teacher has taken on board material, for example, without evaluating it for themselves in the light of their children and the facilities in the school. On the other hand, it is very gratifying when the support teacher is invited to join staff discussions about the policy for supporting these pupils.

Successful support is a two-way process. It occurs at its best when the resolution of problems is seen as a mutual and shared concern (Sayer, 1985). After all, one of the most important functions of the support teacher is to emphasise that mainstream teachers do, in the main, possess the skills and expertise necessary to meet the majority of special needs (Dessent, 1987).

As Bullock observed, the notion of treatment by 'experts' is questionable to say the least. What is required is that all teachers should be sufficiently skilled to adapt their traditional methods and resources to meet individual needs, particularly for those children who have no 'remediable' condition, but who simply find learning slightly more difficult than their peers, who learn at a slower rate or have an uneven capacity for learning (Essex, 1988).

Irrespective of the adopted model, the first priority is for every teacher in the school to understand how the local system works, which in turn requires a clearly understood and effective policy and structure (Mongon 1985). The model adopted will depend on the nature of the pupils in the school, the teachers' own training, experience and willingness to share experiences and expertise with fellow colleagues.

It is interesting that contrary to the expectation of some people, primary schools have been slower to adopt team teaching as the main form of support for learning difficulties (Lorimer *et al* 1987).

Peripatetic staff also need to be aware of the school's approach to special educational needs, and how they can adapt into it. Some peripatetic teachers have an understandable but unhelpful habit of trying to take on board too much, and also matters best undertaken by other people within the school, or other professionals. Balshaw (1987) has found ten areas to be the key components of the support teacher's role: listener, learner, counsellor, confidence giver, practitioner, ambassador, manager, facilitator, disseminator, negotiator. It is important that the vital role of the class/subject teacher is not overlooked. Also, that the support does not conflict with the special needs co-ordinator, tutor, language co-ordinator etc.

Somewhere within the school-focused policy for supporting children with special educational needs, time must be made available for the requisite discussion and liaison by all concerned, within the school, between schools, with all supporting personnel. Much of this occurred naturally in the past, but with the introduction of directed hours is something that cannot be overlooked.

Do the external services satisfy the professionals working in the service?

For those teachers working in a service that has changed its name and function, job satisfaction may need to be considered in the light of the reasons they joined the original service, whether they have kept as up to date as possible with current happenings in education, and whether they feel they have the necessary wide experience and further qualifications to maintain their credibility in the eyes of the class teachers.

A recent NFER survey (Hegarty *et al* 1987) of external support services sees a change towards the teacher rather than the pupil being the client; the support teacher now becomes a consultant (Jones, 1987), providing a service to the teacher in the classroom in modifying teaching approaches and materials, and to the school as a whole in reviewing the ways in which learning and behaviour problems are considered.

It needs to be acknowledged that not all special needs teachers have the necessary skills, expertise or inclination to work in a consultative capacity and that it is only one of several ways forward (Rouse, 1987). McCall in 1977 reminded us, however, that the teacher acting as a withdrawal agent must see the supportive nature of the role and make considerable efforts to gain acceptance as a consultative supporting teacher working with specialist colleagues.

As Bowers (1987) reminds us, not all change is comfortable and policies are more important than the niceties of individuals' work preferences. Change can be fraught with difficulties including changing attitudes, changing roles, new relationships, the loss of certain aspects of security and competence and the change in practices in which one may feel temporarily less competent. In the interim stages there may be feelings of insecurity and taking on an extra work load.

One of the pleasures of working in a peripatetic service is, for me, the objectivity that can be offered, and the opportunity to use the expertise of two teachers for the benefit of the pupils and teachers. The nature of the difficulties is usually recognised by the teachers. The interesting stage is what to do next and perhaps how to find ways round the organisational problems of schools!

As in any position there can be frustrations. These for a support teacher could include: time spent trying to make telephone contact, lack of control of the organisation within schools, constant changes in the timetable, often without warning, conflicts over the use of time while visiting schools, chains of communication in large comprehensives, fitting in with other professionals, traffic, etc.

Do the external services satisfy the school/parental expectations of the service?

Much depends on the policy within the school and how this has been presented to the parents. Parents sometimes find reference in the school brochure to the different services available to the school. It also depends on the stage at which the parents have been involved in discussion about concerns with the head teacher and the staff. Increasingly also the involvement of the service with individual schools and their pupils and teachers will be influenced by the new contexts provided by the ERA and in particular the impact of legislation connected with local management, national curriculum and delegated budgets.

As noted elsewhere in this book, the future manifestation of support to individuals is not a little uncertain.

Functions of the external support services likely to be sought by schools in the future

At this stage it is necessary to reiterate that we are seeking the best possible quality of education for ALL children and students even during periods of change.

If, however, one believes in the principles embodied in the 1981 Education Act, namely:

- integration whenever possible/practicable, and
- full access to the curriculum with exclusion only in the severest cases;

it is to be hoped that these principles will be safeguarded, and that *all* schools will have a 'duty' to *all* children and will not be able to exclude children for fear of lowering standards.

Presumably this is where the LEA will be responsible for setting objectives, with the schools delivering performance which makes those objectives a reality, and with the inspectors of the future checking on the outcome.

Where schools are able to employ additional staff under LMS, one trusts the TGAT (1987) view, that all teachers should be assisted to undertake diagnostic assessment within their work and devise appropriate work with support, will be upheld.

With the advent of local management of schools (LMS) there are certain mandatory exceptions in the draft consultative document, but where LEAs wish to except particular categories of peripatetic or advisory teachers the scheme will need to be submitted for approval (s. 41). This has to be taken in conjunction with the individual LEA plan for the authority may not decide to hold back more than 10 per cent of the total schools budget, and in some authorities it will certainly be a lower proportion.

With this in mind, it is not surprising that many involved in education can see changes in structures and functions for all ahead. These will need to be acknowledged as soon as possible to enable all to plan and train for the future.

Although some external services have a specific brief to cater for statemented pupils, the assistance and monitoring of such pupils in the future will require close attention, as will the children with sensory impairment in mainstream without a statement but supported by the service.

Where grant maintained schools arise they will be able to buy in the assistance of a service if they so decide. The LEA's statutory duties towards pupils with special educational needs will remain and the responsibilities of governors in this field will be crucial and will require monitoring.

The concept of the 'client' will require careful definition!

With the number of meetings, GRIST involvements for some staff and presumably time during the day to assist with the moderation of assessment results, a support teacher's work is going to become more difficult unless there is a permanent increase in the staffing or a permanent 'supply' teacher attached to each school.

Although there is concern about the 'formal' testing (Simmons and Thomas, 1988), any moderation of the observation of practical tasks and oral activities can be only to the benefit of those pupils who have difficulty in getting their thoughts successfully onto paper.

Some concern that children can be opted out of the curriculum for six months, without a statement, at the discretion of the head, has been alleviated by the Education Reform Act 1988 (s. 19) – but the re-entry of the pupil to the system still requires clarification.

The use of profiles, where all concerned with the education of the child/student make contributions on the same paper, can only enhance its purpose, provided they do not become so complex or so simple that their value to the next teacher or employer would be limited.

Difficult though the task may be, the best hope of progress (Essex 1988) for children with special educational needs is dependent upon carefully organised teaching by a skilled teacher who is providing learning experiences that are basically similar to, but adapted from, those experienced by the average child when he was at that stage of learning.

Professional training requirements

Initial training

There is an alarming silence about children with special educational needs in the ERA and the assessment that the majority of children/students will have to undergo in the future. It is of concern to learn (DES 1987) that where weaknesses in initial training were observed, the most common were failure to identify clear teaching objectives; a tendency to identify planning by simply listing tasks or assembling materials; failure to identify the individual learning differences between pupils, a lack of match between content and/or method and the needs of a mixed ability group of pupils. The report did acknowledge that:

> initial training cannot prepare for all that a teacher may be called upon to do throughout a working lifetime. Nor can it be expected to turn out a finished product able to take a full part in the education service and meet all the demands of the day, let alone those that tomorrow will bring.

The survey by Croll and Moses (1985) found that most of the junior school teachers in the study had little or no training in teaching children with special needs or in teaching reading. Although the position had improved through in-service training, Gipps *et al* (1987) found that there still remained a very substantial number of teachers with no training in this field. Yet, according to the press (August 1988) 'Ministers want to bypass the existing training courses . . .' Instead of graduate entrants to college or university education departments, ministers want them to be based in schools, thereby gaining a solid grounding in classroom techniques. Approved universities or colleges would give theoretical instruction on a block release basis.

Yet ACSET (1984) found many teachers in ordinary schools who have pupils with special educational needs in their classes are ill-equipped to ensure that these needs are met! Also, as Thomas and Smith (1985) state, special needs is an area characterised by enormous diversity of practice, provision, policy implementation, and there are opposing camps of diagnosticians and whole-school curriculum believers; behaviour modifiers confront humanistic psychologists; prescriptive teachers disagree with precision teachers and the whole area is replete with sociological and philosophical debates. It is very important that the trainee should be allowed to consider all these approaches without pressure.

DES (1987) indicated that a disturbingly large number of students training for secondary education are not being given a satisfactory preparation to help with meeting the individual needs of pupils.

At the end of the initial (or INSET) course it will be insufficient for teachers to be satisfactory mainstream practitioners whose new insight into special needs is an appendage to their daily strategies and activities. They should have a sense of their own competence and responsibility for meeting them (Mongon, 1985).

Teachers in schools

Some support services have a larger role to play in running courses for teachers, as determined by their job descriptions and time available.

The relevance and effectiveness of training is changing from training for personal development to training as a means of bringing about institutional change, but it will be detrimental to the profession if personal development is not encouraged.

As Hegarty and Moses (1988) endorse, one of the most serious difficulties faced by both the providers of inservice training and heads involved in trying to implement changes as a consequence of an INSET programme, is that these innovations have to be brought about in institutions that are themselves constantly changing, often very rapidly and sometimes in ways that make new ideas very difficult to introduce and even more difficult to sustain.

It must not be overlooked that having an extra teacher in the classroom is a major breakthrough in developing staff co-operation and expertise. Not only does the support teacher assist by developing strategies to ensure the needs of less able pupils are more effectively met, but through his or her presence the class teacher is likely to feel more confident about tackling practical and group work, bringing books into the classroom or turning an extra lesson over to reading and discussion (Wade and Moore, 1987).

It has been suggested (Jones and Jones 1981) that handicap awareness courses organised by LEAs have a useful but limited life if they are to achieve their aims, and much material required to create this knowledge and awareness can just as effectively be made available within schools as part of in-service training.

There will need to be courses for all classroom teachers, one term or equivalent courses for designated teachers with wider responsibilities in one or at the most a very few schools, and one year courses for specialist teachers and advisory personnel who staff an LEA's centralised service (Mongon, 1985).

The best pattern of integrated training is still under discussion, but the ACSET recommendation on subject specialism underlines the involvement of a wider range of tutors than just the 'special needs tutor'.

Together with teacher training there will still need to be specialised support on the inevitable occasions when a sense of inadequacy or failure overwhelms pupils and teachers (Mongon 1985).

Teachers within a service

Besides keeping up to date with special educational needs, in the context of management and organisation of schools and further education establishments, it is vitally important that the implications of recent legislation are taken on board.

It is not surprising that people are being sought for support services who have wide experience and where possible the year's extra training. It is important that the key role of team members is recognised by LEAs and that their attendance at courses is encouraged (Sayer 1985).

Parents and governors

Parents appreciate discussion about methods and materials being used to help them encourage and assist their child. Governors are going to require training in order to fulfil their duties under the 1988 Education Act. These will be ongoing programmes.

PART 3

Supporting and Developing the Curriculum

15 Integrating children and services: a small authority's approach

Mike Dodd, Alex Griffiths, Paul Nicklin and Sharon Shoesmith

The aim of this presentation is to share the apparently successful approach of one small education authority to integrating its services to ensure, in turn, the integration of its children with special educational needs. We will try to specify the philosophy, policies and practice as they have developed, with an extensive section to describe how it works at grass-roots level.

The Metropolitan Borough of Calderdale is a small Yorkshire authority straddling the Pennine hills. Centred on the town of Halifax, it stretches from Brighouse to Todmorden and is little larger in area than Greater London. Since 1984 it has completely re-organised its support services and this has enabled good practice to develop.

By late 1985 the council had agreed a policy statement which embraced not only the 1981 Education Act but also the spirit of Warnock. The policy statement cannot be reproduced here, in full, but we do feel it is worth quoting from it:

> All children live in the same society. The Authority's responsibility is to prepare them to play a useful part in it. It follows therefore that there should be common aims for *all* children regardless of their disabilities. This can only mean that the long term objective should be to give all children some experience of the mainstream setting of education.
>
> The Authority while supporting the philosophy of integration into mainstream education for children with special needs, continues to recognise that if this is to be successful, careful planning is required.

For successful integration into mainstream education of pupils with special needs there must be:

- Positive and optimistic attitudes in school.
- The necessary level of expertise to meet the pupil's needs.
- The resources necessary to support the pupil effectively.

This policy was supported by a document suggesting a far-reaching five-year plan exploring the future of all kinds of provision and support for children with special educational needs. Of particular interest here are the roles the schools' psychological service (SPS) and the assessment learning support service (ALSS) were to play in the future development of special educational needs. In 1984/85 the SPS was re-structured and a team of new educational psychologists appointed. This service is also responsible for a Portage project and has a qualified teacher whose role within the team is that of a specialist case worker.

During this time the ALSS came into being and over the years it has gradually expanded. It has its own head of service and three area heads who each take a geographical portion of the authority. Each of these areas also has two support teachers and a number of resource teachers. The service has a number of specialist teachers who may work in all schools, some of whom have other teachers working with them e.g. the hearing impaired service which has a senior and three other teachers. The ALSS also takes responsibility for the language disorder unit in Calderdale, and a specialist teacher is responsible for this.

There are still four special schools in Calderdale. Currently there are two schools for children with severe learning difficulties, one for children with moderate learning difficulties and one for the physically handicapped. The only other unit existing in Calderdale is the Beaconsfield unit which is a short-term placement for disruptive secondary age children. The team working in this latter area also provide a support service available to secondary schools. It should be pointed out that all the special school head teachers recognise the value of appropriate integration, and support this practically whenever possible.

We have never taken the view that the only important people in special needs are the support teachers and teachers in schools. Others such as school governors have their part to play. Special needs should be on the agenda of all governors' meetings, and on the agenda for in-service training for governors. It is hoped that one governor in every school will take some interest or special responsibility for children with special educational needs. It is this kind of commitment to involve all those concerned, we believe, that has enabled us to deliver a better service to SEN children. We feel the main commitments that the support services give are as follows (no priority order is implied):

- Services need to work together.
- There should be little duplication of work.
- Parental involvement should be a cornerstone of the work of all services.
- The value of teachers in school should always be recognised.
- The integration of SEN children must be regarded as a good aim for all children.
- Everyone should be prepared to pool ideas and share them with others.
- All should try to tolerate the differences between professions and personalities, and look for the strengths of such differences.
- Each child should be respected and valued by all.

- Those involved should look for the most efficient and effective ways to work and deliver services.

Much of this, of course, is self-explanatory. It is critical, however, that people must not only be seen to be working together but must actually work together! Time must be used constructively with as little overlap between people as possible. The need for this led to the planning visit concept.

Each term a school receives a 'planning visit'. This takes places at the school and is attended by the head teacher (or their delegate) with the educational psychologist for the school and a senior member of the ALSS. The agenda for this meeting is largely in the hands of the school which is expected to prepare for the visit by informing parents that their children may be discussed at the meeting, completing initial information forms (this saves a considerable amount of administrative time later) and preparing any other information that may be of interest to the participants in the meeting. The meeting takes 45–60 minutes and has the following main functions:

- To identify the concerns of the school and ensure that those present at the meeting are fully informed of them.
- To establish priorities within the school.
- To ensure that any agreed actions are initiated, and arrange any relevant dates for follow-up visits.
- To co-ordinate the agreed actions.
- To evaluate any actions that have been taken in the past, and to agree on any that need to be taken in the future.

As can be seen, this is a wide ranging but important meeting for the school. What is not discussed at this meeting cannot form the part of any later work. This system has been extremely well received by head teachers who feel they have a direct input into support services and some control over what is or is not done. An important aspect of the meeting is the accountability of all those concerned. The meetings are minuted and the people responsible for any actions do need to explain at the next meeting if those actions have not been taken! These meetings allow the support services to:

- Give support to individual children (or teachers).
- Give support to the whole school.
- Provide in-service training if needs have been identified which could be met in this way.
- Generally encourage change within the school.

Much can be discussed at these planning visits, including the statementing of children under the 1981 Education Act. Of particular importance is the fact that it allows for assessment over a period of time with everyone knowing what is happening at any given time. This is seen as an important aspect of the assessment process by all.

Such visits are followed up as necessary by individuals. It is essential that schools appreciate the stresses and strains that the services are under, and have a full understanding of how large their own piece of cake happens to be. For example, head teachers of primary schools know they are entitled to an average of about three full days of an educational psychologist's time annually. Such shared knowledge helps to sidestep many difficulties which have arisen in other systems. This does not stop all the moaning, but moaning is channelled constructively to meet the needs of children – rather than the needs of teachers and psychologists.

A variety of other initiatives have been taken within the authority, most of which are school based. They have often developed out of school concerns such as a project on encouraging good playground behaviour. Other projects have arisen from a general need, for example, the Calderdale pre-school book project (Griffiths and Edmunds 1987). Such projects add interest to the life of support services, and are certainly not seen as 'fun and games' by the schools but as useful initiatives which add to the richness of primary school experience for children. They also encourage good relationships between services and with schools. Perhaps the pre-school book project is worthy of further consideration here.

Psychologists and an ALSS specialist teacher felt it would be helpful to introduce books to nursery aged children. The aims were to extend and enrich the children's language and introduce them to the world of books, while at the same time consolidating the link between parents and school and stimulating the general environment. Working with four head teachers, a few were introduced into nurseries. By interviewing parents before and after the project as well as testing the children, it was clearly demonstrated that children in the experimental groups made much more progress than children in control groups. At this stage various other members of the teams were involved and an in-service programme across Calderdale developed. Advisers became involved and virtually every nursery class in Calderdale took on board the simple suggestions that this project lay before them. It was a good example of a co-operative project which generated enthusiasm among others, leading to an improvement in educational opportunity for many children.

The systems seem to be working well, but one can never afford to be complacent; indeed the present political clime does not allow one to be complacent! The 1988 Education Reform Act together with other developments such as the 1986 Disability Act, have far-reaching implications which may make it difficult for the present initiatives to be sustained in their current form.

Already the authority is developing the concept of special needs co-ordinators for each school. With proper in-service training and help it should become more and more possible to meet SEN needs within school rather than look to outside provision or support services. In an ideal world we should be educating all our children within the mainstream and this is our aim. The role of the special schools must continue to be developed. For example, the need to use their expertise as outreach workers in mainstream schools has already started – how far should this continue, and what will be the role of such schools in 10 or 20 years' time – will there be a role for them?

We believe all mainstream schools should 'own' their responsibility for SEN children. This should be recognised in the curriculum and in the responsibilities of staff in all departments towards their children. The attitudes of teachers should be positive and welcoming and parental involvement should be the norm.

As the mainstream schools develop integration and this is augmented by 'resourced' mainstream schools supported by staffing resources and physical adaptations, consideration must be given to the closure of special schools at some future date.

Enough of this philosophising and theorising – what is it really like at the coal face? Can such policies really work? Do teachers and educational psychologists get on as well as we suggest they should? Paul Nicklin and Sharon Shoesmith look at how one team gets its act together.

The area team

During 1987/88 the team consisted of an area head, two support teachers, seven resource teachers, 20 support assistants and a resource technician plus clerical support. The teaching staff are based at a resource centre which provides special needs resources for primary schools in the area. The team works in partnership with three educational psychologists led by a senior educational psychologist. The primary school population of the area covered is approximately 7,700 children in 36 schools. The area team is concerned with learning, behavioural and physical difficulties. Children with sensory impairment and language disorders are the responsibility of across-authority specialist teachers.

Roles and responsibilities

Team members have specific roles to play which all contribute to a co-ordinated service for children, parents and schools. The support teachers supported by the area head share the work at the 36 schools and have three broad areas of responsibility:

- Supporting children who are in a period of assessment or who are the subject of a statement of special educational needs.
- Assisting the development of whole-school policy and practice towards special educational needs.
- Providing INSET courses on aspects of special education.

Each resource teacher works in two or three schools, mostly with SEN children who do not require a statement. Resource teachers have a vital role in preventing persistent learning failure for many pupils. This preventative role is expected to reduce the number of children who need a statement.

The support assistants work on a one-to-one basis with children who have a statement. Their work is directed and supervised by a support teacher and in some cases a resource teacher.

The educational psychologists work directly with any member of the team. Our philosophy, our practice and our methods are, for the most part, jointly perceived and endorsed through debate and liaison.

Children with a statement of special educational needs
In line with the LEA policy on integration, there has been a significant increase of children with statements in mainstream schools during the last academic year. At the end of the academic year there were 29 such statements in Halifax for learning, behavioural or physical difficulties. All these children have an allocated support teacher and the majority have a support assistant for a portion of each day. A file is usually kept for each child who has a statement and it remains in the class as the property of the class teacher. It is made available to the head teacher, educational psychologist, support teacher, resource teacher, support assistant and parent(s), all of whom may contribute to it and read the contributions of others.

Children in formal assessment
Support teachers again have a major responsibility towards children, their teachers and their parents during the formal assessment period. They may assist the school in writing their educational advice and may be a 'key worker' whom the parent can contact for advice. In addition they will plan a learning programme and process of monitoring to be followed by the class teacher.

Children with special educational needs (the 18 per cent)
In addition to children in the above groups there is the majority of children with special educational needs who do not require a formal statement. The resource teachers work mainly with this group while others are supported within their mainstream schools by class teachers.

Resource teachers often support up to a maximum of 40 children at any given time. This number may be less if resource teachers are teaching a large proportion of children who need daily one-to-one work.

The team has provided support for 320 children this academic year. This figure represents 5 per cent of the primary school population. This falls short of the 20 per cent of children assumed by the 1981 Education Act to have special educational needs and underlines the wider role schools must play. These numbers emphasise the need for schools to have their own co-ordinators and to develop whole-school policies. ALSS staff in partnership with educational psychologists are able to assist schools in this.

The team perspective

The co-ordination of the differing roles within and between the support services would be difficult if the philosophy and actions of members did not match. The co-ordination of action takes place through planning visits and regular meetings between team members. The philosophical basis of the team has been evolved through discussion and began with a recognition of the elements of policy laid down by council. This was extended to include the following perspectives.

- As most children placed in special provision began their schooling in mainstream schools, our aim was to prevent segregation rather than just promote integration.
- Learning difficulty cannot be investigated or alleviated without reference to the curriculum. Ideally the curriculum should be flexible enough to accommodate all learners contributing at differing levels to common topic areas.
- Good special needs teaching is often the application of good teaching practice, not the application of different approaches.
- The contribution of all learners should be valued.

These ideas are often referred to as the application of a needs-based curriculum enabling slow achievers to succeed and contribute to school and classroom life.

The giraffe syndrome

This type of need-based curriculum has become known within the team and in some schools as the 'giraffe syndrome' following the description, on an in-service course, of a project on giraffes undertaken in a class of mixed ability children. At one end of the continuum some children may deal with aspects of geography and evolution while at the other end of the continuum some children might make books based on zoo animals.

In this way it would be possible for all children to contribute at their own levels – the crucial element is that their work is equally valued by the teacher. Coincidentally some weeks after that example was given a 'giraffe project' was found on display in a class with six children on the school's special needs register, including two children with a statement. The project was an example of how a needs-based curriculum can be put into practice, and a display of the work accompanied this presentation.

Whole-school approach to special educational needs

Such aims and beliefs as stated above clearly indicate the need to work with whole schools rather than with individual children, although team members often need to build credibility by demonstrating success with individuals and groups of children with special educational needs.

Assisting schools towards establishing a whole-school policy is the main aim of the team and is the subject of school-based in-service courses. It is not possible to apply a common policy to all schools or even to groups of schools as their needs are so diverse. But it is possible to present certain common elements. These elements are:

[margin annotation: School issues & instructions]

- Assessing the needs of all children in order to identify those who may have special educational needs.
- Monitoring and recording the progress of such children.
- Involving parents.
- Meeting the needs of children as individuals and within the curriculum.
- Decision-making procedures about whether children need to be discussed further with outside agencies.

These elements fulfil in most respects the first two stages of the five stages of assessment recommended by the Warnock report. Practical examples of initiatives designed to promote the above elements can now be given.

Our approach to the assessment and identification of special educational needs consists of identifying and monitoring the needs of all pupils along a continuum of learning, beginning early in their school careers. In order to achieve this, the 'Early Learning Profile' was developed as a curriculum-based assessment and monitoring tool. It is used by the team members and by teachers, in its original form, or adapted by them to meet the needs of their school.

The profile has several key features and uses:

- It is completed on five occasions beginning at the end of the nursery year and then during each of the first four school terms.
- Often three different teachers complete parts of the profile at different times as the child moves along the continuum represented by the profile.
- Progress as well as rate of progress are indicated.
- At the end of each term a summary sheet is detached for each child and collated to give an overview of a whole age group of children, including those at both ends of the continuum.
- The information gained can give early indications of resource implications.
- The information has implications for curricular planning.
- It ensures that special educational needs are carefully identified over time.

Once special educational needs are identified the progress of children should be carefully monitored. The concept of special needs registers was developed to meet this requirement. Registers are designed differently according to the needs of individual schools but again contain common elements.

The register records for each child:

- Personal details
- The major areas of need, based on information from the profile
- A termly outline of work to be undertaken
- A termly review of progress
- The involvement of all outside agencies.

Several teachers within a school may contribute to the register in addition to the ALSS team members. Ideally it will be organised by the special needs co-ordinator.

Parental involvement at its simplest level of keeping parents informed about the progress of their children is an essential element of the whole-school policy. Hopefully parents are aware of any concerns from the beginning and not when outside agencies become involved. In Calderdale many schools have taken up the PACT Scheme (Griffiths and Hamilton 1984) as a way of introducing shared reading to their schools. Other examples include support groups for parents of children with special needs (Smith 1987) and counselling individual parents and groups of parents. Involving parents in the education of their children is a major aim of the team.

The whole-school approach as we outlined is based on a belief that the special needs of children can be met within a needs-based curriculum. As a team we have developed approaches to literacy for SEN children which are easily encompassed within an overall psycholinguistic approach to literacy. While retaining the necessary structure and over learning to ensure progress, the approach does not segregate children away from the curriculum of their peers. This particular initiative is meeting with considerable interest from the schools.

Finally, our whole-school model gives teachers and schools the tools with which to identify and monitor their own special needs. This allows them to make informed judgments about special needs in their own school. They can therefore fulfill the first two stages of assessment outlined in the 1981 Education Act and can make constructive use of outside agencies through the planning visit system.

Philosophy, belief and planning have all played important parts in the present approach of the Calderdale LEA to provision for its SEN children's needs. The future of the service was under discussion, with a paper on the restructuring and extension of the assessment and learning support service ready for the director of education, when some of the implications of local financial management and the local management of schools became both obvious and urgent.

The result has been a clouding of the future scene and the routes by which we can attain it have now drastically to be reconsidered. Some aspects of the service which are highly valued will be lost. These may, and indeed now must, be replaced by school-based initiatives, with diminished but more specific and supportive central roles that will ensure that all children with special educational needs are accorded their rights to a high quality education. The future looks to be stressful, interesting and demanding and yet with the quality of people involved in the wide range of services available, there are grounds for optimism.

A video illustrating in an infant classroom a number of features discussed above accompanied this presentation.

16 The problem centred approach – an INSET initiative

Pauline Grant, Nicola Mindell, Judith Pettersen and Michelle Sidwell

Introduction

Buckinghamshire schools gave a high priority to 'special needs' when they bid for in-service training under the new GRIST arrangements. Many of the bids highlighted the fact that schools were keen to do the best they could to support pupils with special educational needs within the real resource constraints that existed. The county as a whole holds statements of special educational needs on a relatively high proportion of pupils, so it cannot be argued with any assurance that schools are being asked to deal with pupils who should have access to additional resources.

The pupils identified by teachers as having special needs can be thought of as coming into the Warnock 18 per cent, that is, the children who, although appropriately placed in mainstream education, do from time to time have difficulties which require some sort of extra help. The county psychological service obviously wished to support teachers in helping these children as effectively as possible. At the same time, the difficulties of meeting the needs of individuals while continuing to stimulate the rest of the pupils in the class had to be addressed. It was therefore important that the training was practical for classroom teachers.

Meetings were held with the staffs of the schools concerned, to establish exactly what the teachers needed to help them. There was little enthusiasm for more information about special needs in general, or about particular types of handicaps and difficulties. Instead, teachers were looking for practical procedures that would help them to deal with the problems they were actually experiencing.

The 'problem centred approach' is a well established problem solving technique, designed to address individual problems as well as organisational issues. The approach has been used extensively by Cameron and Stratford (eg 1987). In addition, Levey and Mallon (1984) worked with groups of teachers in the Midlands using a similar process as a basis for individual casework – in this instance the teachers represented different schools.

In the example described here, the participants of each course were the entire teaching staff of the school. This enabled the content of the course to be adapted to the particular circumstances of the school, and to be practised by members of the staff together after the course. This was also in line with the ideas of Georgiades and Phillimore (1975), who described the phenomenon of 'the hero innovator'!

Once the 'problem centred approach' was described in outline to the teachers in an introductory session, they became keen to learn to use it, particularly as the training was to focus on problems they were tackling at that time.

In designing the training, issues related to group dynamics were considered. The objective was to increase the effectiveness of communications between staff during and after the course. To this end, simple ground rules were suggested and negotiated with the teachers. Examples included: 'offer alternatives, not advice' (instead of 'Why don't you . . .?' participants were encouraged to say 'one way might be to . . .'), and recognition of the need for confidentiality. These ground rules were 'modelled' by the tutors and participants were given feedback on their adherence.

Taking these factors into account, it was possible to design a basic framework which included both key objectives and content, which could be adapted within individual schools.

Core objectives of the training

1 To present a model which could be used by teachers with different backgrounds, experience and knowledge.
2 To provide a flexible training opportunity to enable participants to tackle issues and concerns raised during the course.
3 To help teachers to be specific when describing children's behaviour and to provide a focus for their intervention programmes.
4 To combine theoretical input (reduced to a minimum) with support for initiatives within their current class group and classroom practice.
5 To provide and develop general support materials during the training.
6 To provide opportunities for group work among staff, to encourage participants to use each other as 'resources' when solving problems.

Content of the training

The exact details of the training varied from school to school, as each staff identified different goals and problems. The principles remained the same, however, and are summarised as follows:

1 Teachers were asked to think of an issue of current concern to work on and thereby practise the techniques. (Not surprisingly, all chose to work on a problem to do with a child's learning or behaviour.)

2 The problem-centred approach was described and elaborated.
3 Teachers were assisted in using the approach for their chosen problem. At each stage they were given guidance and support, and were encouraged to use colleagues on the staff to help them. Difficulties encountered in implementing plans were discussed, and modifications agreed where necessary.
4 Further rehearsal of the approach involved moving through all the stages, and in some cases choosing different children or different problems to work on. Ways of recording – for baselining and monitoring progress – were discussed. A means of recording the steps through the procedure was suggested.
5 The approach was used for an organisational issue if the staff wished to work on one. Again, this was a real issue of concern to the school.

The duration of the course varied between schools, with some opting for six 'twilight' sessions, while others preferred to make use of 'Baker days'.

The problem-centred approach

The approach was described as follows:

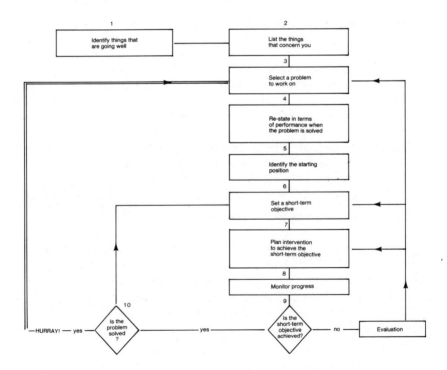

Figure 16.1 The problem-centred approach flowchart.

Notes

1 Thinking about the things that are going well before delving into the problems is a good exercise in thinking positive, but it also has practical value. It helps focus on the aspects of the child's behaviour we wish to retain or build on, and leads to consideration of the situations in which they are happy/interested/motivated. It is equally important to highlight areas in which the child can be rewarded and encouraged.

2 The list can be as exhaustive as you wish. Obviously there is no way all the concerns will ever be tackled, but sometimes seeing them written down together helps in selecting the problem to work on.

3 The first question is, having looked at the list of problems, is there actually one which warrants a more structured intervention? Have the 'softer' methods of drawing it to the child's/parent's attention been tried? A problem to work on does not have to be the most intractable one – indeed, it may be better to achieve some success on one more amenable to change. You may feel there is a priority problem to be tackled first, or merely that there is one you feel most confident in dealing with.

4 Having selected a problem, consideration is given to the situation when the problem no longer exists. What will the child be doing instead of . . .? What will they be able to do that they could not do before? This becomes the target to which the intervention is aimed. It should contain the three elements of performance, condition and criterion.

5 Having decided where we're going, it makes sense to check where we're starting from. What is the child's current skill level? What behaviour is already established in the child's repertoire?

6 The short-term objective takes us one step beyond the starting point towards the target. It helps to think about the time in which this should be achieved – say 1–2 weeks.

7 The intervention is the set of changes made to help achieve the objective. This may be a structured teaching programme, the introduction of rewards for a particular behaviour, or selectively attending to behaviour it is wished to increase. The plan should include consideration of who will implement it and any materials required.

8 A record is kept of progress under the stated intervention.

9 If progress is inadequate, consideration is given to the original selection of the problem, the short-term objective or the intervention. Evaluating a short-term intervention ensures that failure is not continued.

10 Having achieved the short-term objective, it may be necessary to take the next step towards the target. If the target has been achieved, a decision is made as to whether or not to select a further problem to work on.

Teachers needed to set clear targets in terms of what they wanted the child to be doing as a result of their intervention. In order to help them to do this, an exercise was built into the training to write statements that were clear and unambiguous descriptions of performance. Less clear statements (termed 'fuzzies'), although useful as initial steps, were sharpened up into performance descriptions if the teacher wished to act on them.

Evaluation and follow-up

Evaluation of this training initiative was carried out in a number of ways including:

- pre- and post-course questionnaires to elicit information about current practice in meeting special educational needs
- analysis of descriptions of children's behaviour, written before and after the course, to highlight changes in specificity in such descriptions following the course
- discussions with participants about the usefulness of the training.

Evaluation sought to establish the following:

1 Were the 'core objectives' met?
2 Was it effective in changing or confirming practice in the school?
3 Were the materials and methods used robust?
4 Did it meet the teachers' needs?

Core objectives
All the objectives were met to a certain extent. Course participants ranged from probationers to very experienced and long-serving teachers. All problems worked on during training were presented by participants, and interventions were tried out between sessions. Some staff experienced significant success in using the process to tackle concerns. They were able to develop an action plan and carry out an appropriate intervention. This resulted either in the 'problem' being solved, or in first steps being taken towards achieving a satisfactory outcome.

In some cases the participants worked together on an issue concerning the whole school, reaching a successful strategy in a short time. For example, one staff tackled library organisation, in particular the problem of lost books. An action plan was developed during a 'twilight' session, and implementation of this resulted in over two-thirds of the missing books being returned!

Informal analysis suggested that teachers were producing clearer descriptions of children's behaviour and attainments by the end of the course. Staff appeared to find the distinction drawn between 'fuzzy' and 'performance' statements helpful.

Where relevant, the tutors brought in additional materials, or staff shared materials already used in the school – for instance observation schedules and record forms. There was formal and informal evidence that teachers were discussing difficulties and interventions with each other more frequently after training.

School practice
Although it is early to assess this, there was a clear feeling that many components of teachers' current practice were confirmed as being effective, and there were

benefits in having a forum in which these could be shared with colleagues. The quality of discussion within the school staff, and the style of written reports could demonstrate any lasting changes influenced by the training.

Materials and methods

The materials (flowchart, record forms) were presented as being a starting point, and participants in each case were encouraged to make modifications if they wished. In general terms, the flowchart was thought helpful, particularly as participants became familiar with it and were able to go through stages without necessarily recording each step.

The record sheets offered had a mixed reception – some teachers found them helpful while others thought them cumbersome and unnecessary. Nevertheless, it had been regarded as important to offer a means of recording which could be adapted.

The teaching methods employed by the tutors followed a basic format which has been found effective in teaching a variety of skills to many different client groups – adult and child. The approach was demonstrated first, then participants were guided in its use and, finally, support was reduced gradually as staff became more able to use it independently.

Teachers' needs

The initial meetings with staff to explore their concerns led to the training being developed as described. An introductory meeting outlined the whole procedure, and at this point the staff were asked to say if they thought the proposed core course would meet their needs. Modifications to the training could have been made at this time.

Despite the affirmation of this type of training, there remained among some teachers following the course a certain dissatisfaction that they were not given 'the answers'. This was felt to be inevitable, and unlikely to be satisfied by any modification to the programme.

Conclusions

Overall, the educational psychologists involved in this initiative felt that the training had been received well, and had resulted in benefits for the participating schools. The team members believe this course to have been an efficient use of their time, and continue to be committed to supporting schools in this way.

17 Planning for support teaching
Rik Boxer and Dayna Halpin

What is support teaching?

The terminology of support – support in the mainstream, support service, support teaching – now seems firmly embedded in the language of special needs (or should it be individual needs?). Support does have connotations of a one-way relationship (helping to hold up something unsteady), but nevertheless it does represent an important trend in thinking in that it marks a shift away from a predominantly medical model based on 'diagnosis' and 'remediation'.

Support teaching is an umbrella term, covering a wide range of activities, but has acquired a common meaning with the emphasis on:

- Participation in classroom activities, rather than extraction
- Matching curriculum and individual needs, rather than remediation
- Collaboration rather than separation of expertise.

Within this general description, a support teacher's work can lie at different points on a continuum from:

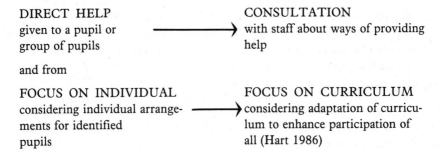

DIRECT HELP
given to a pupil or
group of pupils
⟶
CONSULTATION
with staff about ways of providing
help

and from

FOCUS ON INDIVIDUAL
considering individual arrangements for identified
pupils
⟶
FOCUS ON CURRICULUM
considering adaptation of curriculum to enhance participation of
all (Hart 1986)

Thus, the function of support teaching can extend beyond the individual pupil and has wider implications:

- For other pupils in increasing their participation in activities
- For teachers, regarding adaptation of classroom practice
- For organisations, in helping to highlight areas for further development.

We will argue that the role of the support teacher is highly complex, fundamentally concerned with change and development, and unique to a particular situation.

Analysing your own situation

The successful development of support teaching will be influenced by a variety of factors concerned with the individuals involved, classroom practice and issues at an organisational and LEA level. As a starting-point for planning for support teaching, we would suggest a stock-taking exercise where the positive forces and the potential obstacles are identified at various levels.

Organisational level

Development of support teaching can only realistically be considered within a school and LEA context. While limited opportunities for change at this level may arise, it is important not to lose sight of a 'whole-organisation' or 'whole LEA' approach to delivery of support.

For example, the following factors are likely to be of significance:

- Previous history of collaborative work within the school
- Head teacher's commitment to the philosophy underlying 'support' and how this is communicated to others
- Issues of allocation of resources within the school and within the LEA
- Extent to which a differentiated curriculum is in operation
- Opportunity for in-service training/staff development
- Clarity of LEA policies.

Classroom level

The importance of the overall context must be stressed, but the 'nuts and bolts' of support teaching lie within the classroom. There are many factors involved but the following have been commonly identified.

Extent of pre-planning
Although it is widely agreed that knowledge of content and aims of activities is needed beforehand, little preparation actually seems to take place (Ferguson and Adams 1982). Work involving adaptation of materials e.g. explaining key terms, providing concrete examples, modifying design of tasks (Hodgson 1985) have considerable implications for collaboration between teacher and support teacher.

Activities
The question arises of what type of classroom activities are most suitable for support work. In particular, if a mainly didactic approach is being used there is the danger of a support teacher standing unproductively on the sidelines for long periods. Also, location of facilities and seating arrangements affect the way in which an individual participates in class activities and hence the nature of support work (Clunies-Ross 1984).

Roles and responsibilities
Clear role definitions are likely to enhance teamwork and secure effective working relationships within the classroom (Thomas 1986). In situations where roles and responsibilities are not clearly defined, it may be that pupils will perceive the class teacher as the 'real' teacher and the support teacher as teacher's aide (Ferguson and Adams 1982). Shared responsibilities towards discipline, marking work and addressing the whole group may help to alleviate some of the difficulties.

Individual level

At the heart of support teaching is the nature of the relationship between teacher and support teacher. The role of support teacher seems highly complex, which can perhaps be characterised by a series of balancing acts. For example:

- A respect for current classroom practices, flexibility in adapting to certain situations but being able to open up dialogue about alternative approaches.
- Having skills in matching curriculum and individual needs while avoiding adopting the role of expert.
- To act as a catalyst for change, but with the understanding that the process of change may involve a degree of anxiety and insecurity and is unlikely to bring immediate positive effects.

Generating strategies

Within any particular situation, factors which are seen to help the development of support teaching or to provide obstacles can be identified at different levels. From this analysis, practical strategies may be suggested. Such strategies may arise out

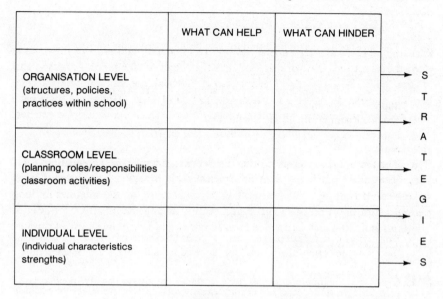

	WHAT CAN HELP	WHAT CAN HINDER	
ORGANISATION LEVEL (structures, policies, practices within school)			S T R
CLASSROOM LEVEL (planning, roles/responsibilities classroom activities)			A T E G
INDIVIDUAL LEVEL (individual characteristics strengths)			I E S

Figure 17.1

of building on the positive forces, but strategies aimed at reducing resistance are likely to be of at least equal importance. Figure 17.1 provides a summary.

One example

The following strategies by support staff are given as an example. They were suggested by a team of support teachers in a primary support teaching service (PSTS), following the exercise 'Analysing your own situation'. As stated earlier, the relationship between class teacher and support teacher underpins effective support work and the strategies listed reflect this (see figure 17.2).

The individual forecast format developed by Jones *et al*, 1986, has been found to be useful in the initial planning stage of support. This would be completed by the class teacher and support teacher early in each term and considers an individual child's needs within the planned classroom activities. Not only does it allow a framework for discussion, but offers ownership of the planning to both parties leading to a commitment to its implementation (see figure 17.3).

Conclusion

In this paper we have attempted to show support teaching as a management of change issue, which has implications for developments at an individual,

POSSIBLE STRATEGIES – Organisational Level

1 The support teacher to be introduced by PSTS co-ordinator to staff.
2 PSTS co-ordinator to talk to all staff about the role of service etc.
3 Service handbook sent to all schools.
4 Involve school co-ordinator at start of support, keep informed.
5 Support teacher must define the boundaries of the role as early as possible.
6 Negotiate support times for benefit of all.
7 Support teacher should help schools to adapt materials for benefit of supported pupil/s.
8 The service to be involved in primary school's staff development programmes e.g. 'Baker days'. Joint planning/involvement with educational psychologist and advisory teacher.

POSSIBLE STRATEGIES – Classroom Level

1 Sensitivity on part of support teacher – support teacher needs to take time to assess the classroom atmosphere, teaching style, do's and dont's etc. Each setting different.
2 Seeing good points in someone else's teaching, not always negative ones – class teachers need praise too!
3 Encourage class teacher to discuss child whenever possible at least every week – ask teacher's advice, as one who knows child best.
4 Set/break down boundaries at the beginning – ask class teacher: Do you want me to help other children, mark their work etc?
5 Avoid putting class teacher under more pressure than already exists.
6 Take a lead in setting work for e.g. home, welfare staff, but not taking over.
7 Trying not to be too disruptive e.g. talking when class teacher addressing class. Classroom manners are important.
8 Offering help in general ways in the classroom without becoming a dogsbody.
9 Keep an efficient filing system which is easily read by class teacher and not too laborious to fill in.
10 Take whole class to relieve class teacher to work with supported pupil/s – gaining recognition as a class teacher again.

POSSIBLE STRATEGIES – Individual Level

1 Engage head and special needs co-ordinator in back-up work and always keep informed – this applies to other professionals involved with child.
2 Always be professional.
3 Arrive at school earlier – stay over break or lunchtime for discussion with class teacher to form a relationship etc.
4 Avoid cliques, discussions about staff. Don't take sides.
5 Leave some follow up activities for supported child.
6 If possible arrange a social get-together with class teacher/other professionals involved e.g. pub lunch!
7 Keep smiling!
8 Share your problems with rest of team.

Figure 17.2 Possible strategies by support staff.

CURRICULUM AREA	INDIVIDUAL SUPPORT	SMALL GROUP SUPPORT	CLASS BASED ACTIVITIES	PARENTS
READING GINN 360	Individual programme based on Ginn 360 level 2. Worksheets, reading games, reading books.	Reading games with 2–3 other children especially Amanda, Caroline and Kerri. Language Master	Ginn Activity book. Gibb family worksheets. Reading from Blackboard. TV follow-up.	Reading games sent home. Flash cards. Back-up reading library
LETTERLAND (phonics)	Workbook. Individual programmes.	Working within Letterland group of 6 other children Letterland stories, phonic games.	Phonic games Phonic card-reader cards, alphabet frieze, colour coded phonic cards.	Phonic games e.g. I Spy. Phonic clues in reading.
NUMBER	Individual Programme on counting consistently to 10 using various real objects.	Number games involving counting with 2–3 other children. Peak Maths in group situation.	Number projects Shape Colour Graphs Counting	Counting real things and pictures in books. Number games.
FINE MOTOR SKILLS	Individual programme to give practice in fine motor areas-cutting colouring, etc.	Games involving handling small objects–jigsaws inset puzzles, etc., cutting sticking general craft activities.	Colouring Copy writing Craft work Sewing Weaving	Cutting Colouring Jigsaws
TOPIC WORK (litter, senses)		Group games based on senses — 2–3 other children. Feely-bag. Guess the taste etc.	Worksheets. TV programmes and follow-up outings.	Reading and interest books. General conversation.

Figure 17.3

classroom and organisational level. We have suggested that the question 'How can individual pupils be supported more effectively?' has no universal answer. A proactive approach where there is an overall strategy or change appropriate to a particular situation is, however, more likely to provide a firmer foundation for the development of support teaching than simply reacting to problems as and when they arise.

18 In-class support – threat or challenge?

Hazel Dodgson

Introduction

Mrs Dodgson? I wonder if you could help us? We are organising a Baker day and we would like some input on in-class support. We have already had an INSET day on special needs to raise the awareness of the staff. We have gone mixed ability in the first three years in most subjects and we have a support system in operation. Our problem is that some teachers will not change, they cannot or won't adapt. Do you know what I mean?

A genuine cry from the heart – but how I dread hearing these words at the other end of the telephone! Unfortunately, the situation is much more complex than taking a step forward towards a management goal.

A 'whole-school approach', 'mixed ability' teaching and 'in-class' support have become generally accepted as the most effective and efficient ways of managing the problem of special educational needs in schools. These beliefs are based on sound arguments to do with providing equal opportunities for all children, ethical issues such as labelling, and the making of pragmatic decisions about the efficient use of limited resources. Rationally and logically this is the obvious answer, so why, despite optimism and enthusiasm from so many for so long, has it proved so difficult to achieve? This paper examines the complex nature of support.

Three models of in-class support have emerged:

1 *The support teacher supports the individual child*
   This requirement is often written into the statements of individual children. However, by identifying children to support within the classroom situation and working with them, we may be changing the location of special education rather than the concept. This model may serve to segregate the child from his peers within the classroom situation.

2 *The support teacher supports individuals or groups of children as the need arises*
   Some teachers find this acceptable, while others, especially over a long

period, find it stressful since their own freedom, creativity and personal power can be limited. As one support teacher put it: 'In some classes I feel I am just there to sharpen pencils.'

3 *A collaborative teaching situation*
The support teacher acts in support of the class or subject teacher in addition to supporting the children. I believe this to be the most satisfactory way to achieve the aims of equality of opportunity and access to the curriculum for all children. It could also prove the most rewarding to the teachers involved. For these reasons I have focused on the collaborative model in this paper.

Defining the nature and function of support

Shumaker and Brownell (1984) define social support as:

... an exchange of resources between two individuals perceived by the provider or the recipient to be intended to enhance the well-being of the recipient.

Support by the support teacher (the provider) for the class or subject teacher (the recipient) is therefore a two-way dynamic process. The reciprocal exchange of resources is important to producing a dynamic relationship in which problems can be perceived as challenges rather than threats. There are two types of factors operating in a support situation.

First, there are factors internal to each person. Everyone has basic human needs which they attempt to satisfy. Second, there are external factors. Support can help the recipient cope with the demands of the environment in which he finds himself or herself.

Internal factors

Glasser (reported by Brandt, 1988) lists our basic human needs as: the need to struggle to survive, to belong, to care and be cared for, to have power and freedom, and to have fun. Survival, in the sense of having enough money to provide the basic necessities in life, has never been a problem in teaching. Many teachers, however, are increasingly asking questions such as 'Will I be next to be redeployed?' 'Should I put in for early retirement?' 'How much longer can I go on without having a breakdown?' or even 'Will I be attacked in school today?' Survival can be perceived in different ways.

Humans are by nature interactive creatures. We have a built-in need for friendship and caring concern. Most teachers, if asked what they most enjoy about work, would say something like: 'We have a good laugh in the staffroom,' or 'The children keep me sane.' Collaborative teaching, if successful, can help satisfy this basic human need. Both teachers, however, need to feel supported and supportive.

Personal power is important to our self-esteem. Every human being needs to feel that he or she has something to offer to a situation. There are three levels of power:

1 Someone we respect listens to us.
2 Someone listens and says: 'You're right'.
3 Someone listens and says: 'You know your way is better than mine. Let's do it your way' (Glasser 1988).

A truly collaborative relationship will never emerge unless the need for power of both the teachers is being met. This need for power also applies to the children.

We all need the freedom to be, at times, spontaneous and creative. In-class support can be restrictive if this aspect is not recognised. As one teacher remarked: 'I feel so tired at the end of a supported lesson. I feel such a sense of relief when the support teacher leaves the room.' Collaborative work can help to satisfy these basic human needs. By working with each other we 'belong and care'. We satisfy our need for power by contributing and discussing our ideas with others. The need for fun tends to follow from having our other basic needs met.

External factors

The second aspect of support is to do with achieving a person–environment fit. We have beliefs about our own personal needs and resources and we also have beliefs about our environment. These interpretations vary from person to person (Lazarus and Launier, 1978). Any demand made upon us can be perceived as having no relevance, as a positive benefit or as a cause of stress. Lazarus and Launier outline three concepts which are significant to a person's 'wellbeing'. These are 'harm-loss', 'threat' and 'challenge'. Both teachers bring to the situation past experiences and the harm or loss that has occurred from them. For example a teacher with a history of discipline problems may feel that they have been time-tabled to be supported because they are being appraised or shown how it should be done. This is threatening to his or her personal power and self-esteem. Alternatively, a teacher may also find himself or herself timetabled to do in-class support as an alternative to redeployment. He feels the management does not know what to do with him. This kind of experience can result in loss of self-esteem, status and commitment.

Threat depends on the 'balance of power between the demands and the resources', (p 288). If a person anticipates that the demands on him exceed his own personal resources then the situation becomes threatening. Ideas about grouping and individualised learning that are put forward by support teachers as coping options may be seen by subject teachers as threatening additions to the demands already put on them by the GCSE etc. In fact support teachers may underestimate the pressures placed on subject teachers as these demands are sometimes not relevant to them.

Support teachers, on the other hand, may ask themselves questions like: 'Am I doing enough?' 'Do I know enough?' 'Can I communicate my ideas?' 'Will I get change?' These questions, however, can equally well be perceived as challenges rather than threats. Lazarus and Launier define challenge 'as the opportunity to overcome hardship and grow' (p 296). Whether these questions become potential threats or challenges probably depends on:

- Each teacher's beliefs about his or her own personal resources, which include the power to adapt
- The degree of shared understanding between them about goals, values, and commitment
- The degree of empathy between them
- Their interpersonal communication skills
- The extent to which they both believe that the support teacher can provide extra resources, both intellectual and emotional, and tangible material help during this adaptation process
- Other contextual factors such as age, race, sex, physical environment and organisational climate.

The extent to which class/subject teachers perceive in-class support as a positive innovation, stressful or irrelevant to them, is possibly determined by the demands made of them, in terms of changes to their existing practices and beliefs. A move away from rigid time-tabling and withdrawal towards in-class support is often viewed in a positive light by teachers but this feeling of joy may be mingled with apprehension about what the change may entail.

If the innovation is seen as compatible with the teachers' values of, for example, equality of opportunity for all children, etc. then they are more likely to perceive the innovation in a positive light. If, however, their beliefs about teaching and learning lead them to consider that children learn better in a small friendly environment with personal attention from a 'specialist expert', they are more likely to find the demands of in-class support stressful.

Incongruency of teacher perceptions

A further problem arises when the recipient's and provider's perceptions are incongruent (Shumaker and Brownell 1984). The two teachers may have different goals and different perceptions about what constitutes help. They may lack the interpersonal skills needed in order to communicate these effectively to each other, or there may be a lack of empathy between them.

Alternatively, the subject or class teacher may be unable to define clearly the kind of resources they require. There may be a lack of ability on the part of the support teacher provider to 'read' the request for assistance, or he may be unwilling to provide the type of help requested. He may feel: 'I am the expert. I know best.'

For example, the subject teacher may feel that the answer to the problem of teaching children with learning difficulties in their classroom lies in the adaptation of worksheets. The support teacher, on the other hand, may believe that nothing less than a rethinking of the lesson content, a change in teaching style and classroom organisation is required. In addition, there may be a lack of knowledge and skill in providing the resources requested on the part of the support teacher.

The support process

The support process involves the exchange of resources between the support teacher and the subject/class teacher. These form three basic types:

1 *Tangible material support*
   This may take the form of providing books, tools, worksheets and behavioural assistance.

2 *Information*
   This may take the form of providing non-judgmental feedback on the behaviours observed in the classroom in order to develop awareness and a shared understanding of the problem. It may be information concerning resources available, classroom management strategies etc. As Shumaker and Brownell (1984) state:

   > Support exchanges can broaden the individual's interpretation of the event and promote its clear understanding. Supportive resources include verbal information about the event and modelled responses to it.

3 *Emotional sustenance*
   This involves listening, being a friend, being reliable and consistent, providing comfort. In other words facilitating and empowering the supported teacher. A real danger of this aspect is that emotional support can often be perceived as an invasion of privacy.

Potential effects of support

The effects of support can be short term or long term. A supportive action, such as the provision of materials, which may be perceived as a benefit in the short term, may in the long term prevent a necessary rethink of curriculum content. There is a real danger of in-class support of this type propping up an ailing system. In contrast, an innovation which may seem of little benefit in the short term such as mixed ability grouping may produce a much more satisfactory situation in the long term. Perceptions of supportive exchanges are therefore not synonymous with effects of exchanges. In addition, if the flow of advice is merely in a one-way direction from the support teacher to the subject/class teacher then this could, in the long term, lead to a loss of personal power on the part of the class teacher.

Effects of support can be negative, beneficial or neutral. A negative effect of support can be an increased dependency of the class/subject teacher upon the support teacher. Also, a feeling of indebtedness may prevent them asking for help in the future. It is also possible that too much support can be offered coming from different directions and 'support that serves one function may interfere with another' (Shinn *et al* p 69). Different kinds of support may be needed at different times. If the response to support is neutral then questions could be asked about the efficient use of expensive resources.

Conclusions

Advocacy of an ideal does not necessarily result in commitment in practice. I found subject teachers on a 'Baker day' quite prepared to accept mixed ability teaching and individualised learning as principles. I also found that they often dismissed them as impracticable and therefore irrelevant to them. The process of support is a complex interaction.

In-service training has a role to play in helping teachers collaborate in this way. However, we cannot 'change attitudes' by lecturing on 'Baker days'. Support has to do with feelings and is only learnt through experiencing being 'supportive' and being 'supported'. Essential to the success of the collaborative teaching process is the ability to communicate these feelings to each other. We cannot control or change others. We only control or change ourselves. Awareness of feelings and the skills of interaction needed to communicate them can only be explored in small group workshops over time.

19   Integration pre-school: a case study

Linda Pound and Michele Moore

Introduction

The emphasis placed on the integration of children identified as having special educational needs by the Warnock Report (1978) and 1981 Education Act, together with the repeated call for equal access to equal opportunities in the Fish Report (1985), has particular implications for young children following the recommendation that opportunity should be available in the early years for those with special educational needs to start their education with other children of their own age in an ordinary class.

The Fish Report, reviewing provision to meet special educational needs for children under five, maintained that

> nursery school and class staff would welcome the chance to accept more children with developmental delays.

A caveat was added, however, in that

> the staffing implications of such placements were made clear. Staff as well as parents felt that extra help was essential if children were to be effectively integrated.

Integration is clearly not seen as an ummitigated good. Harvey (1985) suggests that mainstream classroom teachers feel anxious about taking responsibility for children identified as having special educational needs, despite the fact that perhaps 18 per cent of pupils in the ordinary school population require additional support during their school years (Gipps *et al* 1987).

Evidence that integration is detrimental to normally functioning children is absent from the literature, and some studies demonstrate that integration offers all children cognitive advantages (Odom, Deklyn and Jenkins, 1984). Despite this however, and despite the apparent lack of success of segregated settings (e.g.

Galloway and Goodwin, 1979), some writers express fears that children with special educational needs may be less well served in integrated than in segregated settings (e.g. Gresham 1982).

Such concerns are particularly prevalent in the field of deaf education (e.g. Levy-Shiff and Hoffman 1985, Lindsay and Dickinson 1987). Widespread and misplaced emphasis on the *inabilities* of deaf children is identified by Kyle (1987) as largely responsible for conflicting views on the efficacy of integration for deaf children. Also at the centre of the controversy is the continual debate over the relative merits of oral/aural (speech) or manual/visual (sign) vehicles for education and self expression of deaf children.

Recently public awareness of the rights of minority groups has grown, and so too have knowledge and recognition of signed language (e.g. Reagan, 1985). Paradoxically perhaps for the deaf community, increased awareness of the needs and rights of the deaf as a minority group, and of educationally and politically sensitive issues therein, has coincided with a growing commitment to the principle of integration for all (Fish Report 1985, Swann Report 1985, Booth, Potts and Swann 1987).

Some members of the deaf community, as Lane (1984) has pointed out, have for a long time favoured segregated provision. Others have opposed integration as it is occurring at present, agreeing that the integration of young deaf children is desirable but arguing

because a deaf child does not hear, the traditional method of communication used in the school curriculum where talk, talk, talk is the key technique, will not work.

(Jordan 1981)

Against this background, integration through the development of units within ordinary schools has been initiated for hearing impaired pupils.

This paper reports on attempts made within a case study to enhance practice in the provision of an integrated nursery for young profoundly deaf, and hearing, children.

Background

Occasion for the study arose with the amalgamation of a school for the deaf into an ordinary primary school. In the context of the 1981 Education Act which gave legislative effect in England and Wales to the Warnock Report (1978), amalgamation was seen to offer increased opportunities for integrating deaf and hearing children. Existing nursery provision for deaf children was extended to create an integrated pre-school facility comprising two classes for deaf and hearing children.

During the first year of the study the nursery was staffed with two full-time teachers, one for hearing children, and one for deaf children who had no previous experience of teaching the deaf. During the second study year a probationary teacher, trained as a teacher of the deaf, became the nursery teacher for deaf children. Two full-time NNEB nursery nurses and a part-time helper were based in the nursery. At management level there was a head of primary school, and head of unit for the deaf.

The main empirical focus of the case study involved observations of profoundly deaf children in the period during and preceding their entry into primary school (Sinha *et al* 1988). Alongside this longitudinal observation study, further discussion of which is beyond the scope of this paper, a parallel collaborative programme of staff development was implemented with practical objectives and implications for practice in the early integrated environment.

Three broad aims for a staff development programme were agreed:

1   To develop an atmosphere which would support successful amalgamation and integration among mainstream and unit staff by means of liaison and discussion.
2   To open up discussion of appropriate practice relating to integration issues.
3   To provide opportunity for staff to express views, feelings and any related problems in a constructive climate.

Procedure

Judging the climate

To judge the climate before introducing integrated nursery provision we asked all staff, both directly and through a short questionnaire, how they felt about imminent integration, and what effects they considered integration might have on staff, deaf children, hearing children and parents. We also asked how they thought integration would influence the day to day running of the nursery, and what implications there might be for their own role.

Initial expectations

Staff at all levels envisaged that integration would be a positive experience for all concerned. One of the head teachers felt integration was 'the beginning of children accepting their rightful place in society'.

A nursery nurse, highly experienced with deaf children, thought:

Nothing but good can come from a situation where hearing and deaf children mix normally.

All staff felt that deaf children would benefit from contact with hearing children:

They will benefit from integrating with a larger group with more variety of activities and equipment and not be so isolated in the outside world.

They also felt that hearing children would gain in tolerance and understanding:

Acceptance of others who may at first appear different. Hopefully [hearing children] will improve their communication skills.

This comment, from the teacher of hearing children, is particularly encouraging for those who may share concern that 'since the Warnock Report . . . in the case of hearing impaired children, too much has been expected of them' (Reed, 1981).

The view among staff at this stage was that integration would not markedly affect the day to day running of the nursery, or greatly change individual roles, although careful organisation and planning would be required. Staff felt confident that they would learn from their new experience of integration and did not foresee problems. These responses support Fish *et al*'s supposition that staff in early childhood education would welcome increased opportunities for integration (Fish Report, 1985).

Early impressions

Less than two terms later a follow-up questionnaire revealed that staff now felt far less optimistic about integration. Problems of communication were evident in many aspects of nursery management, principally concerning mode of interaction to be used with deaf children.

At the request of parents it had been agreed that total communication (including use of sign language, amplification, speech, lip reading, finger spelling, reading and writing), would be provided for one deaf child. Other deaf children and several hearing children, particularly those for whom English was a second language, quickly learnt, by observation, to communicate using simple signs and friendships between deaf and hearing children were seen to develop. In line with an LEA directive, however, the use of sign language had to be explicitly discouraged for all children other than the one child. Following this restriction on available communicative strategies, staff became worried that deaf and hearing children were not able to interact in positive ways, commenting, for example:

'I feel the hearing children are almost shocked by the deaf children. They make great efforts and are frequently snubbed. Some of the hearing children have imitated the unusual sounds of the deaf children. Three have stopped talking to me as though they think this is how they should be with me' (teacher of deaf).
'The two year old [deaf children] just seem to ignore the hearing children . . . the four year olds may play with the hearing for a few minutes when there is no one else to play with i.e. no other deaf child. . . . I have seen the

deaf children become very frustrated and sometimes very rude because they are not understanding what is required of them or having what they want.'

At best,

'most [deaf children] appear to play *alongside* the hearing children quite well'.

The issue of communication, which Montgomery (1981) has called 'the key to integration' for deaf and hearing children, had clearly come to the fore.

Each member of staff commented that a great deal of extra work was necessary if they were to realise original high hopes for integration. We were told:

Relationships between staff [have often been] a little strained. We have had many meetings after school to try to sort things out.

Everyone agreed with the teacher of hearing children who said:

From the organisation point of view it means more thought and effort and consequently more co-operation so that the needs of both sets of children are met.

The Fish Report proviso that additional support would be necessary to implement integration in primary schools was by now fully realised.

Enabling a constructive climate

There was a strong feeling that if the staff team could be encouraged to share their views this would be beneficial both to the children and to the process of integration.

To facilitate dialogue and confront difficult issues in a constructive way, opportunities were set up for staff to examine preconceptions and attitudes towards integration, and to reconceptualise if they were prepared to do so. At the beginning of the third term each member of staff was helped to do this individually. Discussions were based on an eclectic interview method originally developed for sharing perspectives within interprofessional groups (Howard, 1986). A similar exercise is described by Rodger and Richardson (1985) as enabling teachers to look at the bases of their judgments of children.

We asked nursery staff to focus on personal experiences of integration, and to write down related words or ideas around the statement 'integration involves me in . . .' Words chosen were then used in an activity designed to elicit each person's own constructs of integration. The final activity was to draw three pictures: 'me involved in integration'; 'something that makes integration work' (a conducive factor); and 'something that makes integration difficult' (a counteractive factor).

Rethinking integration

Staff were now able to base their responses on experience and review of integration in the nursery. They reiterated individually that a great deal was involved in integration, in direct contrast to initial hopes that working in an integrated setting would be 'without much alteration from the usual day to day running . . . in an "ordinary" nursery'. The need to share the workload, plan together, agree on lots of things, maintain co-operation between staff and commitment were all strongly emphasised.

For most staff thoughts that came to mind in relation to integration included positive factors such as 'play' 'opportunity' and 'working co-operatively'. Each person's list included qualifying statements, however, such as 'needing advice', 'needing support', 'hard work', 'extra responsibility', 'frustration', and 'importance of communication'. A nursery nurse had written 'being careful' which, she explained, referred to an increased need for discretion in the face of conflicting messages from senior management. Other comments referred to new skills that had to be accomplished: 'changing ways of talking', 'explanations to hearing children', 'encouraging hearing children', and 'acting play' (meaning play without spoken language).

For all staff the picture of their own involvement in integration showed them facilitating communication between children. The precedence of communication in integration of deaf and hearing children was again reinforced.

Factors identified as supporting integration were other members of staff, praise from other staff, specific areas such as the home corner where communication between children was particularly viable, and the children themselves. Factors which made integration more difficult included conflicting advice from management, staff absence, uncertainty about giving adequate explanations to deaf children, and related to this, interruptions from other children. Commitment to the principle of integration still prevailed, however, the teacher of the deaf saying it was about 'getting the balance right'.

Two years on

At the end of the second year of integrated provision, staff took part in a follow-up appraisal of the situation. This time activities were group based and involved sharing perceptions of integration. Notions of 'what integration *could* mean for children' and 'for me as a professional' were explored. Working around the phrase 'what integration means for me . . .', individuals wrote down personal interpretations. Responses were then pooled in small groups and a schema negotiated which could accommodate them all within a coherent framework.

There were positive responses to what integration could mean for children: tolerance, understanding, breaking down prejudice, widening communication skills and independence were mentioned, but also frustration and resentment.

In relation to what integration could mean for adults, the now familiar themes of extra work, greater responsibility and need for more time were stressed by everyone, with greater accountability emerging as a new theme. Feelings of uncertainty, vulnerability and insecurity were expressed, notably 'the need for support especially if you don't share aims'. These were balanced to some extent by ideas of widening professional horizons, rethinking priorities and the possibility of co-operation.

One group decided the main concerns were curriculum and resource issues; staff; in-service education; organisation; and children, communication and developing social skills. The other group operated on a rather different framework, giving understanding and co-operation priority, and then, communication with children; administration including resources; and organisation. At the end of the session staff proposed to consider ways of assimilating ideas into one overall schema as a way of identifying possible steps forward.

We believe that the staff development programme implemented in the case study school helped to ensure that goodwill towards integration was not dissipated, and enabled staff to feel supported and valued for their contribution to integration in recognisably difficult circumstances. In addition the programme enabled problems to be shared openly and in this way often surmounted.

Discussion

Staff development and research showed the Fish Report to be correct in asserting that staff would welcome integration of children with special needs but would require additional support. That the integrated nursery of our case study was 'provision made . . . originally [as] a relatively *ad hoc* solution to a problem', (Fish Report 1985), however, was reflected in persistent uncertainty among staff throughout the first two years of the initiative.

Gipps (1987) has pointed out the importance of liaison between school staff at grassroots and those who make decisions at LEA level for implementing developments in special needs. Despite this, increasing feelings of dissatisfaction expressed by staff during the two years of this study were not addressed seriously at any senior level. By the end of the first two years of amalgamated provision staff were 'disappointed with integration' and articulating more and more clearly that they needed support to facilitate integration between profoundly deaf and hearing children properly. At no time did commitment to the principle of integration for these children lessen, but there was an increasing feeling that this was not shared at the highest LEA level.

Relatively general issues arising with changes after the 1981 Education Act in provision for children with special educational needs, could be managed within the school. Critical issues in the integration of profoundly deaf children such as mode of interaction for deaf children required communication and partnership between those genuinely concerned with the education of these children at all levels.

It was clear from our involvement in staff development that communication is the single most important issue in the integration of profoundly deaf children. For staff without liberty to communicate in the most effective way with their deaf pupils, however, problems in integration are, predictably, considerable.

The extent to which the picture of integration remains a positive one in the case study school is in spite of the LEA's failure to liaise with staff and provide active support. Difficulties in integration for young deaf, and hearing children, could have been largely overcome had the LEA engaged in two-way communication with school staff. Discussion of particular value would examine the authority's insistence on 'pitching [deaf children] into the oralist wilderness . . . under the guise of 'integration' (Montgomery, 1986).

20 Talking about language with five to seven year olds

Lyn Wendon

Introduction

The importance of talking about language is stressed in the Kingman Report as an integral part of teaching literacy in the primary and secondary school years. Children who are not made aware of the structure of the language are less well equipped to use it. But no teacher expects five year olds to arrive at school able to speak the meta-language required to talk about language (even though we may have underestimated their innate language abilities in the past). So how can we talk to the infant age groups about language in a way that ensures maximum benefit to them?

Our normal verbal currency for talking about language is strikingly cumbersome. The instructional words available might just as well be made of stone – heavy, drab coinage, difficult for children to carry around, joyless for them and for us to exchange with each other. Here are some of our drab 'coins': words, letters, sounds, names, vowels, consonants, syllables, sentences, paragraphs, capitals, hard/soft/long/short sounds – just to name a few.

Do any of these terms arouse a lively picture in a child's mind? Do they trigger a connection? Produce an emotive response? Make them want to know more? How many children use these 'teacher' words themselves, or ask questions about them or their meanings? Do they unite or divide teachers from children? Do they encourage attention, or discourage it?

What do these terms have in common? They are all colourless, devoid of imagery, devoid of prior associations in a child's mind.

They are also all forms of classification. This means they can have full meaning only to those who already know how to use the categories they represent. It is easy but dangerous to assume that infants can readily learn to attach the right collective groups to each term.

Even the alphabet names are classification categories. 'Aee' is the category word for all these shapes: a, α, $\mathbf{a}$, A. It is also the category word for talking about two different sounds (long and short 'aee').

Let's look more closely at our traditional alphabet names, 'aee', 'bee', 'cee', through 'double-u', 'ex', 'why', 'zed'. For centuries this nomenclature has been common coinage for instructing children about letter shapes, sounds, syllables and for talking about how words are spelt. Yet its terms are remarkably flawed. For example, consider the following facts:

- The 21 sounds (the only relevant information which children need for reading and for early creative writing) are at the start of only eight consonant names. They are at the *end* of six, and at neither end of seven. They are, in effect, hidden a full 66 per cent of the time. Many teachers are unaware that the 21 consonant names themselves are never used in reading – only the five vowel names are – and then only intermittently.
- Equally misleading, no less than 15 of our traditional consonant names – almost 75 per cent of them – actually begin with another letter's sound! As a special needs colleague put it, 'It is tragic when a ten year old still thinks that 'duh' is the sound of **w**.'
- A similar flaw is directly responsible for misleading children in spelling, causing them to misplace or leave out vowels (e.g. bgin, for begin). No fewer than 12 consonant names end with a vowel name (57 per cent of them).
- The vowel names are the sources of a further problem – they contain no clue to their sounds. Conversely their sounds give no clue to their five names (100 per cent without clues).

The communication impasse arising just from using our traditional alphabet names can last for months or even years.

It is no secret that the rest of the colourless terminology listed earlier contributes to teacher communication failure. It is well documented in the literature on teaching reading.

A new, narrative form of instruction

For change to be justified it must work. The concept of 'Letterland', a secret place where invisible people and animals reveal themselves within letter shapes, was born of necessity. The necessity was the special needs of children who had fallen behind one or two years or more in reading, and who usually felt totally discouraged about putting pencil to paper for any purpose, least of all for 'creative' writing.

With such children it is essential that they do not fail again. They must somehow catch up instead. So every sentence of instruction must win attention, must be vivid, memorable and quickly understood. Creating Pictogram characters, fused into the plain letter shapes, provided a new way of talking about letters and words.

The first change was to replace temporarily the treacherous alphabet names with reliable alliterative names. Examples are: Annie Apple, Bouncy Ben, Clever Cat, Yo-yo Man and Zig Zag Zebra. The alliterative character names enable teachers to postpone the use of the traditional alphabet name system just long enough to ensure that children do not fall victim to its built-in hazards. Unlike the 'aee, bee, cee' terms, the Letterland names enable infants to select the correct letter sound – without exception – from the start of the character name. Furthermore, descriptive words like Applestand (A) and Duck Door (D) ensure there is no ambiguity when a teacher talks about any of the 17 capital letter shapes that differ from their lower-case shapes.

A second change was handwriting that can be taught by analogy and in verse. The teacher uses rhymes to guide children's hands – and minds – as they chant or sing and stroke (with the whole arm as well as the hand) the correct letter shape on

a large scale in the air. The rhymes refer to the letters' Pictogram body parts. The rhyme for **b**, for example, is:

Brush down Ben's
big, long ears.
Go up, round his head
so his face appears!

The Pictogram might best be described as a piece of 'pictorial language' strategically placed within the abstract shape so that it can simultaneously endorse that shape and symbolise its sound. It enables the letter to become a character in both senses of the word. The children 'see' the secret, bright-eyed brown bunny called Bouncy Ben in their minds' eye. He is alive in the **b**-shape, just waiting to be stroked – motivating them to do him that favour. Even without adding any animating details they know 'who' they have stroked when they have written the **b**-shape.

Contrast this with the traditional instruction language, 'To write the letter **b** correctly start at the top. Go down, up, then around in a circle.'

Once achieved, what do the children have? Simply an abstract symbol, an 'it', a thing called – most incongruously – a 'bee'. They have probably chanted the 'down, up and around', 'around, up and down' type of phrasing with their teacher for every letter. So none of these phrases can linger in a child's mind as unique to one letter.

Another vital difference – from the start the children can speak this instruction language themselves. When five year olds go home and tell their parents that 'The Hairy Hat Man hates noise: that's why he never speaks above a whisper in words,' they are really telling them that 'aitch' is a voiceless consonant. The bare fact has no apparent reason (for adult or child), but in the story version the fact is embedded in a human context and a human reason is provided for it. So the five year old feels at home with the information, happily recounts it and enjoys sharing it.

The greatest shift comes when teaching new values for **a–z** (e.g. **sh, ch, er, aw, igh, tion,** etc). Now, instead of having to convey vital information by the old unpopular, skills-drills approach to reading and spelling the teacher can narrate little stories – stories about the way the Letterland people and animals typically behave when they meet each other in words.

The stories transpose barren rules into brief analogies that can entertain while they teach. Their efficiency as instruction language has been demonstrated in the field in recent years, as more and more teachers have elected to use Letterland, not just as the basis for special needs teaching, but as a central part of their language curriculum. Most schools introduce the system at reception level or even nursery level because the meta-language of instruction invites even very young children to listen and learn, where traditional talk about letters does not.

Many teachers are finding evidence of the effectiveness of this new narrative approach among pre-schoolers. Countless younger siblings now start school already knowing a surprising amount of the Letterland lore, just picked up from their school-aged brothers and sisters.

How does one measure the teaching power of a fantasy? One can probably only take stock of the typical result – a bond between the child and each letter shape, caused by harnessing unique instruction words and ideas to the learning task. A further result is almost invariably curiosity. 'Who is she?' the children ask, eyeing some other Pictogram character on the Letterland wall frieze, and 'What's his name? What's hers?' The shift in pronoun to 'him' and 'her' instead of the perpetual neuter form 'it' is a small change, but it is a change with large ramifications. Blood begins to flow in the veins of a dry subject.

Another point. Traditional instruction language has no method for 'fixing' alliterative words to particular letter shapes. Teachers cannot say that 'ef' is friendly, fond of fishing or fast at fighting fires – but they can do so when 'ef' is transmuted into Fireman Fred, a living embodiment of the **f**-shape. How does he

fight fires? 'Not with water, with foam!' any child in the class will tell you. Why? 'Because *fff*oam begins with Fireman Fred's sound!'

The alliterative fun also leads to vocabulary growth. Before the children 'meet' Fireman Fred they may not know, for example, the words 'force' and 'fist'. But they soon learn them as they play-act being Fireman Fred. They mime **f**eeling the **f**oam *f*orce its way through his **f**lat **f**irehose, **f**illing it out so that he has to hold it very tightly in his **F**ists. The **f** sound is now occurring naturally as the teacher guides the play-acting. No dreary 'word family lists' where we all listen carefully to the 'ef' sound.

Instead the alliterative words help to create a character sketch of one of the heroes of Letterland. They become a means for attending to 'his' letter sound within the living flow of language. The alliterative words also become a mini-exercise in the craft of writing – gathering words (not always alliterative) around a person to create a personality.

Play-acting adds another form of language too, body language, to strengthen the association. When a child has stroked Bouncy Ben's ears, mimed by a friend's upraised arms, there is much more to remember than the tiny finger movements made while holding a pencil and practising the 'bee' stroke.

Any child can 'speak' the pictorial language too, confirming the analogy, in this case, just by adding a face and whiskers. They use their own drawings as a hands-on mapping device, thereby alerting themselves to the letter's shape and orientation.

The whole concept of Letterland is really an extended metaphor. Within each little fiction nestles a little fact, couched in a fable-like narrative. The teacher uses his or her story-telling voice instead of simply stating facts and then requiring the children to state them back. The first stages take the children 'over the wall' into Letterland. Once they have learnt aA–zZ they are awarded a 'Letterland Passport', symbol that now they are free to travel anywhere they choose in the Land of Words.

The second stage includes bigger fictions which harbour bigger facts – major structural principles running through English orthography which can make the pronunciation of most unknown words predictable, and can simultaneously take the mystery out of many seemingly arbitrary spelling patterns.

The problem with the traditional versions of these principles, e.g. 'A final, silent e makes the vowel before it say its name', is that, typically, the children who really need their predictive power don't apply the principles, even when they have learnt the rules. The silent final e rule is easy enough to parrot – but the words are grey. They don't communicate. Even calling the e a 'Magic E' doesn't help very much. The e is still an 'it' and the vowel before 'it' is still another 'it'. The teacher says, 'It says its name.' But if any of the three 'it' categories ('vowel' and 'sound' and 'name') are still amorphous in the child's mind, what can he or she make of it?

In the Letterland story version of the Magic E principle, people are involved – letter people. One person signals for the other one to shout his name. It's a 'naming game' which the children can also play, sing about and act out. They learn by experiencing letter behaviour themselves. The imitation pattern creates the memory pattern. Children in thousands of British infant schools have shown that they can learn this information well enough to benefit their handwriting, their reading and their spelling in their formative reception year.

Kingman's call for the return of an analytical component in the teaching of

English is only justified if it can be done efficiently as a strand which runs parallel to but not in conflict with attention to syntax, contextual clues, to cohesion and all the message seeking strategies which Frank Smith, the Goodmans, *et al* have helped us to see as central to the reading process.

This parallel strand should include a strong element of 'oracy', nourished by hearing stories, learning their content, discussing their messages, and recounting them with understanding.

When the meta-language for instruction about language is stories, children become able, even keen, to speak the instruction language, just as readily as their teacher. So oracy is nourished even as they practise communicating the information to each other.

Furthermore, the new narrative instruction language needs no re-translation. Once it has 'accessed' children into reading, writing, and spelling it has served its purpose. The grey language of traditional instruction has been by-passed, but all its messages have been delivered.

The aim has been to make the meta-language child-centred enough to enhance the 'climate' of learning and the quality of relationships between teacher and children – an aspect which, as Roger Beard says, 'is both under-researched and underestimated in many publications on teacher education'. (*Developing Reading*, Hodder and Stoughton, 1987, pp 3–13).

My hope is that eventually more researchers will turn their attention to the techniques described above so as to produce research data to measure fully the effectiveness of this approach to talking about language in the primary schools.

21   A self-concept approach to dealing with pupils

George Robinson and Barbara Maines

Everyone has inside himself . . . what shall I call it . . . a piece of good news. Everyone is a very great and important character. Yes, that's what we have to tell them. Every man must be persuaded, even if he's in rags, that he is immensely, immensely important. Every one must respect him and make him respect himself too. They must listen to him attentively, don't stand on top of him, don't stand in his light, but look at him with gentleness, deference, give him great, great hopes, he needs them, especially if he's young . . . spoil him. Yes, make him grow proud.

(Burnt Flower Bed, Ugo Betti)

Introduction

Through our many workshops and publications we have attempted to heighten the awareness of teachers and other adults who work with young people to the importance of their role as 'significant others' in the development of the self-concept of the children in their care. In this short article we will give our reasons for believing in the importance of self-concept and suggest some ways in which we can manage to teach and care for young people in ways which will promote their self-concepts.

Why is self-concept important?

We have adopted an interactionist approach, that is, we believe that the way a person feels about himself

- is determined by the way he interprets the messages he receives from 'significant others.'
- determines the way he behaves, learns and relates to other people.

Those of us who work with pupils with learning or emotional and behavioural difficulties often see how the messages are misinterpreted.

Biased scanning is the process by which information which is consistent with the self-image is eagerly accepted; information inconsistent with the child's picture of himself is either ignored, misinterpreted or rejected. Children with low self-concept will look for information to confirm their poor view of themselves. Significant others must constantly offer unambiguous messages of acceptance.

As adults who work with young people we must recognise our role in the formation of their self-concept and we must ensure that the messages we give, both verbal and non-verbal, help a child to feel respected and valued. (Robinson, G. and Maines, B. J. 1988)

"No! Of course I'm not angry."

We speak words but the messages we give with those words are modified and interpreted by the tone of our voices and by the many non-verbal signals we convey through our posture, expression and the environment that we create for the young people in our care.

What we do today influences somebody's self-concept tomorrow.

What do we mean by self-concept?

It is important that we explain our use of the term 'self-concept' because the word 'self' is frequently used in a variety of contexts. Like 'counselling' it can convey a number of meanings. We learnt that from the teacher who offered counselling as an intervention for a difficult pupil. When asked what type of counselling he had used he replied: 'I have counselled him very severely.'

Our interest in self-concept as a determining aspect of children's learning and behaviour led us to read widely (and argue extensively) about the various theories and the terminology. In his book *Improved Reading through Counselling* (1973), Denis Lawrence offers a model on which we have based our thinking.

This is our version: A person's self-concept is his perception of his unique personal characteristics such as appearance, ability, temperament, physique, attitude and beliefs. These determine his view of his position in society and his value to and relationships with other people. The development of self-concept is a continuous process which begins with a baby's earliest interaction with caring adults and continues as the child develops. The significant person in the early years is the parent, but on entering school the child begins relationships with new 'significant others'.

Self-concept has three aspects:

Self-image
A child grows up with all sorts of ideas about himself, his abilities, attributes and appearance. These are acquired and influenced by his perceptions of how he is accepted and valued by the adults who care for him. This self-image goes with him at all times and influences what he does and how he behaves. There can be lots of aspects of self-image – social, physical, intellectual – and they are all influenced by the significant other in the child's life.

A negative self-image is a handicap that we as significant others must recognise and try to alleviate. The environment we create for a child must not reinforce his feelings of failure, rejection and reminders of personal inadequacies. If we could look in on a child's self-image it would resemble an album of self-portraits, sometimes candid, sometimes posed; some are detailed and some enlarged but all are close-ups, all are revealing and all are very personal.

Ideal self
From his interactions with 'significant others' the child forms an impression of the abilities and personal qualities which are admired and valued. From these he can compose a picture of the desirable person, an 'ideal self'.

Self-esteem
This is the total evaluation a person makes of himself and the degree of respect with which he regards himself. If self-image is poor and incompatible with an

ideal self which seems unattainable, self-esteem suffers. Children who have warm, affectionate relationships with parents have higher self-esteem even when they are relatively inadequate at specific skills. High self-esteem provides a child with the confidence to attempt difficult things without an incapacitating fear of failure. A pupil with a low self-esteem finds it difficult to try new strategies. He protects what he has and continues to behave in a manner consistent with his poor view of himself. If he feels rejected and views himself as unacceptable and valueless then he doesn't regard disapproval as a reaction to his behaviour but to himself.

Attempts to work with children to improve self-esteem must offer feedback which counteracts this interpretation under conditions which are accepting and non-judgmental.

We have found the above definition both simple and useful because it offers a basis for change, a hope that we can do something to improve the self-concept of the young people we work with. If we can improve self-image by giving clear and unambiguous messages, and at the same time set realistic and achievable goals so that ideal self is attainable, then we narrow the gap between the two and self-concept is raised.

What we can do about it

In all our work we attempt to encourage adults who work with children to feel positive, to believe that, even in the most adverse circumstances, there is always something that they can do to help the children in their care.

> *An optimist is wrong just about as often as a pessimist,*
> *the difference is that he has a lot more fun!*

It is not our intention to offer you easy answers which will be guaranteed to work for you in your own unique environment. What we do offer are ideas and techniques which we use to create a school environment which enhances the self-concept of the young people we work with. These may interest or challenge you and if you believe that self-concept is important you may find that our work offers you new strategies to try for yourself and make your own.

Bag of tricks
Within the limitations of this article we can only offer a taster of our video film demonstrating the use of these and other strategies which is available with an in-service training manual (Robinson, G. and Maines, B. 1988).

Label the act
Never tell a child he is bad, a liar, a thief. Sure, you are displeased with his *behaviour*, but you still value him. So maintain his self-esteem and tell him that you are disappointed or surprised that a good child like him has done a thing like

that. It's just not like him! That way you can both start to expect that he won't do it again.

Taking the risk yourself

When a child faces a task which puts him at risk of failure you can give him courage by taking the responsibility for possible failure onto your own shoulders. For example:

1 Remove the threat of failure. 'This is very hard but I know you will do your best. Don't worry if you find it difficult, it is my fault for giving you such hard work.'
2 Take the blame for failure. 'I am sorry, I didn't explain that properly. It is my fault. Let me try again.'
3 Offer just enough help and just early enough to prevent failure and consequent breakdown of concentration. It is much easier to intervene when the child is still on task than to rescue a child with low self-concept once he has failed.

Apologise

During a busy working day it is inevitable that occasionally you might have to keep a child waiting, interrupt your attention to him when you are distracted and maybe not manage to do everything you said you would. Make sure that you say you are sorry, that you ask if you may keep them waiting while you attend to some urgent matter. Offer an explanation for your behaviour. That really makes a young person feel important; it lets him know that you care about him as an individual and that he deserves your respect.

Pat on the back

Non-verbal interventions are a very powerful part of the behavioural dialogue. A hand on the shoulder, a pat on the back, a smile or a wink can convey to a child that you recognise him as an individual and that you care about him. A very brief non-verbal message offered fairly frequently when a child is behaving well can keep a child on task and give a very positive signal (Bevan and Shortall 1986).

A whisper in time

A very, very quiet word whispered to a child when trouble is brewing can be an effective way of preventing the situation from escalating. It is private, non-threatening, catches the child's attention and brings you physically close to him. A whisper creates an atmosphere that is calm and quiet and does not inject emotional energy to which the child may react. (It is also a good way to keep your own blood presure down!)

Workshop activities

We are can only offer a very brief description of some of the activities we use with groups of adults to work on topics:

- *Making punishments positive* – an opportunity to examine the use of sanctions, to make them effective while also preserving the self-concept of the children and realising a positive outcome from a potentially alienating situation.
- *Celebrations* – the search for reasons to celebrate each child, not just for achievement or effort, but because they are children.
- *Praise* – the frequent use of praise and positive comments as part of a planned strategy to enhance self-image.

The list of ideas below is one taken from a recent workshop session.

CELEBRATIONS	PRAISE/POSITIVES	DEALING WITH TROUBLE
	Private and public	No hard and fast rules;
SPECIAL EVENTS	Letters home	leave escape routes. Don't
Birthdays, weddings, feasts	Display of work	push pupils into corners from
Home events, holidays	Comments on books	which there is no way out
	Attention	Use negotiation
INDIVIDUAL	Certificates for work,	Discuss with individual, with
Hair, clothes, personal	behaviour	group
attributes, smiles	Control of temper, attitude	Cooling off period, delaying
	Punctuality & attendance	tactics
BEHAVIOUR	Saying hello & goodbye	Diversionary tactics
Helping others Improve-	Winks, smiles, nods, touch	Anticipation
ment in any area of work,		Staff consistency
appearance or behaviour	Communication of adult	Teach coping strategies
	feelings	Clear consistent rules
COULD INCLUDE	Apologising if adult is in the	Stay calm, quiet, polite
Photographs	wrong	Contracts
Pupil of the week	Knowing pupils' names	Ignore
Certificates	Extra playtimes	Humour, NOT sarcasm
Profiles		Know the pupils
Saying hello		Drama role play to explore
Saying goodbye		feelings
Welcome back after absence		Problem solving strategies
Sharing jokes		Label the act
Talking in the playground		Use parents
		Reinforce good behaviour
		'I' messages
		Mild/positive punishments
		Listen to the child's point of
		view

Why don't you . . .?

Use a staff meeting to produce your own list of strategies and techniques that you might use to make punishment positive, celebrate and praise children. Choose one idea from your list which you agree to implement immediately.

Conclusion

We have attempted in this article to suggest why we believe that self-concept is important and how as significant others in the lives of the young people we work with we have an opportunity to influence the way they feel about themselves and consequently the way they learn and behave.

We have formed an organisation called Lame Duck Enterprises which exists to promote this work through lectures, workshops and publications. If you would like more information or if you have work or ideas which you would like to contribute please contact us. Like you we do care about the young people we work with.

A parting thought

. . . you've got to help me. You've got to hold out your hand even when that's the last thing I seem to want or need. . . . Each time you are kind and gentle and encouraging, each time you try to understand because you really care, my heart begins to grow wings, very small wings, very feeble wings – but wings. (Don Peretz Elkins, 1976.)

22 Co-ordinating special needs provision in further education: a personal perspective

Maria Landy

Introduction

Provision for students with special needs in further education is still a relatively new area of work. With few exceptions, young people leaving special schools did not go on to further education colleges until the late 1970s.

As Richard Stowell points out in an early chapter, FE Colleges coped in varying degrees with students who had physical or sensory handicaps before Warnock and the 1981 Education Act. In the absence of controlling legislation much of this early provision was based on goodwill and individual students' aspirations to vocational training.

The situation in further education reflected that which pertains in many ordinary secondary schools in that there was a lack of coherent and co-ordinated policy regarding young people with special learning needs. Since the 1981 Education Act, FE colleges have been forced to examine provision for young people with disabilities and learning needs but as Stowell (1987) points out, quality of response nationwide has been far from even. All the evidence suggests there is a continuing need to raise the awareness of all who work in further education and secondary schools of the need for co-ordinated provision for students with special needs.

This paper is concerned to explore how college policy may be formulated so that educational provision for students with special needs in further education may acquire the characteristics of coherence and responsiveness to individual need. An attempt will be made to focus on the importance and in particular to look at the broader aspects of this role as they might relate to the LEA and the local community. To develop the purpose of the paper the experience of the author within a college of further education will be utilised as part of case study material.

Background practice

Much current practice in schools, notably the move to integration, is also reflected in colleges. Although the further education experience is very different, an adult approach in an adult environment with a vast range of possible opportunities, there are still parallels to be drawn and lessons to be learnt. There are continuing debates concerning funding, resources both human and material, and curriculum development.

The Warnock Report (1981) recommends that:

> A co-ordinated approach to further education for people with special educational needs should be adopted and published by local education authorities against a long-term plan within which arrangements for individual institutions will take their place.
>
> (Recommendations 12 para 10.43)

Effective progress in this area has usually been based on the joint efforts of enthusiastic individuals and enlightened authorities. Provision is still, nevertheless, very patchy and in some areas non-existent. Unfortunately until recently the extent of this development has been difficult to quantify. *Catching Up* (Stowell 1987) is the published results of a survey undertaken jointly by the National Bureau of Handicapped Students and the Department of Education and Science. The survey was designed to find out how many students with special educational needs were being provided for in further education. It highlighted both the gaps in provision and the lack of policy. Less than one in five colleges surveyed had a formal policy concerning SEN students, and there was an under-representation of students with special needs on mainstream courses. Wide geographical differences were reported on the provision available by virtue of students' disability. Those with physical and emotional or behavioural problems appear to be particularly disadvantaged.

Staff awareness of the range of special needs and their educational significance is often patchy. Barriers to integration and change are often related to attitudes held by the more traditional staff in FE colleges. There is much staff development work to be done in special needs and the recommendations of *A Special Professionalism* (1987) need to be implemented throughout the country. There are staff teaching in FE and adult education with no formal teaching qualification and little opportunity presently exists in many colleges to meet the INSET needs of these staff and other providers of educational services. Staff working with students who have special educational needs are constantly requesting in-service training. Existing resources for supplying this are very varied and future provision must consider professional development as a long-term process geared both to the individual and the institution.

The adoption of the multi-agency statementing procedure for some young people with special needs and the changes this has brought in schools is also being reflected in the practice of some colleges. This approach has been adopted as good practice with ongoing involvement of the support services, as well as the careers service and, where appropriate, the community mental handicap team as well as health, adult education, social services and other agencies where appropriate. The aim being a planned long-term coherent approach to educational provision on a local basis.

There are certain problems, however, in that many of the contextual issues recognised by secondary schools as having implications for children's learning have yet to be interpreted fully in the FE context. Important among these would be the attitudes of staff. The development of new strategies within the classroom and the evolution of co-operative support both inside and outside the classroom is still a relatively new approach in some colleges.

Modifying arrangements for teaching and developing appropriate curricular materials remains an exciting challenge for colleges. Indeed some secondary schools have still to take up this challenge. The need for co-ordination, multi-agency approaches, informed policy and the evolution of practice were all matters of high priority for the author in taking up the role of special educational needs co-ordinator within a college of further education in the North East of England. What follows is an attempt to share the particular experiences and challenges faced by this author and some of the solutions found in the process. These solutions relate to policy formulation and to practice.

A case study: towards a college-wide approach

Provision for students with special educational needs within the college was established in 1981. The rapid demand reflected not only the change in educational philosophy but also the demand for further educational opportunities for a variety of students with special educational needs. Provision was seen as an across college responsibility and the college strove to be responsive and flexible, to meet the needs of all students, with a policy of equal opportunities for all.

Development of a policy document: a framework for action

The initial thrust came from the LEA by requesting a college development plan for special educational needs provision. An important early decision was to combine this with a college policy which not only reflected current practice but also led into the development plan considering future provision. In trying to establish a college policy and plan for students with special educational needs, an important early facet was to create the framework of college policy and achieve commitment to a special educational needs development plan. The framework emerged as follows:

1 Visits were made to a number of colleges by the co-ordinator.
2 A cross section of policy documents and statements was surveyed by the co-ordinator.
3 A draft document was produced by the co-ordinator and presented for discussion.
4 An internal college working party was set up to discuss the draft document.
5 Special needs staff were asked for comments – the consultative process included oral and written forms.
6 Group discussions by teaching and non-teaching staff.
7 Careers staff involvement in consultation on agreed policy.
8 Other agencies were consulted for comments.

Many of these took place concurrently. When the consultative process was completed, a second draft of the document was presented to the principal who took it to the academic board. The co-ordinator spoke to the tabled document and the policy and plan were discussed, and, after a few minor alterations, ratified and presented to the governors for their endorsement before being sent to the LEA. This process took approximately a year; it was possible to produce the following policy statements and plan format, ratified at every level within the College.

Agreed policy aims

- To provide for the individual needs of all students.
- To adopt an open door policy for all and to accept students with special needs as any other students with the same rights to college provision.
- To further the process of integration of students with special educational needs.
- To provide relevant, realistic, balanced and broad courses for students with special educational needs.
- To provide pastoral care and ongoing counselling, a continuum of provision, before, during and after college for students with special needs.
- To develop further and refine courses for students with special educational needs in the 16 to 19 age group.
- To develop courses to meet the needs of people with special needs in the community post 19.
- To develop new provision for students with special educational needs within a sufficiently flexible policy framework to allow new ideas to be implemented.
- To make optimum use of existing resources (staff, accommodation, equipment) and to provide the necessary resources for students with special educational needs.
- To liaise closely with parents, other specialist agencies, support services, and voluntary organisations.
- To encourage a continuum of provision for students with special needs

within the area and liaise with other educators and providers. To liaise with adult education, social services, the local health authority, training agency and other groups to avoid unnecessary duplication of courses. The college aims to participate fully in co-operation between all providing agencies.

- To liaise closely with careers services, especially the specialist careers officer for SEN.
- To liaise with feeder schools, building links before entry to college – student, staff and information.
- To publicise available courses and the facilities available for students who have special educational needs at the college.
- To promote in-service training for all staff involved with students who have special educational needs.
- To provide continuous upgrading and review of SEN policy and practice.

Note should be made of the fact that the policy document clarified the use of current descriptions of special needs and set the targets for college recognition within the parameters set by Warnock within the terms of wider definition.

Policy statements regarding students with special educational needs

Agreement was reached as follows:

- *Access*. The college recognises as an ongoing priority the need to maximise access to educational and training opportunities. In this respect, it is particularly concerned to work, as far as possible, towards the situation in which no member of the community who wishes to become a member of the college, is denied access to its courses or otherwise disadvantaged in opportunity or in experience because of disability or handicap. There is a policy and practice of integration.
- *Planning*. This emphasis on access determines the need for planned provision in specific areas and of processes and structures which ensure planning, implementation, monitoring and evaluation of action taken. The college will continually review planned policy and development. An annual review will take place at the beginning of every year.
- *Admissions*. The college will ensure that admission and entrance procedures and requirements acknowledge sensitively and appropriately the circumstances of students with special needs. Applications from disabled students should be judged initially on the basis of academic criteria alone.

  There should be a degree of positive discrimination and some flexibility in the application of normal admissions criteria to disabled students.

  The college leaflets should clearly indicate the support available for disabled students and should also make clear the fact that applications from disabled students would be welcomed.

  Communication networks will be refined so that necessary information reaches those involved with students who have special needs, before, at, and after attending college.

- *Physical access.* The college will actively seek to ensure that all possible barriers to students with special needs are removed or reduced to a minimum level.
- *Health and safety.* The college will respond to the statutory requirements as laid down by the Health and Safety at Work Act to ensure that it caters for problems posed by college members with special needs.
- *Curriculum process.* The college is committed to the adoption of a curriculum which can respond effectively and appropriately to students with special needs. It prioritises the importance of proper assessment, planning and evaluation processes. The curriculum will encompass, on the one hand, the importance of the provision of individual programme planning for students with specific disabilities and, on the other hand, the need to ensure that the 'mainstream' courses do not, as far as possible, deny access or prevent students with special needs from effective participation and opportunity.
- *Support.* The college will endeavour to make a wide range of expertise and skills available within its overall provision (including specialist teaching, counselling and advisory provision) to provide support for students with special needs.
- *Staff development.* The college will encourage and endeavour to implement a wide range of active staff development programmes to enable staff to acquire skills and awareness as appropriate to their professional needs and circumstances relating to students with special needs.
- *Liaison.* The college will take active steps to liaise both internally and with external agencies and authorities and will monitor external advisory and policy statements, and initiate action as necessary. The college is committed to promoting links with all agencies concerned with special needs.
- *Job centre involvement.* The college recognises that for adult students firm links with the job centre are needed, in particular, for SEN students, links with the disablement resettlement officer and the disablement advisory support team.
- *Careers service involvement.* The college recognises that the careers service has an important role to play in

ADVISING	the college on future students and on the future development of present students after college.
PREDICTING	whenever possible a future numbers to aid in planned provision of courses b individuals' special needs with implications for resources, staffing and students' requirements for specialist support services, etc.

PUBLICISING college provision for special needs students and advising on information and publicity materials required by students and parents in the range of courses available at the college for students with special needs, on admission procedures and student services.

LIAISON It is college policy to build close liaison with the careers service, especially with the careers officer for special needs. Liaison is to be achieved by regular meetings:

- *Informally* – ongoing day to day liaison with course tutors, students, support agencies, YTS placement officers, senior lecturer in special needs as and when problems arise as an integral part of monitoring the needs and response of students.
- *Formally* – various team meetings involving the senior lecturer in special needs, college tutors, schools and others as necessary to convey information, build on ongoing monitoring of students, discuss future and present plans, and future students' needs.

This occurs at:

- Special schools review
- YTS special needs meetings
- INSET meetings/courses
- Specific meetings for this purpose.

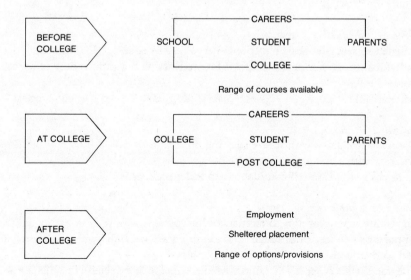

Overview of college and careers involvements

Parental Involvement
The college, in adopting an open door policy, welcomes visits and queries from parents and recognises the concerns they may have about their children becoming students at the college. Positive moves are made to provide information and early ongoing involvement for parents in decision making regarding provision of courses for students with special needs.

Review of Policy
The college will appraise and revise its policies and practices in the light of experience and external developments to improve its provision for students with special needs.

As a precursor to the discussion of a development plan for policy in respect of SEN a thumbnail sketch of existing provision is set out below. Jewers in the following chapter elaborates the characteristics of some aspects of such provision.

Current provision for students with special needs

School link
Arranged for students with SEN in their last year of schooling.
Students come from special schools, special units and mainstream schools.

Mainstream with or without support
Students are enrolled in a variety of mainstream courses.
Students with sensory or physical disabilities and with average or above average ability.

General skills further education
Situated in specially designed special needs resources base, LEA funded.
Individual programmes are designed for students with a wide variety of special needs.
Students join mainstream classes where appropriate, with or without support.

Learning for independence
Course for students with severe learning difficulties.
Discrete with some mainstream integration.
Aims are to increase self confidence and independence.

Two year youth training scheme
For young unemployed who have special needs.
Opportunity to learn full range of practical vocational skills with experience in real work situation.
Integrated with other YTS trainees wherever possible especially in skills areas.

Other courses
Outlined are the main courses which concern this age group but students with special needs are on CPVE, vocational skills and mainstream YTS and other courses such as drop-ins for literacy, numeracy and computing.

Adult evening classes for students with special needs
These are aimed mainly at adults with learning difficulties and cover practical skills.

Drop-ins
LEA funded drop-in workshops for literacy and numeracy (day and twilight and evening sessions).
Some provision for IT awareness.

Adult preparation training
All options available as part of APT programmes, depending on individual circumstances and individual needs (i.e. workshop safety, etc.)
Major areas in APT at present taken up by SEN students are: clerical skills, caring, computing plus some skills areas, e.g. motor vehicle.

50:50 courses
All are available to students with SEN, provided their 'disability' does not cause problems with safety. The major area of provision is in computer courses.

Employment training (ET)
Directed training for qualification, including work placement.

Basic skills training within ET
Four weeks' intensive basic skills tuition (literacy, numeracy, communication) for trainees involved in ET but needing special help in these areas.

Pre-assessment module (PAM)
One complete day of assessment and counselling for those who are unsure whether ET is the right option.

Training link course
An average of five weeks' assessment and 'taster' activity. Including work on basic skills, job getting skills and IT. Designed as a lead into ET for those unsure of which vocational area to enter, but available to anyone who is unemployed.

Job club
Aimed at long-term unemployed over 18.

Restart
Aimed at long-term unemployed over 18.

Mainstream course for adults
An open door policy applies, students with special needs are able to enrol in any course. Their success will depend largely on the individual ability to cope within an integrated setting.

Special educational needs – development plan

It is important to see how the service for SEN students can be developed, refined and monitored to continue to meet their needs within the college and the local community.

Expansion of provision: recommendations
The college should establish an even broader base and extensive provision for students with special educational needs.

A mainstream support service should be established to enable physically and sensory disabled students to integrate fully. It is envisaged that the service will also offer advice and support across the college to students and staff experiencing difficulties.

Discrete provision for students with learning difficulties should be expanded and developed. Integration of students with SEN into mainstream classes and specialist areas across the college must be facilitated.

Special needs provision should be the responsibility of all college staff and all departments should expect to contribute to the maintenance and development of provision for students with special educational needs.

To aid this a framework of college-wide subject specialist tutors who are to monitor and support students with special needs in their area of learning has been established. INSET and awareness raising sessions for these staff are needed. Lists of these named persons within the college sections and across all subject areas were included within the policy document.

Predictions of future student numbers and differing client groups were also included, with an agreed policy for information technology and recognition for the need for further discussions concerning post-compulsory opportunities for students with special needs.

The co-ordinator's role

The co-ordinator's role is not only to manage but to develop and innovate. If progress is to be achieved the framework and structure that such a document provides can be a driving force in this work. The need to influence is also important and finding ways and means within the system is important. The co-ordinator must raise the profile of special needs not only within the college and the community but also within the county. Nothing succeeds like success and raised morale, recognition of good practice, the ripple effect of setting goals and planning provision are reflected in individual course plans, improved curriculum design, improved liaison, local networks and team work.

The co-ordinator is responsible for pulling it all together, guiding and influencing practice. Greater expectations result in greater gains – both for students, staff and other professionals. Making demands for curriculum information not only provides the evidence of work in progress, but makes all involved analyse what is being provided. Inevitably staff abilities and role expectations will vary. The co-ordinator's ability to listen, assimilate and develop is essential. What then are the issues and features of further education that a special needs co-ordinator has to address?

Until recently an important distinction between colleges of further education and schools may arguably have been the funding base. FE is a business where one talks about full-cost courses, part-cost courses, training agency funded, LEA funded, grant aided, European Economic Commission and European Social Fund funding, etc. So where do special needs fit into it all? As a newly appointed special needs co-ordinator with only school experience, an essential early task was to try to clarify this.

It is important, in the first instance, to know where you are before you plan where you are going. This takes time and effort. Any new post brings with it the important decision of how best to use the time, to select priorities, to build relationships with people and discover how the system works and then how best to make it work for your students.

In retrospect, the task was influenced by the starting blocks which had already been set up. There was already provision for schools link, courses for students with moderate and severe learning difficulties, a YTS scheme catering for students with special needs and a history of more able physically handicapped or sensory impaired students coping in mainstream classes. There was much to do and as I share the experience, it is with the realisation that no two co-ordinators would work in exactly the same way but would probably encounter similar problems and in trying to develop strategies to overcome them, would probably achieve similar results.

After primary and secondary school experience, the challenge of further education proved yet another new experience. An attempt at analysing how the task was tackled revealed not only my naïvety but also the lack of a stringent induction to the system. Although my college ran an induction course for all new staff, my need for an in-depth grounding in FE was highlighted. To any new co-ordinator I commend asking the following questions:

Who's who?	*In the College*
	Students and staff across the college.
	Who makes things happen? Who do I go to for support?
	Who do I report to?
	Locally
	In schools, careers, support services, social services, the health authority, in the voluntary agencies.
	Nationally
	Identify areas of good practice. What national bodies are influential? National Bureau of Students with Disabilities, RNIB, RNID, etc.
	Internationally
	Range of provision in Europe, USA, etc.
Where?	*In college*
	Where are courses sited?
	Where are the areas of best/worst practice?
	Where are the strengths and weaknesses?
	Where is the next step?
	Where is the college provision going?
	Locally
	Where are the students coming from?
	Where are they going to?
	Where can I get support?
	Internationally
	Where are the areas of good practice?
	Where can I get new ideas?
What?	What am I trying to do in the short and long term?
	What is my timescale?
	What do I need to do to achieve results?
	What are my criteria for success?
How?	How can I make best use of my time?
	How can we improve provision?
	How can we build teamwork?
	How can we make best use of and improve resources?
	How will we know when we have succeeded?

Co-operation

The philosophy changes and so does the response, but in many cases very slowly. All young people are entitled to education up to the age of 19. The ideal is that education is carried out in the least restrictive environment, so what can colleges offer that schools can't? The chance to go to college like any other youngster, to be treated like everybody else, to choose a range of courses, to continue education or begin vocational training in a vast range of learning areas in an adult environment, a transition to adulthood, at best a progression, at worst a change!

Educational initiatives and opportunities for 14 to 21 year olds comprise a wide choice from TVEI, CPVE, YTS, ET, C and G, GCSE, RSA, college devised courses, EEC funded provision, ESF funded resourcing, etc. All share a commitment to access for all, provide opportunities for students with special needs, practical activity based profiling and preparation for some kind of work or significant living without work. The curriculum changes constantly and quite rightly practitioners must be both clear and accountable. They must document their curricular aims and subsequent outcomes.

Colleges need to be aware of any young person in their own area who is getting extra help within a school or unit and who is likely to require a long-term plan of services and support that may be needed in the post-compulsory and adult education phase.

The role of the careers service and in particular the special needs careers officer cannot be underestimated. They are vital and should have an ongoing involvement in schools when the young person with special needs is given initial guidance regarding the future. They advise the college of future students, predicting, wherever possible, future numbers (an aid to planned provision of courses), and providing information about individual students' needs with the resultant implications for resources, staffing and student requirements. They publicise the college provision by information regarding courses to students, parents and other professionals and they liaise both formally at various team meetings within the college and informally, on a day to day basis while monitoring the needs and response of students.

Schools and the workings within schools for bridging the transition gap towards FE need to be investigated and agreed strategies adopted on a local basis so that heads of year, fifth and sixth years and their tutors, co-ordinators of special needs, special needs teachers, staff responsible for careers guidance and head teachers in schools realise what courses are available and make real links with the college co-ordinator so that all the information reaches the parts. Figure 22.1 provides a framework for transition.

There is a need for co-ordination on a wide scale for the interlinking of agencies providing support and guidance, while aiming for decreased dependence providing real choices and encouraging a self-advocacy approach from the students as well as the perception of needs by the professionals involved. Close interagency co-operation on a local basis is essential if real choice, the aim of a shift towards decreased dependence on support agencies and increasing independence for the individual, is to be achieved.

The liaison part of the SEN co-ordinator's role is presented in figure 22.2. Central to all this is the student. This network outlines available support and information wherever necessary by all the contributing agencies. Co-ordinating the service is an important part of the role as is the ongoing building of links.

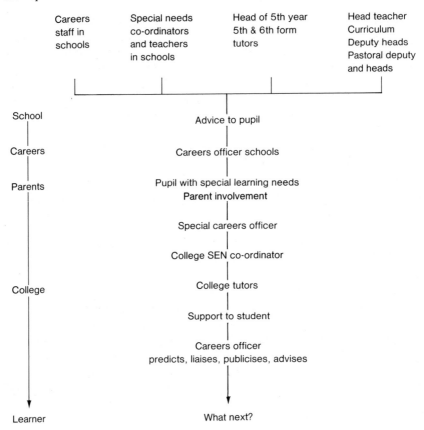

Figure 22.1 The transition from school to college and beyond

Students, with parents and all professionals involved, must develop multi-agency co-operation and a local continuum of educational services, and training opportunities to meet the needs of all learners. The co-ordinator must be aware and able to advise not only on what is available locally and what opportunities exist, but also on equal opportunities for learners with special needs.

Co-ordination

Many colleges now have a member of staff who is identified as the co-ordinator for special needs. The co-ordinator may be at any level, from lecturer to principal and the role varies greatly from college to college. The effectiveness, extent and profile of this role within the college depend greatly on the commitment of senior management to supporting special needs. This is reflected in the different ways in which provision functions within colleges.

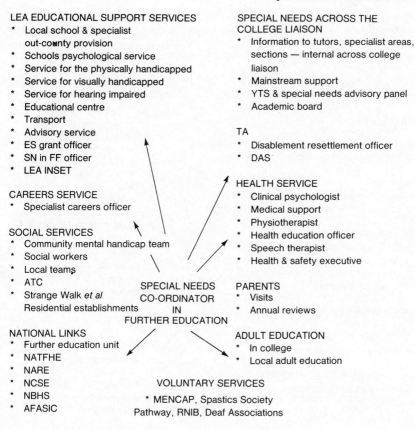

LEA EDUCATIONAL SUPPORT SERVICES
* Local school & specialist
  out-county provision
* Schools psychological service
* Service for the physically handicapped
* Service for visually handicapped
* Service for hearing impaired
* Educational centre
* Transport
* Advisory service
* ES grant officer
* SN in FF officer
* LEA INSET

CAREERS SERVICE
* Specialist careers officer

SOCIAL SERVICES
* Community mental handicap team
* Social workers
* Local teams
* ATC
* Strange Walk *et al*
  Residential establishments

NATIONAL LINKS
* Further education unit
* NATFHE
* NARE
* NCSE
* NBHS
* AFASIC

SPECIAL NEEDS ACROSS THE
COLLEGE LIAISON
* Information to tutors, specialist areas,
  sections — internal across college
  liaison
* Mainstream support
* YTS & special needs advisory panel
* Academic board

TA
* Disablement resettlement officer
* DAS

HEALTH SERVICE
* Clinical psychologist
* Medical support
* Physiotherapist
* Health education officer
* Speech therapist
* Health & safety executive

PARENTS
* Visits
* Annual reviews

ADULT EDUCATION
* In college
* Local adult education

SPECIAL NEEDS
CO-ORDINATOR
IN
FURTHER EDUCATION

VOLUNTARY SERVICES
* MENCAP, Spastics Society
Pathway, RNIB, Deaf Associations

Figure 22.2   Liaison links and special needs support services

Further education must meet the educational needs of all adults in an area. Governing bodies must represent all college users and, as in schools, there should be a governor with a designated responsibility for students with special needs. The co-ordinator should raise the awareness of several of the college governors of the aims, range and future plans of provision for students with special needs. If the governors are making decisions about provision within the college, they should be made aware of the needs of that group of learners and the limitations and aspirations of the provision within their college. The co-ordinator should endeavour to enlist the support and raise the awareness of those local people who are interested and who can assist in not only supporting but promoting and improving provision for students with special needs.

This is particularly necessary now as the changes in college governors are implemented. At least half the members of governing bodies will be business people and it is vital that the provision for students with special needs in further

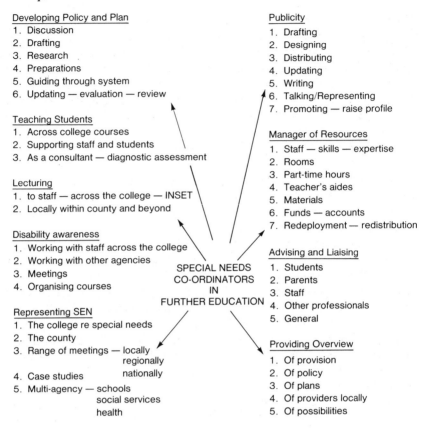

Developing Policy and Plan
1. Discussion
2. Drafting
3. Research
4. Preparations
5. Guiding through system
6. Updating — evaluation — review

Teaching Students
1. Across college courses
2. Supporting staff and students
3. As a consultant — diagnostic assessment

Lecturing
1. to staff — across the college — INSET
2. Locally within county and beyond

Disability awareness
1. Working with staff across the college
2. Working with other agencies
3. Meetings
4. Organising courses

Representing SEN
1. The college re special needs
2. The county
3. Range of meetings — locally
                         regionally
4. Case studies   nationally
5. Multi-agency — schools
                      social services
                      health

Publicity
1. Drafting
2. Designing
3. Distributing
4. Updating
5. Writing
6. Talking/Representing
7. Promoting — raise profile

Manager of Resources
1. Staff — skills — expertise
2. Rooms
3. Part-time hours
4. Teacher's aides
5. Materials
6. Funds — accounts
7. Redeployment — redistribution

Advising and Liaising
1. Students
2. Parents
3. Staff
4. Other professionals
5. General

Providing Overview
1. Of provision
2. Of policy
3. Of plans
4. Of providers locally
5. Of possibilities

SPECIAL NEEDS
CO-ORDINATORS
IN
FURTHER EDUCATION

Figure 22.3 The special needs co-ordinator's role

education is safeguarded. Good quality provision is expensive, with a high staff–student ratio. It serves the community and now is the time to ensure it not only continues to do so, but is developed as an area of good practice. It is essential that students with special needs have several voices of each college governing body. The co-ordinator has a real role to play in awareness raising.

The range of opportunities and options open to all students but especially to those with special learning needs must be understood by the co-ordinator.

Students will benefit if the co-ordinator spends time and effort to build links, has a full grasp of adult education classes or social services, and can set up networks of referral points, regionally and locally. It is important to provide choices, and to open up a range of educational opportunities. The co-ordinator has an important task of guiding the right students on the most suitable course and of addressing the problem of future development.

The co-ordinator must be good with people first, and with paper second; both are important. He or she must be accountable.

The special needs team must have a clear understanding of what it is trying to do and how far along the continuum it has been successful for each student.

The team needs to be accountable and seen to be professional. If the members' work is making a difference, the successes need to be noted even though they may be very difficult to quantify. For instance, it is just as valuable to note that John could not make eye contact or put his coat on when term started but can now do so after following an individual programme, as it is to record that Mark passed his higher diploma with honours. The process is as important as the product.

It is important that the evidence of progress is documented by the team and monitored closely by the co-ordinator. The valuable work done will be invisible and unrelated unless the college as a whole is made aware. The more staff that can be involved, the better. Promoting integration, understanding and acceptance of students on an individual basis with or without support on mainstream courses is probably the best way forward.

The difficulties of getting away from the sink or swim attitude, of teaching students and not subjects is not restricted to further education. The idea of support in the classroom is still relatively new. There is much to be done. The co-ordinator's role is a challenge. Figure 22.3 provides some aspects of that challenge – to manage time, the team, the range of opportunities to the benefit of the community. It is at times a lonely and difficult task but it is also a worthwhile one. I wish, in conclusion, to share a little story which has provided my underlying philosophy, and may help to clarify what we, in this relatively new area of work, are trying to do.

As an old man walked the beach at dawn he noticed a young woman ahead of him picking up starfish and flinging them into the sea. Finally, catching up with her, he asked why she was doing this. She replied that the stranded starfish would die if left until the morning sun.

'But the beach goes on for miles and there are millions of starfish,' countered the old man. 'How are your efforts going to make any difference?'

The young woman looked at the starfish in her hand and then threw it to safety in the waves.

'It makes a difference to this one,' she said.

23 Developments in further education for young people with special educational needs

Avril Jewers

Introduction

Ten years on from Warnock: a good time to consider how far we have come in that time and how much farther we have to go. This paper takes one college and looks at its special needs provision.

The Colchester Institute is a large college of further and higher education on the border between Essex and Suffolk. Its structure is that of a modified matrix with vertical and horizontal lines of management and communication. There are many opportunities for students – CNAA degrees in music, the North East Essex School of Art, Open College and Learning, GCSEs and the many skill training areas associated with technical colleges; there is a strong engineering bias with robotics, CNC, CAD, etc., and since the 1970s the institute has also worked closely with the Manpower Services Commission.

Special needs: provision

The institute has a long tradition of work with the severely mentally handicapped through its involvement with the local adult training centres and hospitals, the vast majority of provision being on a part-time basis. Following the publication of the Warnock Report in May 1978, the first full-time course for school leavers with special needs was offered. Details of this early initiative, the work introduction course, funded by the Manpower Services Commission, can be found in the Hulton/NARE publication, *Planning Effective Progress* (ed Mike Hinson and Martin Hughes 1982).

Since those early beginnings the 1980s have seen huge increases in both demand and in FE provision for special needs. Escalating unemployment, while comparatively insignificant when compared to the north of the country, was nevertheless responsible for greater demand for post-compulsory education and training. The school-leaver with learning and/or behavioural difficulties was most often the first to suffer as unemployment bit deeper.

For these youngsters with special needs, about to leave school but unable to find a job and opting instead to remain in education and training, Essex Education directed that the colleges of FE were, as recommended by Warnock, the most appropriate to meet their needs.

So the first work introduction was added to, until in 1988 we have a wide and varied special needs provision at the institute.

We can classify our special needs work into six broad areas as follows:

1 Part-time courses for severe learning difficulties (previously ESN–S).
2 Link courses with local schools, special and comprehensive.
3 Mainstream courses with handicapped/disabled students fully integrated.
4 Bridge courses for MLD (LEA funded).
5 Training Commission (Training Agency/MSC) funded assessment programmes and initial training.
6 YTS two-year courses for special needs.

The youngsters on courses 5 and 6 (above) are those most likely to gain – and keep – open employment and these courses are described in greater detail. Groups 1–4 are outlined to show the spectrum of institute provision, and figure 23.1 indicates the possible lines of progression for students.

1 Part-time courses for severe learning difficulties

In liaison with the local adult training centres, the health service and social services, courses are held on the institute's campus and through 'outreach'. The work is covered by two full-time lecturers and a substantial number of part-time staff, each of whom works approximately 12 hours a week. With students of this level, including some who are mature in years, it is unrealistic to expect that open employment will be obtained more than rarely. Consequently the aims and objectives of the work provided will concentrate to a large extent on independence training, on social skills and on improving the quality of life outside employment. Literacy and numeracy are taught functionally and related to everyday experiences wherever possible.

2 Link courses with local feeder schools

Pupils in their last year at comprehensives and special schools can experience different skills before leaving school and can benefit from being taught by highly skilled craftsmen in well-equipped workshops, ccTV studios, etc. Sometimes a group keeps together, but quite frequently a single pupil will infill into one of the many institute courses. Special needs youngsters who will be joining a full-time course like the bridge course get to know their way round the site and this gives them greater confidence when they do join us after leaving school.

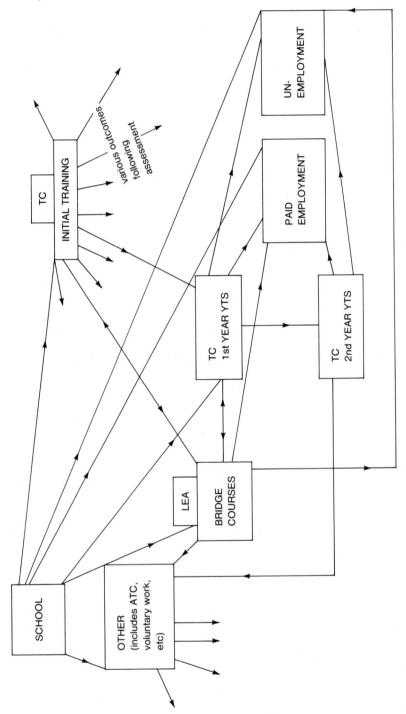

Figure 23.1   Opportunities for school leavers with special needs 1988

3 Mainstream courses with fully integrated handicapped/disabled students

Most of the institute buildings have lifts and ramps where necessary. Over the years very many disabled students have successfully completed courses and gained recognised qualifications. They join mainstream courses and receive additional support as necessary, e.g. there is a 'learning aide' who takes notes for the partially hearing youngster and helps him with his other work.

Blind and partially-sighted students move around on the campus with guide dogs if necessary; wheelchairs are not an uncommon sight.

There is, of course, a limit to the number of quite severely handicapped persons one college can cater for adequately without disrupting the general running of the establishment, but every applicant is treated individually and with empathy.

4 Bridge courses funded by the LEA for MLD youngsters

The bridge courses aim to meet the requirements of post-compulsory school-leaving age youngsters with special needs, most of whom will have been statemented and will wish to receive education and training up to the age of 19.

The majority of bridge students will have attended the three local special schools for MLD; some will have been to out-of-county residential establishments; and reflecting Warnock's recommendations and the 1981 Education Act, an increasing number will have been to local comprehensives.

There is a very wide spread of abilities, personalities and needs, as might be expected. Some students quickly prove they do not need the slower pace of the bridge course and quickly move on to the youth training scheme, and usually the work preparation course at the college. Others will need the full year before YTS, while for the least able a three-year programme must be planned.

These bridge courses are aptly named: they aim to consolidate, re-inforce and build on to that which has been learnt during the compulsory years at school and to prepare for the next stage, whatever that may be, whether YTS, ATCs or another option. There are several advantages that we in colleges have over schools: students attend college because they choose to, not because the law says they must. Parents tend to support us because if they do not like what we are doing they do not have to keep their offspring with us and, of course, because of the mature college environment and atmosphere.

Special schools tend to be relatively small and certainly our feeder special schools are not large. Most cover at least secondary age and many have children of primary age. So instead of being the eldest in a small school a student finds himself the youngest in a large establishment where most people are older than he is, a situation very much like the work place.

Add to this the advantages of well-equipped workshops, ccTV studios and a hairdressing salon, and learning can be made much more fun, which so often produces well-motivated students.

The bridge timetable is designed on a modular basis so that students have the opportunity to experience many different practical tasks and develop independence in a variety of settings.

Literacy and numeracy skills are improved by being taught through functional application. If, after 11 years of schooling, a youngster has achieved a reading ability level of only seven, it is unlikely, to say the least, that he or she will reach fluency or even a reading level good enough to earn a living through literacy skills.

So instead of concentrating on an area of already proven failure, we concentrate on improving his functional literacy application skills, without in any way limiting potential. If he or she wants individual help in college it is available. We also liaise with the local adult basic education classes and a student can join daytime as well as evening classes.

These classes can continue long after he/she has left college, thus giving continuity. Interestingly the youngsters do not seem in the least bit awkward and readily approach one of our team to ask for basic skills help. A year earlier, at school, the same youngsters would have been far more self-conscious. When asked why they didn't mind asking for help, it became clear they felt what was being taught had a direct relevance to the everyday life in college and work experience. They wanted to learn what was useful.

A separate programme has to be designed for students who, for a number of reasons, would not be able to cope with outside work experience, but local firms are willing to assist the most able youngsters by offering places. These usually start with one day weekly and occasionally progress to extra days and blocks. We aim for an insight into what an employer will expect and preparation for the next step which for many will be a youth training scheme course. We are indebted to the local employers for the time, effort and interest spent on our students. Without their support our task would be extremely difficult and at times impossible.

5 Training Agency (Training Commission, MSC) funded assessment programmes and initial training

Essex County Council is the managing agent for these courses, and the institute undertakes mainly everyday administration. These programmes have attracted much interest in the short time they have been running, and visitors from all over the country come to observe and ask questions.

They were started to meet a locally identified need. The old-style work introduction course had been axed and YTS was not yet as flexible as it is today. The sort of people who were being referred to us by the local careers office were those who really did not know what they wanted to do and who would find it difficult to fit into any of the local schemes.

My records showed 11 referrals for whom there was nothing suitable, so we contacted MSC and said the axing of WIC had left a gaping hole in provision and how about letting us fill it! Discussions that followed resulted in a special pilot course being set up. We started with those 11 trainees: one severely and unstably epileptic, one cerebral palsied, one partially hearing, two school refusers, one highly intelligent lad who was still recovering his vocabulary after an operation to remove a brain tumour, a lad who had lost his arm in an accident probably caused by his own maladjustment in the first place, and four with personality problems. Hardly a homogenous group! The only answer was to provide individual programmes for much of the week, coming together as a group for the 'compulsory' areas such as health and safety at work, first aid and computer literacy.

And so the careers assessment programme was spawned.

The jargon on the course leaflet describes the programme as 'providing introductory or interim assessment for young persons often suffering from a physical, mental and/or sensory handicap which puts them at a substantial disadvantage in the labour market. Of 13 weeks' maximum duration, for assessment together with an opportunity for remediation whenever practicable, the CAP provides a means of identifying the interests and aptitudes of youngsters and of exploring their suitability for specific areas of employment.'

The CAPs are not 'courses' with a set or pre-prepared syllabus and perhaps a few deviations. Instead they are exactly what they say, programmes designed individually for each trainee to meet his or her specific needs, and often personal wants. The name has been carefully chosen so that it will be accepted by the prospective trainees. Young people aged between 16 and 21 and in need of assessment are frequently disinclined to enrol on an 'assessment course', so the word 'career' has been added.

The usual YTS training allowance is paid to the CAP trainees, currently £29.50 a week for first years and £35 for second. The travel allowances of any expenses in excess of £3 weekly are also the same.

Any time spent on CAP does not count towards their ordinary two-year entitlement but is additional. When CAP becomes Initial Training the 13 weeks will increase to a possible four months and *will* be counted as part of normal entitlement.

Most of the youngsters referred to CAP have been unable to find work or a local YTS managing agent suitable, able and willing to meet their needs now. One of the administrative difficulties is that most managing agents are in one or perhaps two areas of work, what used to be called 'occupational training families'. So if a girl were to start with one managing agent on, for instance, a catering course, and later decided she could not work in a hot kitchen and wanted to change to care work, she would have to move to another agent.

The CAP is not tied to any one 'family' and can use any field of employment suited to the trainee. Often it is a question of 'can do'. Can the trainee actually do the type of work he has chosen? Is it a realistic possibility? The approach is very much 'let's-have-a-go-and-see-if-this-works' and if it does not work for some reason, it's 'we have-just-chosen-the-wrong-area-so-let's-try-another'.

Occasionally we have to discover if employment is a possibility at all. For example, Colin has spina bifida with the related problems. He had been to an out-of-county residential school and although he was offered further residential skill training he wanted to stay at home with his family because his mother was ill. He walked relatively well but got tired very quickly and his span of concentration was limited. He wanted to work with computers of which he had already acquired some knowledge at school.

He lived near a railway station so we started him with a local firm adjacent to a station a couple of stops up the line. He was to get there by mid-morning to start with, work in the office for two hours, then travel home. It was planned so that his working day would gradually lengthen as (hopefully) his strength improved. Any programme has to be carefully monitored in order to push him, but not too far or too fast.

As we cannot be familiar with every aspect of every problem we always liaise and take advice from the experts, in Colin's case, the local medical officer. We have access to all available records – medical, school, psychological and, if relevant, any police involvement. This is not to say that if the reports were damning we would not accept the youngster: we simply need to know the background in order to plan a programme satisfactorily.

A few years ago I placed a new trainee into a local store to work in the kitchens. She was interviewed and accepted by the restaurant manageress, started work, and then thrown out on the spot the following week when the manager returned from holiday.

Unbeknown to either the manageress – or myself! – my trainee had been caught and prosecuted for shop-lifting in that very store two months previously!

Since that unfortunate and unnecessary incident I always ask the youngster during the interview whether the youngster has had any contact with the police. If we know of any incident we won't make a similar mistake by unwittingly placing a student in an embarrassing position.

When we make approaches to local employers it is always clearly understood that they are not committing themselves for any definite length of time, but to see how it works out. They are not asked to contribute the usual YTS fee of £10–£15 a week for each trainee. Indeed, with our most difficult youngsters we often feel we ought to be paying them!

We work closely with the Essex careers offices whose support we value. The Colchester CAP covers this nothern and central part of Essex, roughly half of the county. We hold case conferences and always give a written recommendation and report to the careers office when a youngster moves on.

The recent Employment Bill directs that 16 to 18 year olds who refuse work or training will no longer be eligible to receive income support. Instead they receive a bridging allowance of £15 a week for a maximum of eight weeks while they are trying to get a job or join a YTS.

We are already feeling the effects of this legislation on the CAP. Youngsters who, it seems, have no intention of working if they can get money doing nothing, are being sent to us to interview. We have all worked with families whose older children are used as cheap labour to look after their younger siblings; who, on leaving school have been able to bring in 'the dole'. The prospect of staying at home and not working has somehow lost some of its appeal now the 'no work, no dole money' ruling is in force.

Most of the youngsters arriving to be interviewed at the institute are of average intelligence or above and street-wise. But being pushed to do a course does not make our life easy, even if it does have its amusing moments.

Debbie was typical. She was neither unintelligent nor slow, and had quite obviously decided that if 'Careers' had put her name forward she might just as well come along and be difficult. She was not rude, merely unable to find anything she was interested in except, to quote, 'reading, swimming, sleeping and screwing'. When she found I was neither shocked nor irritated by her, she told me she had already found a way round the new ruling. If 'they' wouldn't keep her as a single person, she knew they would house and keep her if she had a baby. I found out later that she was already pregnant when she came to see me.

Time will tell just how much success the new ruling brings; in the meantime we are supporting our colleagues in the careers service who have to refer these disaffected youngsters somewhere.

6 YTS two-year work preparation courses (WPCs)

These courses are administered by Essex County Council as managing agents but are given in the institute. The course name no longer reflects adequately the content and aims, since circumstances and extraneous pressures have required response and necessary adaptation. At the height of recent unemployment we widened the content to include more preparation for leisure, for voluntary work and for a 'meaningful life outside employment'.

The introduction of the second year for youth training schemes has made an even greater difference to these courses for special needs than it has for the others. The philosophy of YTS has moved from a one-year generic experience to a two-year specific, with opportunities to obtain a recognised qualification, or in some instances preparations for one. The slower of the special needs trainees would probably not manage to attain a high enough level to pass exams but knowing there are two full years available enables one to design an even richer programme to include better training and more time for reinforcement and consolidation. The extra time available is invaluable for those who find it difficult to assimilate skills readily.

Youngsters with special needs can be accepted on YTS up to the age of 21 although most join at either 16, 17 or, occasionally, 18. The WPC is organised to accommodate two distinct groups of trainees and for all practical purposes two very different courses are running with two separate timetables.

For the MLD youngsters, most of whom will have spent up to a year on our bridge course, we provide WETE (work experience in a training environment). A second course without WETE is for those trainees with specific learning difficulties, etc, and includes many previously on the career assessment programmes.

The WETE group moves at a slower pace and of necessity requires greater initial support than the other group. Work experience starts slowly with only one day a week out with local employers, and the rest of the time spent in college. WETE is heavily workshop biased with 'tasters' in as many different skills as possible in the different tasks. Besides using the mainstream institute workshops we have a multi-skills workshop equipped with materials for the sort of activities the youngsters could do at home. We make terrariums, jewellery, silk flowers, plastic processing objects, enamelling, glass engraving and etching, etc., and also learn DIY including wallpapering. The process is as important as the product although a finished product that has not cost much is a motivator.

During the first two to three months of WETE we concentrate heavily on decision making and problem solving skills in readiness for the time when the trainees are out at work more often. Gone are the days when they were told exactly what to do . . . adult life means making decisions for themselves and being responsible for the result of their actions. Some schools, and parents, have prepared their pupils better than others for this approach. We try to convince over-protective parents that their 'child' is nearly adult.

The WPC course tutor, Zoë, overheard two of her students talking recently. One said:

'I'll have to ask Zoë,' to which the other replied:
'She'll ask you what *you* think you ought to do so you'd better have some ideas ready first.'

One of the great advantages of the YTS courses is that experiences are 'for real', not just learnt in case of future need which can be difficult for some youngsters to appreciate.

All our YTS trainees receive a weekly Essex County Council cheque which is usually paid directly into their chosen bank accounts, since their parents no longer receive child benefit or minor award grants. The young persons who receive the money have to budget it and pay for their keep at home. This involves not only lengthy discussions (and help where needed) on money management, but actually obtaining and handling the money.

Each Friday they have to hand in a completed time sheet showing hours worked and travel expenses. No time sheet, no money. They get paid a week in arrears. On Fridays they are given time to walk in to Colchester to cash a cheque. At first they are accompanied by their lecturer or one of our assistants and later they go with a friend if they still lack confidence on their own. For the less confident and sometimes over-protected youngster, this practical experience is a huge step towards independence and so much more effective when 'for real'.

The WPC group without WETE go out on work experience for at least three days a week from the start. Youngsters who have been school refusers often refuse to come on the course at all if it means coming into the college which they associate with 'school', even if they have never seen for themselves. Rather than leaving them out of a training programme we put them in with suitable work sponsors and we visit them more frequently. We then plan to get them into college gradually. Sometimes we succeed; with more difficult cases where there may be a real phobia, we don't manage to get them to attend classes but we do arrange that rather than have their training allowance paid directly into their bank it is sent to the institute. We've never had anybody who wasn't prepared to come to collect their money! When they do arrive, we can review, counsel, and complete the administration as necessary.

This non-WETE group has widely differing problems and needs. It is this group that gives mainstream lecturers headaches and keeps them on their toes; if we're going to have problems at all it's with this group which includes lads (usually) who are of average intelligence or above, but who have such poor educational standards that they try to overcome their own perceived inadequacies by showing off and causing trouble. Very often we integrate a youngster from the group into our mainstream craft classes and quite often he/she turns out to be as good a craftsman as anyone else. They need to realise that although a lack of literacy skills is a definite drawback at school, there are many other perhaps equally important attributes that employers require.

The 1981 *A-Z Study* conducted by the Industrial Training Research Unit looked at the qualities and characteristics of young people from the lower ability range in their first job. Interestingly one group was from Colchester, using the same employers as we do. The 'A' employees were differentiated from the 'Z' ones by looking primarily at their personal behaviour and attitudes as identified by the employers (see figure 23.2 and figure 23.3).

Let us take just one factor listed high up on the list of Z type 'complaints' – timekeeping. At school, being late is taken as a personal misdemeanor; at work it can disrupt a whole production line and repeated lateness will usually result in the sack. Employers expect that by the age of 16 the foundations of self-reliance should have been laid and are seldom tolerant if facts prove otherwise.

One of the problems is that some youngsters find it very difficult to realise just what it is the boss wants. Equally not all employers are skilled in explaining clearly. Result: lack of communication and dissatisfaction all round. We always have lengthy discussions with our trainees before they go out on work experience and explain to them not only employer expectations but the 'hidden' aspects of starting a job.

Particularly difficult areas of adjustment are:

- Coping with the longer-than-school working day and travelling to get to work. You *will* get tired, so expect to be.
- Coping with unfamiliar social situations, such as a mixed age group; working with and for older people who don't understand them (frequently); the 'things-weren't-like-this-when-I-was-young' syndrome; and subtleties in personal relationships in a working group of which a newcomer cannot be expected to be aware, and of which the existing staff themselves may hardly be aware.
- Coping with other employees who lack empathy towards just about

A type

	1st	2nd	3rd	4th	5th	6th	7th	8th
Versatility	8	6	2	5	2	3	—	—
Pride in job	6	5	3	3	5	1	—	1
Takes initiative	6	4	6	4	3	1	—	—
Good personal relations	6	4	3	5	—	2	2	—
Wide viewpoint	4	4	4	3	5	—	1	—
Seeks work when slack	4	3	4	—	2	1	—	—
Asks questions	4	—	2	6	—	—	1	—
Listens to instructions	3	7	5	2	3	1	—	—
Quality conscious	3	4	5	—	—	1	—	—
Methodical and neat	3	3	2	—	3	—	3	—
Reports faults	—	4	1	3	3	2	—	—
Remedies problems	—	2	2	5	1	1	—	—
Good timekeeper	—	1	5	2	2	4	1	1

Z type

	1st	2nd	3rd	4th	5th	6th	7th	8th
Doesn't follow instructions	10	5	4	2	2	—	—	—
Bad timekeeper	10	5	1	3	—	—	—	—
Can't concentrate	6	3	2	—	1	—	—	—
Over-confident for ability	5	2	1	2	—	—	—	—
Personal problems	5	—	4	—	2	1	—	—
Bad personal relations	4	2	2	2	—	1	—	—
Dislikes supervision	3	5	4	6	1	—	—	—
Chats, gazes around	1	7	2	2	—	—	—	—
Doesn't pull weight	1	3	2	2	1	—	—	—
Doesn't report faults	1	1	2	—	1	—	—	—
Doesn't like change	1	1	1	1	3	—	—	—
No loyalty to company	1	—	2	—	—	—	—	—
Careless about quality	—	5	8	2	—	—	—	—

Figure 23.2 Number of times a Behaviour Factor was mentioned in East Anglia, at each order of priority

everyone, particularly the young, the 'he's-always-like-that-on-Mondays' type.

- Coping with 'ragging'. Schools are mostly quite serious places and do not tease their pupils. At work the newcomer is often the butt of the group. We warn our youngsters of the most common ploys, such as going for a long weight/wait, striped paint, sky-hooks, left-handed hammers, etc. and we encourage them not to fly off the handle or get too upset if they are made to feel silly.
- Stickability. So few people seem to have warned the school leaver just how boring work can be! We work out the number of hours they will probably work between 16 and 65 years (over 90,000) and tell them not to expect every one to be exciting. Starting at the bottom with jobs within their new capabilities, they're often bored after three days. And I often reply: 'I get bored with you sometimes!'

- Finally, the parents. Most are marvellous, but occasionally parents go in to work placements or keep their son at home because one of the foremen has told their little cherub to 'bugger off', 'pull your finger out' or similar words of endearment. We have had to pour plenty of oil on troubled waters.

The future?

How far have we got with introducing special needs into our colleges of further education? What are the problems and are they being looked at in more than just a cursory way?

As with so many new initiatives the work began before the subject was thought through or properly prepared for, and special needs youngsters entering colleges were no exception. Apart from perhaps one or even two people experienced and qualified, nobody in the FE college understood the very different aims, objectives and methods needed to teach these 'new FE' students. There was no formal staff development programme so it was left to the course tutor to liaise and support the mainstream lecturers. In the early days any existing staff development was often taught by the existing staff developer who had little experience and no qualifications in this specialist field.

The staff development problem was finally both recognised and something done about it. FHE3 (DES) undertook a survey and special needs became one of

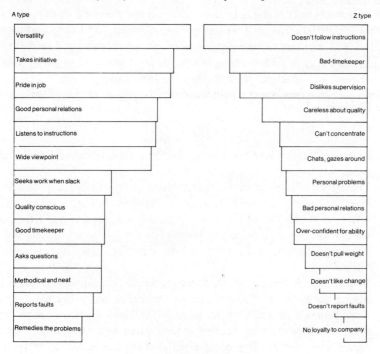

Figure 23.3

the priority areas. GRIST (grant related in service training) money helped with releasing staff for training; RSA, City and Guilds, etc., provided qualifications to be gained.

One of the major barriers to having special needs work accepted in colleges is the salary structure. Unlike schools where the additional skills required to teach pupils with special needs are recognised or special schools where for years teachers were paid an additional allowance, in colleges it is all low-grade work paid for at the lowest level, the cheapest rate.

This lack of status has serious repercussions in FE establishments where salary depends upon the grade of work taught, and 'bars' exist that can only be crossed if 'high grade work' is taught. How many times have excellent lecturers confided that they would be quite willing to teach special needs but they are not prepared to take on low grade work which will have a detrimental effect on their salaries and on their promotion chances. It is difficult to disagree with this viewpoint, which is well recognised by the National Bureau for Handicapped Students in their publication, *Burnham: the biggest barrier of all?*. It concluded with the damning statement:

> Present regulations militate against suitable provision for students with special needs . . . Burnham (and NJC) regulations must therefore be changed to incorporate the points made in this paper.

The very hard work being done in our colleges and the empathy of many of the staff are recognised, but until we can get formal policies at county and national levels we will continue to have patches of excellence only and will be dependent upon the empathy of senior management. We need and want to be professional and 'efficient and effective' rather than treated as a charity.

In ten years we have come a long way but there is still further to go.

Bibliography

Chapter 2

Cicourel, A. V. and Kitsuse, J. I. (1963) *The Educational Decision Makers*, Bobbs-Merrill.

Department of Education and Science (1988) *Mathematics for Ages 5 to 16*.

Her Majesty's Inspectorate (1963) *Curriculum 11–16: Towards a Statement of Entitlement* HMSO.

McPherson, A. and Willms, J. D. (1988) 'Comprehensive schooling is better and fairer' in *Forum for the Discussion of Trends in Education* January 1988.

Maughan, B. and Rutter, M. (1987) 'Pupils' progress in selective and non-selective schools' in *School Organization* vol 7 (1) pp 50–68.

Moon, B. (ed) 1988) *Modular Curriculum*, Paul Chapman.

Rawls, J. (1972) *A Theory of Justice* Oxford University Press.

Reynolds, D. and Sullivan, M. (1987) *The Comprehensive Experiment* The Falmer Press.

Steedman, J. (1983) *Examination Results in Selective and Non-Selective Schools*, National Children's Bureau.

Warwick, D. (1987) *The Modular Curriculum* Blackwell Education.

Chapter 3

Apter, S. (1982) *Troubled Children, Troubled Systems*, Pergamon.

Bradley, M. (1982) *The Coordination of Services for Children Under Five*, Windsor, NFER-Nelson.

Calder, P. (1986) 'Children in Nurseries', in New, C. and David, M. (eds) *For the Children's Sake*, Harmondsworth, Penguin.

Celestin, N. (1986) *A Guide to Anti-racist Childcare Practice*, VOLCUF.

Chazan, M., Laing, A. F., Shackleton Bailey, M., Jones, G. (1980) *Some of our Children* Open Books.

Chazan, M. and Laing, A. (1982) *The Early Years*, Open University Press.

Clark, M. (1988) *Children under Five: Educational Research and Evidence*, Gordon and Breach.

Cleave, S., Jowett, S. and Bate, M. (1982) *And so to school, A study in Continuity from Preschool to Infant School*, Windsor, NFER-Nelson.

Curtis, A. (1986) *Curriculum for the Preschool Child*, Windsor, NFER-Nelson.

Davie, C.E., Hutt, S.J., Vincent, E., Mason, M. (1984) *The Young Child at Home*, Windsor, NFER-Nelson.

DES (1982) *Young Children with Special Educational Needs*, London, HMSO.

DES (1988) *Combined Provision for the Under Fives: The Contribution of Education*, London, HMSO.

Fish, J. (chair) (1985) *Equal Opportunities for All?* Report of the committee reviewing provision to meet special education needs, Inner London Education Authority.

Gilkes, J. (1987) *Developing Nursery Education*, Milton Keynes, Open University Press.

Jowett, S. and Sylva, K. (1986) 'Does Kind of Preschool Matter?' in *Educational Research*, vol 28 (1).

Lazar, J. (ed) (1979) *Lasting Effects after the School*, Washington, US Printing Office.

McGlynn, N. and Phillips, G. (1987) 'Integrated Preschooling: An Overview of the Literature', *Educational Psychology in Practice*, vol 3 (2) July.

Mortimore, J. and Blackstone, T. (1982) *Disadvantage and Education*, Heinemann Educational Books.

Moss, P. (1987) *A Review of Childminding Research*, Working and Occasional Paper No 6, Thomas Coram Research Unit, University of London Institute of Education.

Moss, P. (1988) *Childcare and Equality of Opportunity*, Commission of the European Communities.

National Foundation for Educational Research/School Curriculum Development Committee (NFER/SGDC) (1987) *Four Year Olds in School: Policy and Practice*, NFER, Windsor.

National Union of Teachers (1988) *Guidelines on Negotiating for Special Needs*.

Osborn, A.F. and Milbank, J.E. (1987) *The Effects of Early Education, A Report from the Child Health and Education Study*, Oxford, Clarendon Press.

Potts, P. (1987) *Integrating Pre-School Children with Special Needs*. Centre for Studies on Integration in Education, 415 Edgware Road, London NW2 6MB.

Pugh, G., Aplin, G., De'Ath, E., Moxon, M. (1987) *Partnership in Action: Working with Parents in Preschool Centres*, London, National Children's Bureau.

Raven, J. (1980) *Parents, Teachers and Children*, Hodder and Stoughton.

Sandow, S., Stafford, D. and Stafford, P. (1987) *An Agreed Understanding? Parent-Professional Communication and the 1981 Education Act*, Windsor, NFER-Nelson.

Select Committee, House of Commons (1987) *Special Educational Needs: Implementation of the Education Act 1981*, 3rd Report from the Education, Science and Arts Committee, vols 1 and 2, HMSO.

Smith, T. (1980) *Parents and Preschool*, Grant McIntyre.

Swann, M. (Chair) (1985) *Education for All* Report of the Committee of Inquiry into the Education of Children from Ethnic Minorities, HMSO.

Sylva, K., Smith, T. and Moore, E. (1986) *Monitoring the High/Scope Training Programme 1984-1985*, Final Report, Department of Social and Administrative Studies, University of Oxford, January.

Tizard, B. (1974) *Early Childhood Education, a Review and Discussion of Research in Britain*, NFER.

Tizard, B., Mortimore, J., Burchell, B. (1981) *Involving Parents in Nursery and Infant Schools*, Grant McIntyre.

Tizard, B. and Hughes, M. (1984) *Young Children Learning*, Fontana.

Tizard, B. (1986) *The Care of Young Children, Implications of Recent Research*. Working and Occasional Paper No 1, Thomas Coram Research Unit, London University Institute of Education.

Topping, K. (1986) *Parents as Educators*, Croom Helm.
Warnock, M. (chair) (1978) *Special Educational Needs*, HMSO.
Wolfendale, S. and Bryans, T. (1980) 'Intervening with Learning in the Infants' School' in *Remedial Education*, vol 15, No 1.
Wolfendale, S. (1983) *Parental Participation in Children's Development and Education*, Gordon and Breach.
Wolfendale, S. (1987a) *Primary Schools and Special Needs; Policy, Planning and Provision*, Cassell.
Wolfendale, S. (1987b) 'The Evaluation and Revision of the *All About Me* Preschool Parent-Completed Scales', in *Early Child Development and Care*, vol 29.
Wolfendale, S. (1987c) 'Developing Services to meet the special needs of Children Under Five' in *Children and Society*, vol 1 (3).
Wolfendale, S. (1988) 'The Parental Contribution to Assessment,' in *Developing Horizons* No 10, National Council for Special Education, Stratford upon Avon.
Woodhead, M. (1985) 'Preschool Education has Long-term Effects; but can they be generalised?' in *Oxford Review of Education*, vol 11 (2).
VOLCUF, 40 Brunswick Square, London, WC1N 1AC.

Chapter 5

Ainscow, M. and Tweddle, D. (1988) *Encouraging Classroom Success* Fulton.
Bell, P. and Best, R. (1986) *Supportive Education* Blackwell Education.
Dessent, T. (1987) *Making the Ordinary School Special* The Falmer Press.
FitzGerald, A. (1988) 'Summer Specials' *The Times Educational Supplement* (26 August 1988).
Inner London Education Authority (1985) *Educational Opportunities for All* ILEA.
Warnock, M. (1988) 'Special Needs Threatened with Relegation', in *The Times Educational Supplement*, 11 March 1981.

Chapter 8

Booth, T., Potts, P. and Swann, W. (1984) *Preventing Difficulties in Learning* Basil Blackwell.
Britton, R. (1981) 'Re-enactment as an unwitting professional response to family dynamics, in Box, S. (ed) *Psychotherapy with Families* Routledge and Kegan Paul.
Caplan, G. (1970) *The Theory and Practice of Mental Health Consultation* Basic Books.
Daines, R. *et al* (1981) *Child Guidance and Schools – A Study of a Consultation Service* Department of Social Work, School of Applied Social Studies, University of Bristol.
Department of Health and Social Security (1988) *Working Together – A guide to inter-agency cooperation* HMSO.
Hanko, G. (1985) *Special Needs in Ordinary Classrooms – An Approach to Teacher Support and Pupil Care* Blackwell Education.
Hanko, G. (1986) 'Social Workers as Teacher Consultants' *Journal of Social Work Practice* vol 2 (2).
Hanko, G. (1987) 'Group Consultation with Mainstream Teachers' in *Educational and Child Psychology* (BPS/DECP) vol 4 (3,4).
Hanko, G. (1989) 'Joint Problem-solving Approaches to Behavioural, Emotional and Learning Difficulties' in Widlake, P. (ed) *Special Needs, The Latest Thinking* Hutchinson (to be published).

Hegarty, S. (1987) *Meeting Special Needs in Ordinary Schools* Cassell.

Laslett, R. and Smith, C. (1984) *Effective Classroom Management* Croom Helm.

National Association for Remedial Education (1985) *Teaching Roles for Special Educational Needs, Guidelines 6* NARE Publications.

Quinton, D. (1987) 'The Consequences of Care' in *Maladjustment and Therapeutic Education* vol 5 (2).

Quinton, D. and Rutter, M. (1988) *Parenting Breakdown* Avebury.

Sayer, J. (1987) *Secondary Education for All?* Cassell.

Warnock, M. (chair) (1978) *Special Educational Needs* HMSO.

Wolfendale, S. (1987) *Primary Schools and Special Needs* Cassell.

Chapter 9

Bayliss, S. (1986) 'Twelve rungs on ladder to success' in *The Times Educational Supplement* 5 April 1986.

Bernstein, B. (1970) 'Education cannot compensate for society' *New Society*, 387, 344–7.

Bird, C. *et al* (1980) *Disaffected pupils*, Brunel University.

Butt, N. (1986) 'Implementing the Whole-School Approach at Secondary Level', in *Support for Learning* vol 1; 4.

Coard, B. (1971) *How the West Indian Child is made Educationally Sub-normal in the British School System*, New Beacon Books.

Coleman, J.S. *et al Equality of Educational Opportunity*, Government Printing Office, Washington, US.

DES (1977) *Ten Good Schools: A Secondary School Enquiry*, HMSO London.

DES (1977) *A New Partnership for our Schools (Taylor Report)*, HMSO London.

DES (1978) *Special Educational Needs: Report of the Committee of Enquiry into the Education of Handicapped Children and Young People* (Warnock Report), HMSO London.

DES (1984) Slow learning and less successful pupils in secondary schools, HMSO London.

DES 1981 Education Act, HMSO London.

DES 1986 Education Act, HMSO London.

DES 1988 Education Act, HMSO London.

Eggleston, J. (1986) *Education for Some*, Trentham Books.

Evans, M. (ed) (1980) *Disruptive Pupils*, Schools Council Publ.

Furlong, V.J. (1985) *The Deviant Pupil*, Open University Press.

Galloway, D. (1982) *Schools and Disruptive Pupils*, Longman.

Gipps, C., Goldstein, M. and Gross, M. (1987) *Warnock's eighteen per cent*, The Falmer Press.

Hargreaves, D.H. (1975) *Deviance in Classrooms*, RKP.

Hargreaves, D.H. (1984) *Improving Secondary Schools, Report of the Committee on the Curriculum and Organisation of Secondary Schools* ILEA London.

Jencks, C. *et al* (1972) *Inequality: A Reassessment of the Effect of Family and Schooling in America*, Basic Books, New York.

Mortimore, P. (1988) *School Matters*, Open Books.

Pack, D.C. (1977) *Truancy and Indiscipline in Scotland* (Pack Report), HMSO/SED.

Power, M.J. *et al* (1967) 'Delinquent Schools' in *New Society* 542 19 Oct.

Reid, K. (1986) *Disaffection from School* Methuen.

Reid, K., Hopkins, D. and Hully, P. (1988) *Towards the Effective School*, Basil Blackwell.

Reynolds, D., Hammersley, M. and Woods, P. (eds.) (1976) *The Delinquent School in the Process of Schooling*, Open University Press.
Reynolds, D., Sullivan, M. and Gillham, B. (ed) (1981) *The Effects of School: A Radical Faith Re-stated in Problem Behaviour in the Secondary School*, Croom Helm.
Rutter, M. *et al* (1979) *Fifteen Thousand Hours*, Open Books.
Thomas, N. (1985) *Improving Primary Schools* (Report of the Committee on Primary Education), ILEA London.
Tomlinson, S. (1982) *The Sociology of Special Education*, RKP London.
Widlake, P. (1984) 'Beyond the Sabre-Toothed Curriculum', *Remedial Education* vol 19 (1).
Wilson, M. and Evans, P. (1980) Education of disturbed children.
Wragg, T. (1987) 'Time Travel' in *The Times Educational Supplement* 25 September 1987.

Chapter 11

Anderson, E.M. (1973) *The Disabled School Child*, Methuen.
Brennan, W.K. (1985) *Curriculum for Special Needs*, Open University Press.
Clunies–Ross, L. (1984) 'Special Needs in Ordinary Classrooms' *Special Education Forward Trends* 11 2, 11–14.
Department of Education and Science (Plowden Report) (1967) *Children and Their Primary Schools: A Report of the Central Advisory Council for Education (England)* vol 1. HMSO, London.
Department of Education and Science (Warnock Report) (1978) *Special Educational Needs. Report of the Committee of Enquiry into the Education of Handicapped Children and Young People* HMSO, London.
Dessent, T. (1987) *Making the Ordinary School Special* Falmer Press, London.
Duthie, J.H. (1970) *Primary School Survey. A Study of the Teacher's Day* HMSO, Edinburgh.
Goacher, B., Evans, J., Welton, J., Wedell, K. (1988) *Policy and Provision for Special Educational Needs* Cassell Educational, London.
Hegarty, S., Pocklington, K., and Lucas, D. (1981) *Educating Pupils with Special Needs in the Ordinary School* NFER Nelson, Windsor.
Hodgson, A., Clunies-Ross, L., and Hegarty, S. (1984) *Learning Together. Teaching Pupils with Special Educational Needs in the Ordinary School.* NFER Nelson, Windsor.
Kennedy, K.T., and Duthie, J.H. (1975) *Auxiliaries in the Classroom.* HMSO, Edinburgh.
Kolvin, I., Garside, R.F., Nichol, A.R., MacMillian, A., Wolstenholme, F., and Leitch, I.M. (1981) *Help Starts Here* Tavistock, London.
National Union of Teachers (1962) *The State of our Schools – A Report of the Findings of the National Survey of Schools Part 1* NUT, London.

Chapter 12

'Working'. DHSS, HMSO (1988) *Working Together for the Protection of Children from Abuse. Report of the Inquiry into Child Abuse in Cleveland 1987. DES Circular 4/88.* HMSO.
Dowling, E. and Osborne, E. (1985) *The Family and the School* Routledge and Kegan Paul.
Goffman, E. (1962) *Presentation of Self in Everyday Life.*

Chapter 13

Bornstein, M. R., Bellack, A. S. and Hersen, M. (1977) 'Social-skills Training for unassertive children. A multiple-baseline analysis' *Journal of Applied Behaviour-analysis* 10.

Brown, R., Wynne, M. and Medenis, R. (1985) 'Methylphanidate and Cognitive Therapy: A comparison of treatment approaches with hyperactive boys' *Journal of Abnormal Child Psychology* 1985, 13.

Camp Bonnie, W. (1977) 'Verbal Mediation in Young Aggressive Boys' *Journal of Abnormal Psychology*, vol 86 (2).

Chazan, M., Laing, A. F., Jones, J., Harper, G. C. and Bolton, J. (1983) *Helping Young Children with Behaviour Difficulties* Croom Helm.

Cross, J. and Goddard's (1988) 'Social Skills Training in the Ordinary School Setting' in *Educational Psychology in Practice* vol 4 (1) April 1988.

Davies, G. (1983) 'An introduction to Life and Social Skills Training' in *Journal of Maladjustment and Therapeutic Education*.

Elardo, P., Caldwell, B., (1979) 'The Effects of an Experimental Social Development Program on Children in the Middle Childhood Period' in *Psychology in the Schools*, vol 16 (1) January 1979.

Ellis, S. (1985) 'The Work of the DO5 School Support Team' in *Maladjustment and Therapeutic Education* vol 3 (2).

Flavell, J. H., Beech, D. H. and Chinsky, J. M. (1966) 'Spontaneous verbal rehearsal in a memory task as a function of age' in *Child Development* 1966, 37.

Jackson, N. (1983) *Getting Along with Others* Res Pres 1983.

Lloyd–Smith, M. (1985) 'Off site, out-of-mind?' *Times Educational Supplement* 13 September 1985 pp 53–54.

Long, M. (1988) 'Goodbye Behaviour Units, Hello Support Services: Home-School Support for Pupils with Behaviour Difficulties in Mainstream Schools', in *Educational Psychology in Practice*, vol 4 (1) April 1988.

Meichenbaum, D. (1985) 'Cognitive Behaviour Modification with Hyperactive Children' Paper presented at the International Conference on Hyperactivity as a Scientific Challenge, held in Grannger, The Netherlands, 13–14 June 1985.

Meichenbaum, D. and Goodman, J. (1971) 'Training impulsive children to talk to themselves. A means of developing self-control. *Journal of Abnormal Psychology* 1971, 77.

Rutter, M., Maughan, B., Mortimore, P. and Austin, J. (1979) *Fifteen Thousand Hours – Secondary Schools and their Effects on Children* Open Books.

Spence, S. (1980) *Social Skills Training with Children and Adolescents. A Counsellor's Manual.* NFER Windsor.

Spence, S. H. (1983) 'Teaching Social Skills to Children' *Journal of Child Psychology and Psychiatry* vol 24 (4).

Spivak, G. and Shure, M. B. (1976) *Social Adjustment of Young Children. A Cognitive Approach to Solving Real Life Problems* Jersey Bass London.

Stott, D. H. (1974) *The Social Adjustment of Children* ULP Ltd.

Topping, K. (1983) *Educational Systems for Disruptive Adolescents* Croom Helm.

Van Hasselt, V. B., Hersen, M., Whitehill, M. and Bellack, A. (1978) 'Social Skill Assessment and Training for Children. An Evaluative Review', in *Behaviour and Res. and Therapy* vol 7.

Weissberg, R. P. and Gesten Ellis, L. (1982) 'Considerations for Developing Effective

School-Based Social Problem-Solving SPS Training Program', in *The School Psychology Review* vol 11 (1), Winter 1982.

Wheldall, K. and Merrett, F. (1987) 'Training teachers to use the behavioural approach to classroom management, the development of BATPACK' in Wheldall, K. (ed) *The Behaviourist in the Classroom*, Allen and Unwin, London.

Chapter 14

ACSET (1984) *Teacher Training and Special Educational Needs* DES London.

Ainscow, M. and Tweddle, D.A. (1988) *Encouraging Classroom Success* David Fulton London.

Balshaw, M. (1987) 'Mainstream support work – What is it all about?' in Bowers, T. (ed) *Special Educational Needs and Human Resource Management*.

Bell, P. and Best, R. (1986) *Supportive Education* Blackwell Education, Oxford.

Booth, T. and Potts, P. (eds) *Integrating Special Education* Basil Blackwell, Oxford.

Booth, T., Potts, P. and Swann, W. (eds) (1987) *Preventing Difficulties in Learning. Curricula For All* Basil Blackwell in assoc with Oxford University.

Bowers, T. (ed) (1987) *Special Educational Needs and Human Resource Management* Croom Helm.

Croll, P. and Moses, M. (1985) *One in Five. The assessment and incidence of special educational needs* Routledge and Kegan Paul London.

DES (1975) *A Language for Life* (Bullock Report) HMSO.

DES (1981) *Education Act* HMSO London.

DES (1987) *National Curriculum. Task Group on Assessment and Testing* DES London.

DES (1987) *Quality in Schools: The Initial Training of Teachers*. HMSO London.

Dessent, T. (1987) *Making the Ordinary School Special* The Falmer Press, East Sussex.

Essex CC Education Department (1988) Special Needs Information Pack (SNIPS) Essex CC.

Fish, J. (chair) (1985) *Educational Opportunities for All?* ILEA.

Gipps, C., Gross, H. and Goldstein, H. (1987) *Warnock's Eighteen Per Cent. Children with special needs in the primary schools* The Falmer Press, London.

Gross, H. and Gipps, C. (1987) *Supporting Warnock's Eighteen Per Cent. Six case studies.* The Falmer Press London.

Gulliford, R. (1987) 'Meeting individual needs' *Support for Learning* vol 2 (4) pp 5–10.

Hanko, G. (1985) *Special Needs in Ordinary Classrooms* Blackwell Education, Oxford.

Hart, S. (1986) 'In-class support teaching: tackling Fish' *British Journal of Special Education* vol 13 (2), June.

Hegarty, S. (1987) *Meeting Special Needs in Ordinary Schools* Cassell, London.

Hegarty, S. and Moses, D. (1988) *Developing Expertise. INSET for special educational needs*. NFER–Nelson Windsor.

Hinson, M. (ed) (1987) *Teachers and Special Educational Needs*. Longman in assoc with NARE Essex.

House of Commons (1987) *Education Reform Bill* HMSO.

Jones, K. (1987) *The Consultant Teacher. Special Educational Needs*. NCSE Stratford-upon-Avon.

Jones, N.J. and Jones, E.M. (1981) 'Oxfordshire looks towards the future', in *Special Education. Forward Trends* vol 8 (2) June.

Jowett, S., Hegarty, S. and Moses, D. (1988) *Joining Forces. A study of links between special and ordinary schools*, NFER Nelson.

Lorimer, E., Potts, P. and Swann, W. 'Support in operation: the Linksfield area special needs team' in Booth, T., Potts, P. and Swann, W. *ibid.*

Mongon, D. (1985) 'Patterns of Delivery and Training Implications' in Sayer, J. and Jones, N. *ibid.*

Moses, D., Hegarty, S. and Jowett, S. (1988) *Supporting Ordinary Schools. LEA initiatives*, NFER-Nelson, Windsor.

Postlewaite, K. and Hackney, A. (1988) *Organising a School's Response* Macmillan.

Rouse, M. (1987) 'Bringing the special needs department out of the cupboard' in Bowers, T. (ed) *ibid.*

Sayer, J. (1987) *Secondary Schools for All? Strategies for Special Needs* Cassell London.

Sayer, J. and Jones, N. (1985) *Teacher Training and Special Educational Needs*, Croom Helm London.

Simmons, K. and Thomas, G. (1988) 'Testing times for special needs', *Special Children* June.

Thomas, D. and Smith, C. (1985) 'Special Educational Needs and Initial Training' in Sayer, J. and Jones, N. *ibid.*

Thomas, G. and Feiler, A. (1988) *Planning for Special Needs. A Whole School Approach* Basil Blackwell.

Wade, B. and Moore, M. (1987) *Special Children . . . Special Needs. Provision in ordinary classrooms*, Robert Royce London.

Wolfendale, S. (1987) *Primary Schools and Special Needs* Cassell, London.

Chapter 15

Griffiths, A., Edmunds, E. (1987) *The Calderdale Pre-School Book Project* Available from the SPS, Northgate House, Halifax HX1 1UN.

Griffiths, A., Hamilton, D. (1984) *Parent, Teacher, Child* Methuen.

Smith, B. (1987) 'A Wonderful Idea' *Special Children* No 14.

Chapter 16

Cameron, R.J. and Stratford, R.J. (1987) 'A Problem Centred Approach to Applied Psychology Practice', *Educational Psychology in Practice*, 2(4) pp 10–20.

Georgiades, N.J. and Phillimore, L. (1975) 'The Myth of the Hero Innovator and Alternative Strategies for Organisational Change' in Kiernan, C.C. and Woodford, F.P. (eds) '*Behaviour Modification and the Severely Retarded*', Oxford Associate Scientific Publications.

Levey, M. and Mallon, F. (1984) 'Support and Advisory Groups in Primary Schools' *AEP Journal*, 6 (4) pp 25–9.

Chapter 17

Clunies–Ross, L. (1984) 'Supporting the mainstream teacher' in *Special Education: Forward Trends* vol 11 (3).

Ferguson, N. and Adams, M. (1982) 'Assessing the advantages of team teaching in remedial education: The remedial teacher's role *Remedial Education* vol 17 (1).

Hart (1986) 'Evaluating support teaching' *Gnosis* (ILEA).

Hodgson (1985) 'Meeting special needs in mainstream classrooms', in *British Journal of Special Education* vol 12 (3).

Jones, K. *et al* (1986) 'Support for learning in service children's schools', in *Support for Learning* vol 1 (4).

Thomas G. (1986) 'Integrating personnel in order to integrate children', in *Support for Learning* vol 1 (1).

Chapter 18

Brandt, R. (1988) 'On Students' Needs and Team Learning. A Conversation with William Glasser' *Educational Leadership* vol 46 (6) pp 38–48.

Lazarus, R.S. and Launier, R. (1978) 'Stress-Related Transactions between Person and Environment' in L.A. Pervin and M. Lewis (eds) *Perspectives in Interactional Psychology* Plenum Press, New York.

Shinn, M., Lehmann, S. and Wong, N.W. (1984) 'Social Interaction and Social Support', *Journal of Social Issues* vol 40 (4) pp 55–76.

Shumaker, S.A. and Brownell, A. (1984) 'Towards a Theory of Social Support: Closing Conceptual Gaps, in *Journal of Social Issues* vol 40 (4) pp 11–36.

Chapter 19

Booth, T., Potts, P. and Swann, W. (1987) *Preventing Difficulties in Learning: Curricula For All*. Basil Blackwell.

Department of Education and Science (1978) *Special Educational Needs. The Warnock Report* HMSO.

Department of Education and Science (1981) *Education Act*, HMSO.

Galloway, D. and Goodwin, C. (1979) *The Education of Slow Learning and Maladjusted Children*, Longman.

Gipps, C., Gross, H. and Goldstein, H. (1987) *Warnock's Eighteen Per Cent: Children With Special Needs in Primary Schools*, Falmer Press.

Gresham, F.M. (1982) 'Misguided Mainstreaming: The Case for Social Skills Training With Handicapped Children', in *Exceptional Children* vol 48 (5).

Harvey, D.H.P. (1985) 'Mainstreaming: Teachers' Attitudes when they have no Choice about the Matter', in *The Exceptional Child* vol 32 (3).

Howard, J. (1986) *Attitudes of Professionals Towards Teenage Parents*. M Phil Thesis, University of London, Institute of Education.

ILEA (1985) *Educational Opportunities for All? The Fish Report*. London, ILEA.

Jordan, K. (1981) 'Integration and Total Communication in the Education of Deaf Children' in G. Montgomery (ed), *The Integration and Disintegration of the Deaf In Society*, Scottish Workshop Publications.

Kyle, J. (ed) (1987) *Sign and School*, Multilingual Matters.

Lane, H. (1984) *When the Mind Hears*, Souvenir Press.

Levy-Shiff, R. and Hoffman, M.A. (1985) 'Social Behaviour of Hearing Impaired and Normally Hearing Preschoolers', in *British Journal of Educational Psychology*, 55.

Lindsay, G. and Dickinson, D. (1987) 'Integration of Profoundly Hearing-Impaired Children into a Nursery Setting,' in *British Journal of the Association of the Teachers of the Deaf* 11.

Montgomery, G. (ed) (1981) *The Integration and Disintegration of the Deaf in Society,* Scottish Workshop Publications.

Montgomery, G. (1986), 'A Comparison of Limited and Total Communication Approaches to Language Attainment of Deaf Children', in G. Montgomery (ed) *Beyond Hobson's Choice: The Appraisal of Methods of Teaching Language to Deaf Children,* Scottish Workshop Publications.

Odom, S.L., Deklyen, M. and Jenkins, J.R. (1984) 'Integrating Handicapped and Non-Handicapped Preschoolers: Developmental Impact on Non-handicapped children', in *Exceptional Children* vol 51 (1).

Reagan, T. (1985) 'The Deaf as a Linguistic Minority: Educational Considerations' in *Harvard Educational Review* vol 55 (3).

Reed, M. (1981) 'The Strategy of Integration' in G. Montgomery (ed) *The Integration and Disintegration of the Deaf In Society,* Scottish Workshop Publications.

Rodger, I.A. and Richardson, J.A.S. (1985) *Self-Evaluation for Primary Schools* Hodder and Stoughton.

Sinha, C., Moore, M. and Pound, L. (1988) 'Coding Communicative Strategies and Development : Issues, Methods and a Preliminary Report of a Naturalistic Study', *International Journal of Sign Linguistics Monograph* in press.

Swann, W. (1985) *Education for All,* DES/HMSO.

Chapter 21

Bevan, K. and Shortall, K. (1986) *Educational Review* vol 38 (3).

Canfield, J. and Wells, H. (1976) *100 Ways to Improve Self-Concept in the Classroom* Prentice-Hall.

Elkins, D.P. (ed) (1976) *Glad to be Me,* Prentice-Hall.

Lawrence, D. (1973) *Improved Reading through Counselling,* Ward Lock.

Robinson, G.S. and Maines, B.J. (1988) *They Can Because . . . A Workshop in Print* AWMC, c/o Redhill School, Maidstone ME17 3DG.

Robinson, G.S. and Maines, B.J. (1988) *A Bag of Tricks . . . The Video* Lame Duck Publishing, 71 South Road, Avon BS20 9DY.

Chapter 22

HMSO (1978) *Special Educational Needs: Committee of Enquiry into the Education of Handicapped Children and Young People,* HMSO.

Department of Education and Science (1987) *A Special Professionalism,* FEU/DES.

Stowell, Richard (1987) *Catching Up? Provision for Students with Special Educational Needs in Further and Higher Education,* National Bureau of Handicapped Students.

Notes on contributors

Dr Roy Evans is a past President of NARE, and currently Assistant Dean (INSET) at Roehampton Institute, London, SW15.

Dr Ron Davie trained and worked as a teacher and then as an educational psychologist for his first thirteen professional years. Moving to the National Children's Bureau in 1964 to take charge of the National Child Development Study, he spent his next nine years mostly in research. He was then appointed Professor of Educational Psychology in Cardiff. Nine years later, in 1982, he was back at NCB as Director, since when he has been grafting onto the Bureau's established research reputation a strong action component designed to improve services and influence policy.

Philip Robinson is Dean of the School of Education, Roehampton Institute, London SW15.

Professor Sheila Wolfendale has been a primary school and remedial teacher and educational psychologist in several LEAs, and is currently in charge of a postgraduate professional training course for educational psychologists. She has written extensively. Recently publications include *Word Play* with Trevor Bryans (published by NARE), *Primary Schools and Special Needs: Policy, Planning and Provision* (Cassell) and *The Parental Contribution to Assessment* (NCSE 1988).

Mr Peter Smith is Primary Adviser for Hounslow LEA and has been President of UKRA.

Mr Phil Bell has worked in the field of special needs for sixteen years and currently holds the posts of Head of Supportive Education and TVEI Co-ordinator at The Rickstones School, Witham, Essex. He has written several publications including *Spellmaster, Help at Home, Spelling* (Holmes McDougall) and is co-author of the significant publication *Supportive Education* (Blackwell).

Richard Stowell is Director, National Bureau for Students with Disabilities, London, SW9.

Sue Abell is Senior Advisory Tutor, Adult Basic Education, Essex County Council Education Department, Colchester.

Ms Gerda Hanko previously Head of Education, Thomas Huxley College,

Ealing. She now works as Special Needs consultant and organising tutor of Teacher Support Workshops for LEAs, Teachers' Centres, School Psychological Services and voluntary educational organisations. She is Hon. Secretary of the Forum for the Advancement of Educational Therapy.

Mr John Atkinson is Senior Lecturer in Education at Bretton Hall College of Higher Education, West Bretton, Wakefield.

Mr John Harrington is Assistant Education Officer, Royal County of Berkshire, Department of Education, Shire Hall, Reading.

Mr Terence Clayton is Specialist Senior Educational Psychologist, Wiltshire Education Authority.

Mrs Eva Gregory has an Honours Degree in Social Science. She trained first as a Probation Officer and then as a Psychiatric Social Worker. She then spent ten years working in Community Mental Health Services and Psychiatric Hospitals. This was followed by ten years in research and some years in a London Social Service Department. She is currently responsible for social work services to about two-thirds of the ILEA special day and boarding schools.

Mr Bernard Levey and **Mrs Susan Miller** are Educational Psychologists with Humberside Local Education Authority.

Miss Lois Hockley is Head, Teaching and Support Service, West Berkshire.

Mr Alex Griffiths is Head of Psychological Services, **Mr Mike Dodds** is a Special Needs Adviser, **Mr Paul Nicklin** is Educational Psychologist and **Ms Sharon Shoesmith** is Head of ANA (ALSS) – all at MBC Calderdale.

Mrs Judith Pettersen is Senior Educational Psychologist, **Mrs Michelle Sidwell, Ms Nicola Mindell,** and **Mrs Pauline Grant** are Educational Psychologists, Buckinghamshire County Psychological Service.

Mr Rik Boxer is Educational Psychologist, London Borough of Havering, and **Ms Dayna Halpin** is Co-ordinator of Primary Support Teaching Service, Inkersall Green School, Derbyshire.

Mrs Hazel Dodgson is Lecturer in Special Educational Needs (In-Service Faculty), Edge Hill College of Higher Education, Ormskirk, Lancs.

Mrs Linda Pound is Senior Lecturer in Education and **Ms Michele Moore** is Lecturer in Communication Studies – at Roehampton Institute of Higher Education, and at City of Sheffield Polytechnic respectively.

Mrs Lyn Wendon is author of *Letterland*.

Mr Barbara Maines is a Psychologist and **Mr George Robinson** is a Head Teacher with Avon Education Authority.

Maria Landy is Adviser, Special Education, in Gloucestershire.

Mrs Avril Jewers is Senior Lecturer at Colchester Institute and Co-ordinator of YTS and SEN. She has previously taught all age groups and has been a member of a remedial department and advisory teacher in a remedial team.

Index